The
Primary
Care
Consultant

Application and Practice in Health Psychology Series

The
Primary
Care
Consultant

The Next Frontier
for Psychologists in
Hospitals and Clinics

EDITED BY
LARRY C. JAMES AND
RAYMOND A. FOLEN

American Psychological Association · Washington, DC

Published by
American Psychological Association
750 First Street, NE
Washington, DC 20002
www.apa.org

To order
APA Order Department
P.O. Box 92984
Washington, DC 20090-2984
Tel: (800) 374-2721
Direct: (202) 336-5510
Fax: (202) 336-5502
TDD/TTY: (202) 336-6123
Online: www.apa.org/books/
E-mail: order@apa.org

In the U.K., Europe, Africa, and the Middle East, copies may be ordered from
American Psychological Association
3 Henrietta Street
Covent Garden, London
WC2E 8LU England

Typeset in Goudy by World Composition Services, Inc., Sterling, VA

Printer: Sheridan Books, Ann Arbor, MI
Cover Designer: Naylor Design, Washington, DC
Editor/Project Manager: Debbie Hardin, Carlsbad, CA

The opinions and statements published are the responsibility of the authors, and such opinions and statements do not necessarily represent the policies of the American Psychological Association. Any views expressed in chapters 1, 3, 4, 6, 9, and 14 do not necessarily represent the views of the United States government, and the authors' participation in the work is not meant to serve as an official endorsement.

Library of Congress Cataloging-in-Publication Data

The primary care consultant : the next frontier for psychologists in hospitals and clinics / edited by Larry C. James and Raymond A. Folen.—1st ed.
      p. cm.—(Health psychology series) (Application and practice in health psychology)
   Includes bibliographical references and index.
   ISBN 1-59147-212-1
   1. Clinical health psychology—United States. 2. Primary care (Medicine)—United States. 3. Mental health services—United States. 4. Integrated delivery of health care—United States. I. James, Larry C. II. Folen, Raymond A. III. Series. IV. Series: Health psychology series (American Psychological Association)

   R726.7.P75 2005
   616'.001'9—dc22   2004016291

British Library Cataloguing-in-Publication Data
A CIP record is available from the British Library.

Printed in the United States of America
First Edition

To
Drs. Ursula Delworth,
Daniel W. Fullmer,
and Patrick H. DeLeon:
Visionaries, mentors, colleagues, and friends.

CONTENTS

CONTRIBUTORS

Curt Buermeyer, PhD, Department of Clinical and Medical Psychology, Uniformed Services University of the Health Sciences, Bethesda, MD

Daniel L. Clay, PhD, Counseling Psychology, University of Iowa, Iowa City

Jay E. Earles, PsyD, ABPP, Department of Psychology, Eisenhower Army Medical Center, Ft. Gordon, GA

Joseph R. Etherage, PsyD, ABPP, Malcolm Grow Medical Center, Andrews Air Force Base, MD

Raymond A. Folen, PhD, ABPP, Department of Psychology, Tripler Army Medical Center, Honolulu, HI

Corey J. Habben, PsyD, Department of Psychiatry, Walter Reed Army Medical Center, Washington, DC

Diane E. Isler, PhD, San Antonio, TX

William C. Isler III, PhD, Lackland Air Force Base, San Antonio, TX

Larry C. James, PhD, ABPP, Department of Psychology, Walter Reed Army Medical Center, Washington, DC

Robert D. Kerns, PhD, Psychology Service, VA Connecticut Healthcare System, Westhaven, CT, and Psychiatry Department, Yale University, New Haven, CT

Willem J. Kop, PhD, Department of Clinical and Medical Psychology, Uniformed Services University of the Health Sciences, Bethesda, MD

Wendy A. Law, PhD, Department of Clinical and Medical Psychology, Uniformed Services University of the Health Sciences, Bethesda, MD

John D. Otis, PhD, VA Boston Healthcare System; Department of Psychiatry and Psychology, Boston University, Boston, MA

Alan L. Peterson, PhD, ABPP, Department of Psychology, Wilfred Hall Medical Center, San Antonio, TX

Ellen L. Poleshuck, PhD, Departments of Psychiatry and Obstetrics and Gynecology, University of Rochester School of Medicine and Dentistry, Rochester, NY

M. Carrington Reid, MD, PhD, Division of Geriatrics and Gerontology, Weill Cornell Medical College, New York

John D. Robinson, EdD, MPH, ABPP, Departments of Surgery and Psychiatry, Howard University Hospital, Washington, DC

Anderson B. Rowan, PhD, ABPP, Malcolm Grow Medical Center, Andrews AFB, MD

Christine N. Runyan, PhD, Air Force Medical Operations Agency, Brooks Air Force Base, TX

Marilyn Stern, PhD, Departments of Psychology and Pediatrics, Virginia Commonwealth University, Richmond

Meg I. Striepe, PhD, Independent practice, Concord, MA; University of Minnesota Medical School, Minneapolis

Mark Verschell, PsyD, Department of Psychology, Tripler Army Medical Center, Honolulu, HI

Joel E. Williams, MPH, Norman J. Arnold School of Public Health, University of South Carolina, Columbia

Dawn K. Wilson, PhD, Norman J. Arnold School of Public Health, University of South Carolina, Columbia

SERIES FOREWORD

Division 38 (Health Psychology) of the American Psychological Association presents a new volume in its series focusing on the application and practice of health psychology. One of the primary objectives of the division has been an ongoing interest in health promotion, disease prevention, and treatment through application of principles and procedures that have emerged in the research arena. The vitality of health psychology depends on an active dialogue between researchers and practitioners and the interdependence between the scientific and the applied aspects of the discipline. A primary goal of this series is to continue to expand this dialogue. Accordingly, attempts to translate research findings into applications and interventions, to test and evaluate the effectiveness of these interventions with patient populations, and to denote important clinical experiences and research needs of the practice of health psychology are important foci of these volumes.

It is intended that the volumes in this series will serve as vehicles for translating research into practice, with an analysis of issues related to the evaluation, prevention, and treatment of health behaviors and health problems. These goals are met by conceptualizing clinical and applied health psychology as broadly as possible, including community and public health assessment and intervention methods and problems of health care use. Topics are covered across a wide variety of applied and practice settings, such as hospitals, the practitioner's office, community clinics, the work site, and school environments. Each volume provides direction in areas of need and populations to be served by health psychology intervention. After identifying the population, each volume critically examines issues and problems involved in clinical evaluation, prevention, and treatment of specific disorders and illustrates the effectiveness of clinical approaches to prevention, diagnosis, and treatment that may guide future research and practice. Each volume focuses on seminal topics and synthesizes research from a range of areas to reinforce the theoretical and scientific rationale for the practice of health psychology.

Dawn K. Wilson and Perry M. Nicassio
Series Editors

ACKNOWLEDGMENTS

We would like to thank our spouses, Joan L. James and Allene E. F. Chun, for their encouragement, love, and patience with this project. We are also grateful to our many colleagues for their consistent and inspiring support. We thank the Army Medical Department, a hub of health care innovation, and in particular Tripler Army Medical Center, for offering us the opportunity to engage in exciting research and clinical practice over the past two decades. Our thanks also to our book editor, Debbie Hardin, for her patience, attention to detail, and ability to keep things on track.

The views expressed in this book are those of the authors and do not reflect the official policy of the Department of the Army, Department of Defense, or the U.S. government.

The
Primary
Care
Consultant

INTRODUCTION

LARRY C. JAMES AND RAYMOND A. FOLEN

We began this book by asking questions about the health psychologist's role in addressing the United States's extensive health care needs. We had long ago arrived at the conclusion, now shared by a great many of our colleagues, that fully integrated services provided by psychologists in primary care settings constitute the most challenging and interesting opportunities, with the most impact, offered to the psychology profession. The psychologists who first cultivated this new primary care landscape are now well established in their field. Training programs are slowly turning their wheels toward this new direction as well. Many questions still remain, however: Can we provide effective interventions within the 15-minute time frame the primary care setting often demands? Does the traditional 50-minute therapy hour serve us or diminish us in the long run? Will our scope of practice narrow or expand as a result of our move into primary care? With increasing stress on the American family, can we effectively meet the escalating service demands by providing preventative and remedial programs to children within the primary care setting? Is there a need for women's and men's health programs that are managed by primary care psychologists? As the demand for primary care psychologists exceeds availability, can technology offer some practical solutions?

To address these questions we began to draw on relevant experiences from the national health care system that exists within federal health care agencies such as the Department of Defense (DoD) and the Veterans' Administration (VA). Unique health care systems, the DoD and VA are often the testing grounds for innovation in health care. This is particularly true in the primary care setting, where federal health psychologists are leading the way with clinical and technological innovations. These opportunities have also led to an expanded scope of practice. DoD health psychologists, for example, are now prescribing psychotropic medications within primary care clinics, as an integrated component of specific treatment programs such as tobacco-use cessation or weight management. They also conduct medical and health assessments and order lab work as part of their comprehensive psychological evaluations. In addition, the DoD and VA have expanded delivery of these unique services to isolated facilities located thousands of miles from the health psychologist by using high and low bandwidth telehealth technologies.

Given the dramatic changes in health care and technology over the past decade, this book is not intended to be a restatement of the many well-established and now considered traditional tasks that health psychologists engage in. Rather, by highlighting innovative DoD and other programs, we offer new ways of thinking about health psychology that may serve as a guide for the future. The first chapter in this book, for example, provides a new conceptual model and practical primer for the delivery of services in a primary care setting. Imbedded in this and other chapters are paradigm shifts the reader is encouraged to make. The hallowed 50-minute therapy hour, for example, is replaced with an effective 15- to 30-minute session that complements the primary care physician. Where appropriate, authors provide the reader with helpful hints on how to make the transition to these new models a smooth one.

In most training programs, it is the psychosocial aspects of the biopsychosocial model that are emphasized. Unfortunately, the *biological* aspect invariably gets short shrift. Psychological assessment in primary care and other medical settings demands a greater emphasis on medical history, medical assessment, and medical symptomology, and the authors of chapter 2 address this often missing link. In keeping with the expanding themes of the first two chapters, the third chapter further extends the influence of primary care psychologists through the use of telehealth, with specific attention to the clinical, ethical, and technical issues that emerge with the use of this technology.

Next the book presents interventions and treatment models specific to the adult primary care setting. Chapter 4 addresses the importance of a multidisciplinary primary care approach in the treatment of pain management, and this is followed by chapters on treating cardiovascular disease,

HIV/AIDS, diabetes mellitus, and insomnia. Pediatric behavioral health consultation, pediatric psychology in primary care, and school-based pediatric psychology models and interventions are presented in the next three chapters. The final three chapters in the book address the role of primary care psychology in women's health, in sexual issues related to women's health, and present future applications of primary care psychology to men's health.

As editors of this volume, we had the freedom to solicit manuscripts from the most experienced and most capable psychologists working in primary care settings. To our great pleasure, all responded enthusiastically to our requests. The result is an exciting and challenging collection of cutting-edge health care treatment models written by some of the most innovative thinkers in primary care. We hope these chapters will provide the reader with new models for the delivery of psychological services, present new skill sets that will expand the reader's role in health care, and provide some direction for training the next generation of primary care psychologists.

I

A NEW WAY OF CONCEPTUALIZING HEALTH PSYCHOLOGY IN THE PRIMARY CARE SETTING

1

A PRIMER ON THE CONSULTATION MODEL OF PRIMARY CARE BEHAVIORAL HEALTH INTEGRATION

ANDERSON B. ROWAN AND CHRISTINE N. RUNYAN

In both scientific and health care administration venues, there has been an explosion in writings about the integration of mental health services into primary care clinics over the past decade. The dramatic increase in models for integration and research in this area parallels the substantial change that has occurred in primary care medicine. Specifically, the nature of primary care has shifted from an acute care model to providing "integrated, accessible health care services by clinicians who are accountable for addressing a large majority of personal health care needs, developing a sustained partnership with patients, and practicing in the context of family and

This chapter was authored or coauthored by an employee of the United States government as part of official duty and is considered to be in the public domain. Any views expressed herein do not necessarily represent the views of the United States government, and the author's participation in the work is not meant to serve as an official endorsement.

The authors gratefully acknowledge Mountainview Consulting and Kirk Strosahl for helping to develop, train, and implement the model of consultative behavioral health care that is currently used in the Air Force Medical Service and was the basis for this chapter.

community" (deGruy, 1996, p. 33). To meet the demands of this shift, mental health providers and services have become increasingly more important in the delivery of primary medical care as a means to effectively and efficiently address the myriad of mental health complaints that commonly occur in primary care settings. This chapter briefly describes the rationale for a consultative model of integrated behavioral health care, draws on a clinical example to further illustrate this model of care, and discusses typical pitfalls encountered when transitioning from the specialty mental health role to the primary care behavioral health consultation role. The goals of this chapter are to expose the reader to a nontraditional model of mental health care delivery, to demonstrate how and why a consultative model of behavioral health care is symbiotic to the goals of today's primary care environment, and to provide a foundational understanding of what this model of care looks like in actual clinical practice.

RATIONALE FOR INTEGRATION

The benefits of mental health programs integrated with primary care in a variety of practice settings, patient populations, and clinical modalities have been well documented. Previous studies have shown that integrating mental health services into primary care clinics can improve patient satisfaction (e.g., Katon et al., 1996), improve provider satisfaction (e.g., Corney, 1986; Katon et al., 1996), improve patient outcomes (Balestrieri, Williams, & Wilkinson, 1988), and decrease health care costs (e.g., Von Korff et al., 1998). Numerous studies have also found that collaborative care models designed to improve the recognition and management for specific diseases or conditions within primary care are both clinically effective and cost-effective. For example, several successful collaborative care models have been developed for depression and have uniformly demonstrated improved recognition of depression that, if followed by multidisciplinary, multicomponent interventions, improve both disease-specific as well as overall health outcomes (Bower, Richards, & Lovell, 2001; Pignone et al., 2002; Schoenbaum et al., 2001; Unutzer et al., 2002; U.S. Preventive Services Task Force, 2002). Improved patient satisfaction, increased adherence to medications, decreased medical utilization among "high utilizers," and cost offsets (Brown & Schulberg, 1995) have also been reported using collaborative care models. Behaviorally based lifestyle interventions delivered in primary care are also likely to have cross-cutting beneficial effects because unhealthy lifestyle habits such as smoking, sedentary lifestyle, and high calorie diets are known risk factors for multiple chronic illnesses such as diabetes, ischemic heart disease, and chronic obstructive pulmonary disease (COPD). In fact, evidence is currently mounting that self-management for these chronic conditions can be effectively taught in non-disease-specific primary care based groups, leading to significant impact on aspects of health status, health behaviors, and fewer hospital days (Lorig et al., 1999).

Integrated care can take many forms, ranging from a minimal combination of behavioral health and physical medicine services to providers regularly working together in delivering health care services as a unified team. Merely colocating mental health providers into primary care does not equate to integrated care and has been found to be an insufficient solution. In the absence of changed processes, colocated mental health providers are likely to revert to delivering specialty services and to treating only the small proportion of the population that are easily identified by primary care providers as needing clinical intervention. Rather, the common elements of successfully integrated programs appear to be full integration of mental health providers within the clinic, behavioral and lifestyle interventions, a structured program of treatment, an emphasis on follow-up care, and a focus on depression (Simon & Von Korff, 1995).

Moreover, if integrated care is also being used as one means to make an impact on the entire population of interest, this requires yet another echelon of integration. For this to occur, the model of integration must be consultative in nature and rooted in a public health perspective of service planning and delivery. In this type of model, behavioral health providers support improved detection of behavioral health problems through targeted or universal screening, focused assessment, brief interventions, and follow-up. Such a model of integration requires a fundamental shift away from many of the basic tenants of specialty mental health care, as shown in Table 1.1.

In the integrated care model, the focus is on brief behavioral health services that are provided to patients at an earlier point in their progression along the health continuum, in a setting that minimizes resistance to care and provides different types of services to more closely match patients' needs. The focus is on resolving problems within the primary care service structure, as well as assisting patients to engage in health promotion activities. Because integrated care allows symptoms to be more easily recognized and treated when they first emerge, it is also likely to reduce the duration and intensity of treatment required to move individuals back toward the healthier end of the continuum. Integrating behavioral health providers on the front lines of primary care to deliver consultative behavioral health care allows for a shift toward a population-based approach.

TABLE 1.1
Key Differences Between Behavioral Health Consultation and Specialty Mental Health

Dimension	Primary care behavioral health consultation	Specialty mental health care
Primary goals	• Performs appropriate clinical assessments • Supports primary care provider decision making • Builds on primary care provider interventions • Teaches primary care provider core mental health skills • Educates patient in self-management skills through exposure • Improves primary care provider–patient working relationship • Monitors, with primary care provider, at-risk patients • Manages chronic patients with primary care provider in primary provider role • Assists in team building	• Delivers primary treatment to resolve condition • Coordinates with primary care provider by phone • Teaches patient core self-management skills • Manages more serious mental disorders over time as primary provider
Appointment structure	• Limited to one to three visits in typical case • 15- to 30-minute visits	• Session number variable, related to patient condition • 50-minute visits
Intervention structure	• Informal, revolves around primary care provider assessment and goals • Less intensity; between-session interval longer • Relationship generally not primary focus • Visits timed around primary care provider visits • Long-term follow-up rare, reserved for high-risk cases	• Formal, requires intake assessment, treatment planning • Higher intensity, involving more concentrated care • Relationship built to last over time • Visit structure not related to medical visits • Long-term follow-up encouraged for most clients
Intervention methods	• Limited face-to-face contact • Uses patient education model as primary model • Consultation is a technical resource to patient • Emphasis is on home-based practice to promote change • May involve primary care provider in visits with patient	• Face-to-face contact is primary treatment vehicle • Education model ancillary • Home practice linked back to treatment • Primary care provider rarely involved in visits with patient

continued

TABLE 1.1   *(Continued)*

Dimension	Primary care behavioral health consultation	Specialty mental health care
Termination/ follow-up	▪ Responsibility returned to primary care provider ▪ Primary care provider gives relapse prevention or maintenance treatment	▪ Therapist remains person to contact if in need ▪ Therapist provides any relapse prevention or maintenance treatment
Referral structure	▪ Patient referred by primary care provider only	▪ Patient self-refers or is referred by others
Primary information products	▪ Consultation report goes to primary care provider ▪ Notes made in medical record only	▪ Specialty treatment notes (i.e., intake or progress notes) ▪ Part of a separate mental health record with minimal notation to medical record

Note. From "A Novel Approach for Mental Health Disease Management: The Air Force Medical Service's Interdisciplinary Model," by C. N. Runyan, V. P. Fonseca, J. G. Meyer, M. S. Oordt, and G. W. Talcott, *Disease Management, 6,* p. 179. Copyright 2003 by Mary Ann Liebert, Inc. Adapted with permission.

THE PRIMARY CARE BEHAVIORAL HEALTH CONSULTATION SERVICE

In general, the goal of a primary care behavioral health consultative service is to position the behavioral health provider in the second tier of the primary care delivery system (Population Health Support Division, 2002). *Behavioral health consultant* (BHC) is a term used to describe any behavioral health provider who (a) operates in a consultative role within a primary care treatment team and within primary care and (b) offers recommendations and care delivery regarding behavioral interventions or psychotropic medications. Second-tier providers support the primary care provider, bringing more specialized knowledge to bear on problems that the medical provider believes require additional support or that are identified through systematic screening processes. In some cases, the BHC may only provide consultation to the primary care provider but more commonly will also see the patient for a limited assessment and intervention. The consultant's interventions are always designed and delivered to support the medical provider's impact on the patients' overall health. The BHC is, in essence, working on behalf of the physician because he or she can offer more specialized knowledge and skills in behavioral health, but these interventions are never in contradiction to or irrelevant to the physician and patient's overall health care plan. Ongoing communication with the physician regarding recommendations and the patient's status is key to the consultant's role. In contrast to specialty mental health settings, consultation by the BHC does not require a separate informed consent document because behavioral assessment and intervention are a part of the primary health care team's service. Moreover, documentation is recorded only in the medical record rather than in a separate mental health chart. In summary, both patients and providers experience the consultant and the care provided as part of the overall approach to primary health care. The primary care behavioral health consultation model is tailored to and integrated within the process of normal primary health care services. The consultation model has been implemented effectively in the Air Force Medical Service (AFMS) and has been well received by its primary care providers and patients alike (Runyan, Fonseca, & Hunter, 2003).

ROLE OF THE BEHAVIORAL
HEALTH CONSULTANT

The BHC is typically a social worker or a psychologist with specialized clinical training in consultative behavioral health care. The consultant's role is to provide support and assistance to both primary care providers and their patients without engaging in any form of extended specialty mental health care. The model and associated interventions rely heavily on cognitive–behavioral theory because cognitive–behavioral interventions flow out of a problem-focused assessment, can be implemented quickly using handouts and other instructional aids, and have strong empirical support. Some consultations are single visits with immediate suggestions for intervention strategies made to the referring provider. Other times the consultant will meet with the patient for a few additional appointments to help establish momentum toward change. Interventions with patients tend to be simple, "bite-sized," and compatible with the types of interventions that could be provided or reinforced in a typical 15- to 20-minute health care visit (i.e., interventions that can be done in 2 to 3 minutes). It is also clear to the patient that the consultant is being used to help the physician and patient come up with an effective plan of attack to target the patient's concerns. Follow-up consultations are choreographed to reinforce provider-generated interventions. The goal over time is to maximize what often amounts to a limited number of visits to either the consultant or the medical provider. Thus, the consultant is able to follow patients who need longer term surveillance at arm's length, in a manner that is consistent with how primary care providers manage many of their at-risk patients. At all times, care is coordinated by the medical provider, who is still responsible for choosing and monitoring the results of interventions. In other words, the primary care providers "own" these cases. Integrating behavioral health providers into the primary care setting in

EXHIBIT 1.1
EXHIBIT 1.1
Expected Benefits of Integrated Behavioral Health Care

- Immediate access to behavioral health care
- Improved recognition of behavioral health needs
- Improved collaborative care and management of patients with psychosocial issues in primary care
- An immediate and internal resource for primary care providers to help address a patient's psychosocial concerns or behavioral health issues, without referring the patient to a specialty mental health clinic
- The provision of rapid feedback to the medical provider
- Improved fit between the care patients seek in primary care and the services offered
- Prevention of more serious mental disorders through early recognition and intervention
- Triage into more intensive specialty mental health care by the BHC
- Facilitation of the transfer of empirically supported treatments into primary care
- Improved efficiency in the delivery of empirically supported treatments

this manner is expected to yield the beneficial results demonstrated by other collaborative models over time (see Exhibit 1.1).

CLINICAL PROCESSES

The remainder of this chapter provides a foundational overview of what this model looks like in actual clinical practice and references the case of Mrs. Smith to illustrate these processes:

> Dr. Jones consulted the BHC on Mrs. Smith, a 29-year-old female with migraine headaches that have been refractory to standard medications. Dr. Jones informed the consultant that Mrs. Smith reports significant stress in her life and Dr. Jones believes this is contributing to her headaches.

The Initial Appointment

The initial appointment, which is typically 25 to 30 minutes, can be broken down into three distinct phases, with a bridge between each. These phases, which are discussed in turn, are the introduction, the assessment, and the intervention (see Table 1.2).

Introduction

The first few minutes of the initial appointment are spent introducing the BHC's role and what the patient can expect to happen in the appointment. In addition, patients are informed of the following: (a) the consultant

TABLE 1.2
Phases of the Initial Evaluation Appointment

Stage	Time
Introduction	1–2 minutes
Bridge to assessment	10–30 seconds
Assessment	10–15 minutes
Symptoms	
Functioning	
Bridge to intervention	1–2 minutes
Intervention	5–10 minutes

has the same reporting requirements as the patient's doctor; (b) the consultant will give feedback to the patient's provider; and (c) the appointment will be documented in the patient's medical record (see sample introduction in Appendix 1.1). In addition, most providers give patients a brochure about the BHC service that contains much of this information at the time they discuss the initial referral to the consultant.

Bridge to Assessment

The consultation assessment is problem-focused; therefore, the bridge seeks to move the patient quickly into a discussion of the referral question. The transition to the assessment will usually be a single question that directs the patient to the reason for referral. The bridge used with Mrs. Smith was the following:

> In talking with Dr. Jones, it sounds like you have tried extensive medical interventions with insufficient effect and she is wondering if stress may be contributing to your migraine headaches. Is that your understanding of why Dr. Jones wanted me to see you, or do you have another take on this?

Sometimes, the physician is not able to inform the BHC of the specific referral question in advance. In this case a BHC might say the following:

> I wasn't able to talk with Dr. Jones before I saw you today, so can you tell me what you and she were talking about when she mentioned it might be a good idea to have you talk with me?

Questions such as these focus the session much more effectively than traditional mental health bridges such as, "So, what brings you in today?" The traditional bridge, when used in primary care, often prompts patients to talk about things not related to the consultation problem, leading to several minutes being wasted as a consultant tries to redirect the patient to the referral question and still maintain rapport.

Assessment

The assessment phase usually lasts about 15 minutes, depending on the complexity of the problem and the tendency of the patient to get side-tracked. Although 15 minutes may not sound like much time, once BHCs become skilled in the model, this is usually plenty of time to assess the referral problem. In addition, the primary care setting, combined with the BHC's introduction, sets the patient's expectations to be consistent with this type of interview and generally makes it easier to get and keep the patient focused. During this phase, the consultant seeks to obtain information regarding symptoms and functioning.

Symptom assessment is based on the referral question and the patient's presentation. Thus, with Mrs. Smith, the consultant focused on information regarding her headaches and stress. For referrals that suggest a possible psychiatric disorder, a diagnostic scan should be done for disorders consistent with this information. If a cursory assessment suggests a possible disorder, a more thorough but directive evaluation is in order to make the appropriate diagnosis.

An assessment of the patient's daily functioning gives the consultant a picture of how the symptoms are affecting the patient's life and often leads to the identification of possible intervention(s). Typical functional areas assessed include impacts on work, marriage, family roles, social roles, leisure time, exercise, and so forth. An initial question that often yields an abundance of information quickly is, "Tell me what you do in a typical day."

An important and often neglected part of the assessment is inquiry regarding what the patient has already done to try to reduce or manage the symptoms and their impacts. This information enables the consultant to avoid heading down an intervention road the patient has already tried (and thus will reject with only a few minutes left in the appointment). In addition, the BHC may be able to identify the reason a previous intervention failed (e.g., patient gave up too early or did not practice the technique properly), enabling the consultant to address these factors when proposing the intervention.

The assessment of Mrs. Smith revealed that her primary stressors were work related (pressure of deadlines, long hours, and hectic pace). She usually developed a migraine by mid-afternoon on about 50% of workdays, which lasted until she went to sleep, but she rarely developed a headache on her days off. About once per week she would have to leave work early because of a headache, but they had little impact on her personal life. She had tried multiple medications with little success. Mrs. Smith recognized stress as a contributor to her headaches and had tried a relaxation tape, which she did three times when her headache was particularly unrelenting. She stated that the relaxation exercises did not help so she threw the tape away. She works 10 hours, 6 days per week, and does not take a lunch break (eating at her desk). She exercises when she gets home, which reduces tension, but she is unable to exercise on days she has a headache. She has good social support, does not smoke or drink alcohol, denies illegal drug use, reports good adherence with her medications, and denies other notable triggers for the headaches.

Bridge to Intervention

An effective way to shift into the intervention is to summarize the assessment. As part of the summary, the BHC should provide a conceptualization of the problem, focused on the areas of potential intervention. Summarizing the things the patient has already done that have been helpful can provide a positive, encouraging quality to the intervention. In this way a consultant can build on or enhance what the patient is already doing. The bridge with Mrs. Smith was as follows:

> Okay, it sounds like you clearly see how stress is making your headaches worse. You recognize your primary stress is at work and the tension builds up through the workday. You exercise when you get home which relieves the tension, at least on days you don't have a headache, but you don't have any ways to reduce the tension during the workday or in the evening when you have a headache. Thus it sounds like it would be helpful to develop a way to more effectively manage work stress throughout the day so that you could reduce the tension that contributes to your headaches. Would you be interested in pursuing something like this?

Intervention

The intervention phase typically lasts about 10 minutes. The proposed intervention flows directly from the conceptualization provided to the patient and should be concrete and practical. The focus should be on effective symptoms reduction techniques when possible. When symptom reduction is not possible, the intervention becomes focused on improving functioning. The intervention needs to be supportable by the primary care provider in that it is both consistent with the medical interventions being conducted by the physician and easy for them to reinforce during follow-up medical visits.

If the patient has agreed with the BHC's conceptualization, the patient will usually be receptive to interventions that are clearly tied to this conceptualization. Therefore, it is important not to move into the intervention phase until the patient concurs with the conceptualization. Also, it is beneficial to provide a menu of options to address the identified problem. Finally, the patient can be asked if he or she has ideas of changes or strategies that would be helpful and doable. Having choices increases the patients' involvement in and control over the process and often increases their investment in the chosen intervention or helps them to be open to interventions in the future if they choose not to pursue change at the present time.

Mrs. Smith was offered the options of (a) doing nothing, (b) working together to develop a plan to take brief breaks at work or to take a short lunch break to go for a walk, or (c) learning a relaxation technique and how to use it appropriately. Relaxation training was recommended because she had not previously given it an adequate trial. When these recommendations were given, the BHC first said the following:

> You've tried a relaxation technique before, which we know helps the majority of headache patients; however, it sounds like you didn't receive good training or instruction on how to use the technique to reduce your headache. Therefore, it might be helpful to try relaxation again.

She opted to learn a relaxation technique. The consultant briefly explained how relaxation techniques work, introduced the key components of the diaphragmatic breathing technique, and taught her how to breathe with her diaphragm. The rest of the education and instruction was done through a detailed five-page handout covering the sympathetic and parasympathetic responses, the rational for the technique, instructions in all components of the technique, and instructions for practice and trouble-shooting.

Follow-Up Appointments

Follow-up appointments can range anywhere from 5 to 25 minutes, with the length of the session based on clinical necessity rather than the scheduled time allotted. Thus, even though the appointment slot was scheduled for 30 minutes when Mrs. Smith came in, she was doing much better and the consultant determined no further intervention was needed. The appointment ended after 7 minutes. Follow-up appointments can be scheduled every 15 to 30 minutes, depending on the skill level of the BHC and the needs of the population. Follow-up intervals are also based on clinical necessity rather than historical convention. For example, some patients may have an initial follow-up visit 3 to 4 weeks following their initial BHC encounter to allow sufficient time to practice a newly learned technique, whereas others may be seen within the same week or at their next scheduled medical visit. For some, follow-ups may only be done if a patient has problems using a newly learned skill or if it does not help. In such cases, the primary care provider may simply include a progress check at the next scheduled medical visit. The consultant typically involves the patient in collaboratively determining both the timing and method of follow-up. Schedulable appointment slots are available for about 75% of the consultant's time; the remaining

25% is typically left open for same-day walk-in appointments or to "catch up" on note writing, phone follow-ups with patients, and giving feedback to referring physicians.

Other than these differences, follow-up appointments are similar in structure to a typical cognitive–behavioral therapy (CBT) follow-up in specialty mental health treatment. Specifically, the appointment begins by assessing how the patient did on the tasks from the last appointment. The impact of these efforts on their symptoms is then determined and the need for additional skill training assessed. If there is a need for additional intervention, it will be conducted and the task for the next follow-up period discussed. Given the similarity with standard CBT, new consultants typically find the practice adjustments necessary for follow-ups much easier to make than those required for doing the initial assessments. Although structured similarly, these appointments are briefer because of the focus on the referring problem, the selection of "bite-sized" targets of intervention, and the use of "self-help" oriented educational materials.

FEEDBACK TO THE PRIMARY CARE PROVIDER

Communicating back to primary care providers is one of a BHC's highest priorities, even if it means handwritten notes or staying late to have a face-to-face conversation. Feedback is best given the same day the patient is seen. Ideally this feedback is given verbally and in person. When this is not possible, a phone call, voice mail message, secure e-mail, or a copy of the consultant's note will suffice.

The feedback given to Dr. Jones regarding Mrs. Smith was as follows:

> Dr. Jones, I just saw Mrs. Smith today. Her headaches do appear to have a significant stress component, primarily work stress. I trained her in a relaxation technique she can use at work and will follow up in 1 month. When you see her again, you might ask her how the practice of the technique is going and encourage her progress toward better management of her work stress. If she has problems or is not making progress, feel free to re-consult me and I can teach her some additional skills.

PITFALLS TO AVOID

Introduction Phase

A common pitfall for new consultants is to significantly abbreviate the introduction phase. The introduction script in Appendix 1.1 was carefully crafted to quickly but fully inform patients of key information related to their care. Therefore, we recommend new BHCs memorize this introduction or a similar script suitable for the health care setting of practice. The consultant should seek to present this information in its entirety, using a smooth, natural communication style.

Informing the patient about the length of the evaluation and that it will be problem focused are often neglected by new consultants. However, these parameters serve to decrease the likelihood of the patient bringing up minor concerns or issues peripheral to the chief complaint. Neglecting to provide this information often results in the patient spending several minutes discussing tangential information and the BHC losing valuable time as he or she tries to refocus the patient on the problem.

Assessment Phase

There are two primary pitfalls to avoid during the assessment phase. The first is a tendency to "go fishing" for problems. The role of the BHC is to expound and clarify the nature of the referral problem and develop recommendations to help the physician address the particular health issues pertinent to the consultation. As in all types of primary health care, although other problems are likely to exist, they are not the target of this visit or consultation. Primary care providers do not do a complete physical each time the patient comes with a new complaint. In primary care, the physician assesses and treats the factors causing the current symptoms, knowing that as new problems arise or surface, the patient will come back. By being present in primary care, the BHC will be available to assist with future problems as they arise. For example, in evaluating Mrs. Smith, the consultant did not inquire about neurovegitative signs of depression, suicidality, homicidality, or full mental health and physical health treatment history because no indicators of such were included in the consultation, revealed in the assessment, or observed in the patient.

The second primary pitfall is the tendency to move too fast to the intervention phase. Because of the time pressures in this environment, there is a natural tendency to start an intervention as soon as any problem that the BHC has an intervention for is identified. This is the opposite of the first pitfall, in that in this case the consultant fails to gather enough information. For example, as soon as the he or she heard Mrs. Smith acknowledge "stress," the consultant might quickly recommend training in a brief relaxation technique. When this happens, the BHC typically meets resistance from the patient. Even if the consultant has successfully identified the issue, completing the assessment phase enables a more effective bridge to be made to the intervention. Therefore, it is best to complete an adequate, yet focused, assessment before identifying the intervention target.

Intervention Phase

Cognitive–behavioral therapists often have an extensive array of hand-outs that they will bring into the primary care setting. However, given the short appointment times in primary care, more extensive handouts than the ones typically used in specialty mental health practice are useful. In traditional mental health care, a full 45 to 50 minutes is usually available to do the intervention. Thus the therapist can take the time to explain, demonstrate, or practice whatever is being trained in that session. As a consequence, handouts are usually brief and focused on providing reminders of what was trained. In contrast, handouts used in the primary care setting are more similar to traditional self-help literature. Specifically, they should be concise but provide all the details necessary for patients to do it on their own. In the appointment, especially the initial one, the consultant will often only have time to introduce the technique and possibly discuss/demonstrate a few key points. Most of the teaching will be done through the handout.

Similarly, new consultants often tend to limit interventions to those they have handouts about. However, not all interventions require handouts. For example, if Mrs. Smith opted to work on increasing breaks at work and taking a walk at lunch, the consultant would work with her to develop a specific plan to accomplish this goal. In these cases, the BHC will often write down the plan or have the patient write it down. In our practice, we have developed "behavioral prescription" pads in which we record the plan and follow-up appointment time and give it to the patient.

Another pitfall is for the consultant to be overly conservative about who can be managed at the primary care level. One of the goals of the initial consultation is to determine the likelihood that the patient's behav-ioral health needs can be supported in primary care. In general the BHC is available to see any patient for an initial consultation, unless the initial discussion with the physician indicates the patient's needs clearly exceed the scope of care for consultation. If the initial assessment reveals a serious psychiatric disorder, the medical provider should be given the recommenda-tion to refer directly to specialty mental health services. For patients in crisis, the BHC should initially take the person off the physician's hands, thereby allowing the physician to stay on schedule. If the crisis cannot be quickly managed in the clinic or if the patient is imminently suicidal and thus beyond the scope of the consultation service, an immediate referral to a specialty mental health service should be recommended. The BHC can help facilitate the transfer. Aside from these situations, the primary indicator for a recommendation to specialty mental health care is the patient's failure to respond to a reasonable collaborative treatment effort between the consul-tant and physician. Mrs. Smith did not have a serious psychiatric disorder and was not in crisis; therefore, no referral was recommended. However, if after attempting these recommendations, her headaches were not significantly improved, the consultant would likely recommend a referral to a specialty clinic that would conduct a full evaluation and provide a more intensive regime of CBT for headaches.

Follow-Up Phase

A common pitfall in the follow-up phase is having too brief of an interval between appointments and scheduling follow-ups when unnecessary. The default follow-up time in specialty mental health care is typically 1 week. In contrast, the BHC follow-up default is approximately 1 month, with modification based on clinical need. Thus some patients may come back in a week or less, some in 3 months or more. The benefits of the delayed follow-up include (a) more time for the patient to have practiced and benefited from the intervention; (b) the patient develops a greater sense of responsibility for carrying out the intervention; and (c) appointment availability is maintained for the entire population without compromising the clinical care provided to each individual patient. Consultant follow-ups are typically used for patients with whom additional interventions are planned when the accountability provided through a follow-up is expected to help the patient maintain behavior change motivation, when it is expected the patient will encounter problems in implementation, when it will save the physician time, or when the patient prefers it.

The BHC will sometimes do an intervention and not schedule a follow-up, similar to when a patient sees his or her medical provider, is given a medication and told to come back if he or she does not get better. If the consultant working with Mrs. Smith assessed that she had a high motivation level, was responsive to the instruction in the initial appointment, and seemed like she managed other aspects of her life well, the BHC might conclude it would be reasonable to have Mrs. Smith come back only if she had trouble learning the technique or if it was not helpful but would otherwise follow-up with her doctor at the planned 3-month follow-up visit. Dr. Jones could reconsult if Mrs. Smith needed further assistance. However, in discussing follow-up options with Mrs. Smith, if she indicated it would help her to follow up earlier, the consultant would usually agree to follow-up with her in 1 month rather than recommend Dr. Jones use one of her appointments to schedule an additional follow-up, thereby saving the physician an appointment slot.

Physician Feedback

Case presentations in the mental health field tend to be in-depth (i.e., full history, psychosocial factors, etc.). However, primary care providers are busy and the consultant typically is catching providers between patients. Therefore, feedback should be brief, usually a minute or less, concise, free of psychological jargon, and limited to essential information. If the BHC presented cases in the style typically done in a specialty mental health setting the provider would begin avoiding the consultant because he or she would take up too much time. In general, the BHC should seek to mimic the way physicians present cases to each other. Key feedback to providers includes a statement of the problem, the intervention conducted by the consultant, and recommendations for the physician. The recommendations the consultant gives to the provider should be specific, behavioral in nature, and doable in 1 to 2 minutes during the provider's follow-up with the patient.

CONCLUSION

Integration of behavioral health providers into primary care offers an incredible opportunity to identify and intervene with problems before they develop into significant pathology, to reach people with effective treatments who would not otherwise seek out mental health treatment, to increase access through more efficient use of providers, and to enhance the behavioral health care that is already being provided by primary care providers. In the consultation model, clinical services mirror those delivered by the physician, enabling true integration into the primary care clinic. However, this requires BHCs to adapt their service delivery methods to the rapid, problem-focused primary care environment. Because primary care based behavioral health consultation differs substantially from traditional specialty mental health care, an adaptation of existing skills and the development of new skills requires time and training.

As this model has been implemented throughout the Air Force Medical Service, it is apparent that reading about the model is not sufficient. Obtaining clinical training is critical to becoming a BHC and especially to developing the understanding and skills necessary to maximize the effectiveness of the consultative model of integration. As previously mentioned, the model relies heavily on CBT. Thus solid CBT skills are necessary to function effectively in this model, but they alone are not sufficient. Even established CBT providers require practice at being flexible as they apply existing clinical skills in new and challenging ways. For providers not yet trained in CBT, extensive behavioral training is necessary as well as learning how to use these newly developed skills in the primary care clinic. In conclusion, although a foundation is presented, we strongly recommend organizations that already have or that are seeking to implement a model of integrated care invest in a didactic and clinical training program for their providers.

APPENDIX 1.1
SAMPLE SCRIPT OF BEHAVIORAL HEALTH CONSULTANT INTRODUCTION (U.S. AIR FORCE MEDICAL OPERATIONS AGENCY, POPULATION HEALTH DIVISION 2002)

Hello, my name is _____. Before we get going today, let me explain to you a bit about who I am and what I do here.

I'm a behavioral health consultant for the clinic and a psychologist by training. I work with the medical providers here in situations where good health care involves paying attention not only to physical health, but also to emotional and behavioral health and how these things interact with each other. Whenever a provider is concerned about any of these things, they can call me in as a consultant. As a consultant, I help you and your provider better address things that are affecting your health or sense of well-being. To do this, I want to spend about 20 minutes with you to get a quick snap shot picture of what's going on in your life—what's working well and what's not working so well. Then, we'll take this information and come up with some recommendations that might help and that are doable for you.

The recommendations might be things you begin to do differently or they might include things we can do differently here at the clinic. Often they will involve some self-help materials. Additionally, we may decide it would help to have you come back to see me a couple of times if we think it would get some positive momentum going on specific skills. Sometimes, we decide that people might benefit from more intensive specialty services. If that were the case, I'd make that recommendation to your provider and help them arrange the referral.

After we're done today, I'll go over with your provider the recommendations we came up with so they can be incorporated in your overall health care plan. Also, I'll write a note in your medical record so in case you see other providers they can follow up on how the plan is going.

Finally, I want you to be aware that I have the same reporting requirements to ensure your and other's safety as other providers in this clinic.

Do you have any questions about this before we begin?

REFERENCES

Balestrieri, M., Williams, P., & Wilkinson, G. (1988). Specialist mental health treatment in general practice: A meta-analysis. *Psychological Medicine, 18,* 711–717.

Bower, P., Richards, D., & Lovell, K. (2001). The clinical and cost-effectiveness of self-help treatments for anxiety and depressive disorders in primary care: A systematic review. *British Journal of General Practice, 51,* 838–845.

Brown, C., & Schulberg, H. C. (1995). The efficacy of psychosocial treatments in primary care: A review of randomized clinical trials. *General Hospital Psychiatry, 17,* 414–424.

Corney, R. H. (1986). Marriage guidance counseling in general practice. *Journal of the Royal College of General Practitioners, 36,* 424–426.

deGruy, F. (1996). Defining primary care. In M. S. Donaldson, K. D. Yordy, K. N. Lohr, & N. A. Vanselow (Eds.), *Primary care: America's health in a new era. Report of a study by a committee of the Institute of Medicine, Division of Health Care Services* (pp. 27–51). Washington, DC: National Academy Press.

Katon, W., Robinson, P., Von Korff, M., Lin, E., Bush, T., Ludman, E., et al. (1996). A multifaceted intervention to improve treatment of depression in primary care. *Archives of General Psychiatry, 53,* 924–932.

Katon, W., Von Korff, M., Lin, E., Walker, E., Simon, G., Bush, T., et al. (1995). Collaborative management to achieve treatment guidelines: Impact on depression in primary care. *Journal of the American Medical Association, 273,* 1026–1031.

Lorig, K. R., Sobel, D. S., Stewart, A. L., Brown, B. W., Bandura, A., Ritter, P., et al. (1999). Evidence suggesting that a chronic disease self-management program can improve health status while reducing hospitalization: A randomized trial. *Medical Care, 37*(1), 5–14.

Pignone, M. P., Gaynes, B. N., Rushton, J. L., Burchell, C. M., Orleans, C. T., Mulrow, C. D., et al. (2002). Screening for depression in adults: A summary of the evidence for the U.S. Preventive Services Task Force. *Annals of Internal Medicine, 136,* 765–776.

Population Health Support Division (PHSD). (2002). *Primary behavioral health care services: Practice manual version 2.0.* San Antonio, TX: Air Force Medical Operations Agency, U.S. Air Force.

Runyan, C. N., Fonseca, V. P., & Hunter, C. (2003). Integrating consultative behavioral healthcare into the Air Force medical system. In N. A. Cummings, W. T. O'Donohue, & K. E. Ferguson (Eds.), *Behavioral health as primary care: Beyond efficacy to effectiveness* (pp. 145–164). Reno, NV: Context Press.

Runyan, C. N., Fonseca, V. P., Meyer, J. G., Oordt, M. S., & Talcott, G. W. (2003). A novel approach for mental health disease management: The Air Force Medical Service's interdisciplinary model. *Disease Management, 6,* 179–188.

Schoenbaum, M., Unutzer, J., Sherbourne, C., Duan, N., Rubenstein, L. V., Miranda, J., et al. (2001). Cost-effectiveness of practice-initiated quality improvement for depression: Results of a randomized controlled trial. *Journal of the American Medical Association, 286,* 1325–1330.

Simon, G. E., & Von Korff, M. (1995). Recognition, management, and outcomes of depression in primary care. *Archives of Family Medicine, 4,* 99–105.

Unutzer, J., Katon, W., Callahan, C. M., Williams, J. W., Jr., Hunkeler, E., Harpole, L., et al. (2002). Improving mood-promoting access to collaborative treatment. Collaborative care management of late-life depression in the primary care setting: A randomized controlled trial. *Journal of the American Medical Association, 288,* 2836–2845.

U.S. Preventive Services Task Force. (2002). Screening for depression: Recommendations and rationale. *Annals of Internal Medicine, 136,* 760–764.

Von Korff, M., Katon, W., Bush, T., Lin, E., Simon, G. E., Saunders, K., et al. (1998). Treatment costs, cost offset and cost-effectiveness of collaborative management of depression. *Psychosomatic Medicine, 60,* 143–149.

2

ASSESSING THE PATIENT'S NEED FOR MEDICAL EVALUATION: A PSYCHOLOGIST'S GUIDE

JOHN D. ROBINSON AND LARRY C. JAMES

Practicing in a medical or primary care setting provides a tremendous opportunity for psychologists to reduce psychological symptoms and hospital costs. Sweet, Rozensky, and Tovian (1991); Cummings (1991); Cummings, Cummings, and Johnson (1997); and Belar and Deardorff (1995); as well as others (Kelleher, Talcott, Haddock, & Freeman, 1996; Young, Bradley, & Turner, 1995) have described well how psychological interventions can serve to assist patients and control costs. Not only do they provide a detailed discussion of psychological interventions in medical settings, but these researchers also underscore the close link between physical disease and mental health.

Psychologists are well aware of the close link between physical disease and mental health. Therefore, it is vital that psychologists in health and in primary care settings be able to make a gross distinction between physical illnesses that may have a psychological component and those that are entirely psychological in nature. This can be done in the initial contact with the patient. For psychologists to check for these possible medical conditions, it is necessary to provide them with a simple template to assist in the assessment of physical disorders. A referral to a physician can be made with a better understanding of the physical condition and the treatment that is necessary for the health of the patient. Psychologists in primary settings should have a good working relationship with a physician who can provide medical consultation when needed. There are several medical conditions that may present initially as psychological disorders. Assessment and treatment of these physical–medical disorders is vital.

Taylor (1990) and Morrison (1997) conservatively estimate that at least 10% of psychological symptoms are caused by medical or physical conditions. Barnes and Galton (1976); Folen, Kellar, James, Peterson, and Porter (1998); and James and Folen (in press) have offered data and clinical information to highlight how diseases may cause psychological symptoms. Barnes and Galton (1976) discuss in detail the role hypothyroidism plays in symptoms associated with depression, energy level/fatigue, obesity, and cardiovascular symptoms, to name a few. Morrison (1997), in his book *When Psychological Symptoms Mask Medical Disorders*, provides case illustrations. Morrison described how medical conditions such as anemia, mitral valve prolapse, thiamin deficiency, infections, lupus, tumors, and other disorders can be missed because psychological disorders mask or dominate the presentation of the disorder. In addition, Haley et al. (1998) asserted that many patients seen in primary settings really are physically ill. The authors add that it is important for psychologists to understand how the patient's physical disease may affect the psychological symptoms and that it would serve one well to have a good understanding of the patient's medical illness and condition.

Being cognizant of the fact that most graduate programs in clinical and professional psychology do not provide instruction on how to conduct medical histories, the MINTS model (discussed later in the chapter) can be used as a guide to understand the connection between a patient's medical condition and the presenting psychological symptoms. A thorough understanding of this will allow the attending psychologist to obtain the necessary information to make the appropriate medical referral so that the patient may receive adequate and appropriate medical treatment that could be life saving.

THE MINTS MODEL

The acronym MINTS draws attention to five words or phrases that remind the reader of terms central to asking the appropriate questions and getting the necessary information while conducting a psychological examination in a medical setting: *m*etabolic, *i*nfections, *n*eoplasts, *t*rauma, and psychological. All too often, psychologists may ask only cursory questions related to the patient's disease or medical condition, assuming that a physician has addressed these. This is not always the case because psychologists can frequently be the patient's first contact, especially if the patient is displaying "psychological" symptoms. As a result, for example, a connection between the patient's depression and an actual medical disease process can be missed. Thus, the patient can continue to deteriorate. A preliminary review of the patient's medical systems with the MINTS acronym in mind will assist the examiner in ascertaining the cause of the psychological sequealae.

Metabolic Abnormalities

Disorders of metabolism can cause a variety of medical disorders that can have a psychological appearance. Some of these are end stage organ disease, various forms of diabetes, uremia, thyroid disorders, hypoxia, hyper/hypoglycemia, alcohol and drug intoxication, encephalopathy, anemia, poisons, and so forth. These involve chemical and cellular changes that interfere with the body's ability to produce energy, utilize food, and eliminate waste products. Disorders such as electrolyte imbalances, kidney and liver disease, certain blood disorders (anemia), dehydration, difficulty utilizing oxygen (e.g., anoxia, hypoxia, etc.) or perhaps endocrine disorders (e.g., diabetes, hypothyroidism, etc.) can alter the body's ability to function, and the first signs can mimic symptoms of a psychological disorder. Patients who present with fatigue, lightheadedness, or shortness of breath, for example, may actually have an electrolyte imbalance, diabetes, or a common anemia. These patients may present to the health care professional as being anxious or in a panic state that would cause them to be referred to a psychologist for initial treatment.

Case 1

Jay is a 35-year-old single, Black, male professional. He reported to the mental health clinic because friends told him that he must be depressed. He could not understand that, in spite of doing well at his engineering job, positive dating relationship, and healthy family relations, he began to sleep 14 hours a day. This was an abrupt change for him; he was accustomed to 5 hours of sleep per day. He described his sleep as nonrestorative, no matter how much he slept. He remained fatigued. Jay began to feel tired during the day and had difficulty remaining awake at work. He reported that his thoughts were slow and he had trouble concentrating on his job.

After 3 months of psychotherapy, his "depressive symptoms" did not improve. Jay began to notice daily rectal bleeding but took no action. After 3 months, he mentioned it to his psychologist because he began to experience lightheadedness when he either exercised or walked up-stairs. His psychologist referred him to his family physician immediately. Bleeding hemorrhoids were discovered and his red blood cell count, hemoglobin, and hematocrit were very low. His physician treated Jay medically and surgically and his presenting psychological symptoms disappeared.

Jay's case provides an example of how a patient's mental status can be affected by changes in physical health. Questions associated with a history of rectal bleeding or abnormal menstrual cycles or discharges (for female patients) would assist the examiner in identifying causes for an abrupt change in mental status. This is frequently seen in medically ill and chronically ill patients. Hypomagnesaemia, hepatic encephalopathy, and uremia are frequently seen in organ transplant patients. Toxicity to medications often presents with signs of confusion, anxiety, delirium, depression, and psycho-logical symptoms. Psychologists who work with pilots or patients who fly frequently often see signs of confusion, disorientation, and so forth, which may be signs of hypoxia as a result of altitude sickness. Patients who appear in a panic, anxious, or depressed may be suffering from a thyroid disorder (hypothyroidism or hyperthyroidism). When a psychological etiology is not clear, or a patient does not respond to psychological treatment, it is always wise to get a medical consultation. The etiology of the patient's psychological disorder may in fact be physiological.

Infections

Some of the leading causes of disordered mental status are infectious processes. HIV/AIDS dementia is commonly seen in clinics and hospitals. Patients with abscesses (abdominal, brain, head–neck, pancreatic, spinal cord, etc.) may present with signs of dementia, delirium, anxiety, agitation, and so forth. Patients who are hypoxic as a result of a disease process, such as pneumonia, often present in an agitated state. Seldom do we see cases of tertiary syphilis in the United States. However, in some parts of America and in other countries, these patients are usually in psychiatric facilities and present as demented. Rabies is seen in rural areas and patients present as highly agitated and combative, frequently the same as patients with an acute psychotic episode. Patients who are encephalopathic can appear agitated, demented, confused, and so forth.

Infections can be of several different forms. A patient may have an abscess, a viral infection, pneumonia, a cytomegalovirus (CMV) infection, or numerous other infections that may cause disorientation, confusion, severe fatigue, or other physical symptoms that mimic a psychological change in mental status. A case will provide an example of how an infection can complicate psychological treatment and evaluation.

Case 2

Jimmy is an 18-year-old college freshman football player at a local
university. He was doing well socially, academically, and at football
practice. Over the weekend he began to feel ill. His roommates noticed
that he was agitated and restless. Jimmy began to complain of difficulty
breathing and his roommates decided to take him to the local hospital
emergency room. By the time he got there, he was very agitated and
somewhat combative. The emergency room personnel noticed that he
was a well-muscled young man who was highly agitated and combative,
thus, probably difficult to handle. They immediately signaled for the
health psychologist on call to see this young man and possibly admit
him for observation and treatment on the inpatient psychiatry unit.
When the psychologist came to the ER to evaluate Jimmy, he noticed
that he was agitated, combative, and threatening. The psychologist also
noticed that Jimmy was gasping for air and breathing heavily. On closer
observation, the psychologist noticed that the mucosa in Jimmy's mouth
was slightly blue, which could be a definite sign of oxygen deprivation.
Because of this, he alerted the emergency room personnel, who re-
strained Jimmy so they could give him oxygen. Chest x-rays revealed
that Jimmy had bilateral pneumonia that was causing him to have
difficulty breathing, thus becoming hypoxic. Within minutes of receiving oxygen supplementation, Jimmy became calm, settled down, and
responded to antibiotic treatment.

As this case illustrates, patients may present with psychological symptoms that may mask physiological disorders. Sometimes the patient may be
at high risk for medical–health complications if he or she is not assessed
properly when his or her behavior or change in "normal" mental status is
assumed to be of a psychological origin. Abrupt changes in mental status
or behavior without psychosocial stressors may be indicative of underlying
medical etiology.

Neoplasts

Tumors or "new growths" can produce noticeable changes in behavior
and mental status, especially when located in the cerebral or pancreatic
areas. Renal and hepatic tumors or cancers frequently cause these changes.
Patients may present initially with fatigue, which can be misinterpreted as
depression. Frequently psychological symptoms of tumors present before
overt physical symptoms. This is especially true of adenocarcinoma at the
head of the pancreas. Early physical diagnosis is difficult, and often patients
with these tumors present with what appears to be depression that is not
responsive to psychotherapy or psychotropic medications. Cancer of the liver
(hepatoma or hepatocellular carcinoma) may cause mental status changes in

patients. These patients may also present with physical symptoms that are often misdiagnosed as psychophysiological or psychosomatic by mental health professionals.

Trauma

Blunt traumas to the head come to mind in the context of illness that could manifest itself as "psychological." Postconcussion syndrome can be a perplexing condition. A patient may experience a mild head injury and physical diagnostic procedures may be within normal limits, yet the patient may present with unusual behaviors. These can include vision difficulties, memory deficits, and motoric disorders. Blunt traumas to internal organs can be more subtle. Bruises to the kidneys or liver can affect the metabolic process and, thus, affect a patient's mental status.

Psychological

After the psychologist is sure that all of the physical aspects of the evaluation have been performed and the patient has no physiological reasons for the change in behavior or mental status, then it is safe to assume that this change is a result of a psychological reason. At that point, we can perform the necessary psychodiagnostic assessment needed to obtain a differential diagnosis.

When psychological symptoms do not improve within a reasonable time frame, it would be prudent to seek medical consultation for the patient. Once the patient is medically cleared, then it may be safer to assume that the psychological symptoms are not driven by a medical disease.

INTEGRATING MINTS INTO THE INTERVIEW

The examining psychologist should remain cognizant of the MINTS concept when conducting a psychological evaluation. Each component of MINTS should be reviewed with the patient and tailored to specific questions. It is always wise to have a patient medically cleared before embarking on a course of psychological treatment. The following questions will provide assistance for integrating MINTS into the interview. They may serve as a guide to uncovering the link between the patient's disease process and psychological symptoms.

1. *When was the last time you were well and without symptoms?*
   This will serve as a marker and can provide significant information about the connection between the current symptoms, stressors, and a medical condition.

2. *Do you have a family history of a medical disorder?* Family histories of medical problems become important in regard to conditions such as diabetes, hypertension, cancer, psychological disorders, and so forth. Hereditary disorders of the thyroid may be responsible for family histories of obesity or depression. Symptoms of a hyperactive thyroid may present as a panic disorder, chest palpitations, cardiac disorders, or anxiety symptoms.

3. *Have you had a change in weight (gain or loss) within the past year that is not due to diet?* When patients abruptly gain or lose weight (without being on a diet) this can be a sure sign of a physical disorder requiring medical attention.

4. *Are you currently taking any medications?* This question should also include over-the-counter medications as well as vitamins and food–dietary supplements. The presenting symptoms may be related to a change in medications, a dosage that is inappropriate, or a combination of medication side effects. This also gives the psychologist an opportunity to discuss any medical conditions for which the patient is being treated. One should inquire about the exact names of prescription medications, dosage, and length of treatment.

5. *When was the last time you had a physical examination?* Reasons for this question may appear obvious, but it is often overlooked and should be addressed with all patients. If there were significant physical–medical findings, the psychologist should be aware of these and any possible psychological sequela. If a patient has not had a physical examination in more than a year, it would be prudent to refer the patient for a complete medical evaluation.

6. *Can you tell me about your medical condition?* If a physician refers a patient, ask questions about the medical condition for which the patient saw the physician. Having an understanding of the symptom cluster associated with a disease or medication side effect related to the patient's medication can aid in therapy. The average physician spends about 15 minutes with each patient. Thus, patients frequently leave the physician's office with unanswered questions. The more the psychologist learns about a patient's medical condition and that patient's understanding of his or her medical condition, the more one will be able to explain symptoms and side effects to the patient.

7. *Do you have a history of head trauma or loss of consciousness?* Many patients have domestic accidents such as falling off of roofs, falling down stairs, or minor accidents. They do not see the physical results of the injury and assume that there is

none. Head trauma or trauma to an internal organ may be the cause of many symptoms that appear to be psychological.

8. *Can you tell me how you are sleeping?* Chronic sleep loss is related to mood changes, disorientation, fatigue, and other symptoms. If psychosocial stressors cannot be identified in the interview, the underlying cause for a sleep disturbance takes on greater importance.

9. *How is your appetite?* If a patient is not on a planned diet and has a sudden loss of appetite and weight loss, this should be explored in detail. Eating patterns should be discussed to assess the possibility of an eating disorder. Fluid intake should also be discussed because dehydration, hence electrolyte imbalance, can precipitate visual hallucinations, disorientation, delirium, and fatigue.

CONCLUSION

By asking these questions, a psychologist can better assess the overall functioning of the patient to provide optimal care. Collaboration and consultation with other health professionals is essential when the etiology of a disorder is not clear and when medical care is needed.

If any of these physical conditions are present or if the psychologist feels that the patient could benefit for a complete physical assessment, a referral to a properly trained physician should be done. It is important that the psychologist has a good working relationship with the physician to provide the best care to the patient. If the psychologist is aware of some of the physical–medical conditions that may present as psychological conditions, she or he will be able to communicate this to his or her medical colleagues to ensure proper care. For this care to be given, the psychologist must rule out any medical conditions that may complicate the psychological treatment.

REFERENCES

Barnes, B., & Galton, L. (1976). *Hypothyroidism: The unsuspected illness.* New York: Harper & Row.

Belar, C., & Deardorff, W. (1995). *Clinical health psychology in medical settings: A practitioner's guidebook.* Washington, DC: American Psychological Association.

Cummings, N. (1991). Arguments for the financial efficacy of financial services in health care settings. In J. Sweet, R. Rozensky, & S. Tovian (Eds.), *Handbook of clinical psychology in medical settings* (pp. 113–126). New York: Plenum Press.

Cummings, N., Cummings, J., & Johnson, J. (1997). *Behavioral health in primary care: A guide for clinical integration.* Madison, CT: Psychosocial Press.

Folen, R., Kellar, M., James, L., Peterson, D., & Porter, R. (1998). Expanding the scope of clinical practice: The physical examination. *Professional Psychology: Research and Practice, 29,* 155–159.

Haley, W., McDaniel, S., Bray, J., Frank, R., Heldring, M., Johnson, S., et al. (1998). Psychological practice in primary care settings: Practical tips for clinicians. *Professional Psychology: Research and Practice, 29,* 237–244.

James, L., & Folen, R. (in press). *Training health psychologists to be primary care managers.* Washington, DC: American Psychological Association.

Kelleher, W., Talcott, G., Haddock, K., & Freeman, R. (1996). Military psychology in the age of managed care: The Wilford hall model. *Applied and Preventive Psychology, 5,* 101–110.

Morrison, J. (1997). *When psychological problems mask medical disorders.* New York: Guilford Press.

Sweet, J., Rozensky, R., & Tovian, S. (Eds.). (1991). *Handbook of clinical psychology in medical settings.* New York: Plenum Press.

Taylor, R. (1990). *Distinguishing psychological from organic disorders: Screening for psychological masquerade.* New York: Springer.

Young, L., Bradley, L., & Turner, R. (1995). Decreases in health care resource utilization in patients with rheumatoid arthritis following a cognitive behavioral intervention. *Biofeedback and Self-Regulation, 20,* 259–268.

II

TREATMENT APPLICATIONS: ADULT INTERVENTIONS

3

MULTIDISCIPLINARY APPROACHES TO PAIN MANAGEMENT IN PRIMARY CARE SETTINGS

JOHN D. OTIS, M. CARRINGTON REID, AND ROBERT D. KERNS

Primary care strives to be an accessible service in which effective early intervention and continuity of care is provided. It aspires to address patients' most common health complaints and to manage specialty care in a responsible and cost-effective manner. Of all problems reported by primary care patients, pain is one of the most common complaints made to primary care providers (Gureje, Von Korff, Simon, & Gater, 1998; Mantyselka et al., 2001), accounting for significant suffering on the part of patients and more than $100 billion in lost productivity and disability per year (*NIH Guide*, 1998). Although most acute pain episodes resolve on their own without the need for intervention, there is a small percentage of patients for whom pain persists or reoccurs on an intermittent basis. Among these individuals, pain-related disability and emotional distress may develop, adding to the

This chapter was authored or coauthored by an employee of the United States government as part of official duty and is considered to be in the public domain. Any views expressed herein do not necessarily represent the views of the United States government, and the author's participation in the work is not meant to serve as an official endorsement.

complexity of the problem and the challenge to primary care providers in their efforts to reduce pain and suffering.

Over the past 25 years, the development of a greater understanding of the functional, psychological, and social problems commonly associated with chronic pain has had a significant impact on the field of pain and the delivery of treatment. Long aware that some of their chronic pain patients were also depressed, out of shape, in financial crisis, or abusing medications, purely medical and unidimensional approaches to pain management (e.g., sole reliance on the use of analgesic medications) have increasingly been called into question.

Health care providers now more commonly make use of a range of health care disciplines for assistance in managing these problems. Integrative, multimodality programs that address the complexity of problems commonly associated with the chronic pain experience have been developed to provide a more sophisticated and organized approach to pain management. These programs typically involve several health care disciplines (e.g., physical therapy, occupational therapy, nursing, anesthesiology, and psychology) in an integrative assessment and treatment approach for pain, while also fostering interdisciplinary research and training. The cost effectiveness of multidisciplinary approaches for chronic pain management has been convincingly documented (Flor, Fydrich, & Turk, 1992; Turk, 1996).

Psychological interventions are increasingly offered as a component of these multidisciplinary efforts. One particularly common psychological approach is cognitive–behavior therapy (CBT; Turk, Meichenbaum, & Genest, 1983). This approach targets patients' maladaptive cognitive and behavioral coping and promotes the adoption of perceptions of enhanced personal control related to the pain condition and an adaptive and active problem-solving approach to pain management. The efficacy of CBT has been reliably demonstrated (Morley, Eccleston, & Williams, 1999). Unfortunately, despite the availability of CBT for chronic pain, many patients fail to be successfully engaged in these treatments, drop out prematurely or fail to adhere to therapist recommendations, or fail to maintain treatment gains following the completion of treatment (Turk & Rudy, 1991). Efforts to enhance patients' interest and motivation for participating in multidisciplinary efforts that incorporate CBT through improved integration of these approaches in the primary care setting represents a potentially important strategy for improving outcomes for a larger proportion of patients.

The primary aim of this chapter is to describe potential approaches for promoting the integration of multidisciplinary chronic pain management in the primary care setting. The specific roles of the clinical health psychologist are highlighted in several of these integration approaches, including the ways in which a clinical health psychologist might function in a stepped care model to managing pain in the primary care setting and the roles a clinical health psychologist might take on in a comprehensive pain management center. In addition, a specific integration model currently under investigation by a clinical research group overseen by the authors is described in detail. PRIME-Cognitive–Behavioral Therapy (PRIME-CBT) seeks to enhance the successful engagement and full participation of patients in CBT, within the context of a multidisciplinary clinical, research, and training program for chronic pain, to promote improved outcomes. The chapter closes with a brief discussion of future directions for theory building and research.

THE PRIMARY CARE PROVIDER PERSPECTIVE

Chronic pain can be difficult for primary care providers to manage within the limitations of the primary care setting. Given that patients with chronic pain often have comorbid medical conditions that must be addressed and monitored, there is often insufficient time during a routine medical appointment for providers to rule out disease as a cause of pain, provide patient education, and create a treatment plan for pain. Also, the reliance by providers on a medical model (e.g., medications or standard medical interventions alone) for the treatment of chronic pain may not be appropriate or sufficient, because there are often psychosocial factors that contribute to the experience of pain. In addition, extensive use of medical diagnostic tests and procedures and a sole reliance on medical interventions may contribute to a patient's belief that a medical cure for his or her pain exists, making the individual less likely to take personal responsibility for pain management and more reliant on his or her provider. When a patient's expectations for a cure are not met, anger, frustration, and depressive symptoms often follow. The lack of clear and consistent guidelines for chronic pain management, the relative lack of provider education and clinical expertise in managing pain, and a range of additional provider, patient, and health care system barriers represent significant challenges to providers in their efforts to manage this complex problem.

Analgesic medications are by far the most common treatments recommended for chronic pain in the primary care setting. A careful history and physical examination are mandatory to define, if possible, the underlying etiology of a patient's pain condition. Pain is most often classified as either nociceptive (i.e., pain that results from stimulation of peripheral nerve receptors such as from tissue inflammation) or neuropathic (i.e., pain that occurs as a result of abnormal processing of peripheral or central nerve signals such as postherpeutic neuralgia) in origin. Certain analgesic medications are more effective for nociceptive pain (e.g., nonsteroidal anti-inflammatory agents), whereas other medications (e.g., tricyclic antidepressants, anticonvulsants) appear to be more effective for pain of neuropathic origin. A growing array of analgesic and adjunctive medications is available for pain management, and guidelines for the use of pharmaceuticals in managing specific pain disorders (e.g., sickle cell pain, arthritis) are increasingly available.

Opioid medications are sometimes used to treat pain that does not respond to first-line medications. Of note, the use of opioid medications for the treatment of chronic pain remains controversial, largely because the safety and efficacy of this treatment approach have not been well established. Patient and provider concerns about these medications represent additional barriers to their effective use. If a trial of an opioid medication is planned, a patient's concern about the possibility of addiction to the drug often represents a substantial barrier to compliance and should also be discussed. Primary care providers' concerns about opioid use often focus on the possibility of patient misuse of these medications (e.g., diversion or overuse). In a recent study of chronic pain patients receiving long-term opioid therapy in two primary care settings, an earlier history of substance abuse (either alcohol or drugs) was found to be a strong and independent factor associated with an increased likelihood of misusing opioid medications, whereas increasing patient age was found to be associated with a lower likelihood of misusing opioid analgesic medications (Reid et al., 2002).

Several strategies for the effective and safe use of opioid medications for chronic pain have been promulgated. Round-the-clock dosing and the use of extended release or long-acting preparations have been encouraged. Prescribing short-acting opioids on an as-needed basis for break-through pain is also advocated for optimal pain management. Specific attention to common side effects of opioids, especially constipation, is another important strategy. Routine and random toxicology screens to confirm use of the medications or to identify other illicit substance use are also recommended. Opioid agreements—which are written agreements between patients and providers that specify the manner in which patients will receive opioid medications (e.g., prescriptions filled by only one provider) and the terms under which the medication will be promptly discontinued (e.g., reports of lost or stolen medications)—may help to reduce the risk for opioid analgesic misuse in the primary care setting (Oliver & Lee, 2003; Veterans Health Administration, 2001).

A frank discussion regarding patient expectations, treatment goals, as well as the potential adverse side effects of an analgesic medication is required before instituting any therapeutic trial of a pain medication. Potential barriers to compliance should also be explored with the patient before undertaking such a trial, including drug costs, unrealistic patient expectations regarding the ability of an analgesic medication to totally eradicate all pain, as well as the potential for interactions with other drugs.

Consultation with specialists is another option for primary care providers in their efforts to address patients' pain concerns. Referral for physical or occupational therapy represents the second most common option used by primary care providers. Numerous rehabilitation therapy modalities are often used, including education regarding body mechanics and energy conservation, manipulation, transcutaneous electrical nerve stimulation, and ultrasound, among others. Graded physical exercise, sometimes including aerobic conditioning, is also frequently recommended. Exercise approaches, however, require active participation of the patient and a commitment to maintain exercise on a long-term basis to promote reconditioning, improved functioning, and reduced pain. Unfortunately, many patients fail to adopt a lifestyle that incorporates regular exercise, often because of experiences of pain exacerbation that is attributed to the exercise.

The availability of medical pain specialists for consultation is also increasingly common. The pain specialist may assist with differential diagnosis of the underlying painful medical condition, provide expert pharmacological advice, and discuss the many complex issues of pain management. Referral to other medical and surgical specialists for addressing specific painful conditions is also routine.

Relatively new to the primary care providers' armamentarium is the availability of specialized psychological treatment services designed to promote the use of adaptive pain coping strategies (e.g., activity–rest cycling and pacing, avoiding pain-contingent rest, use of mental relaxation strategies). As described later, models for the integration of these services within the primary care setting are being developed and implemented in efforts to more directly support the primary care providers' efforts at addressing the complexity of psychological and social concomitants of the experience of chronic pain.

Referral to a multidisciplinary pain management program that incorporates the services of several of these specialists is also sometimes available. As already noted, these programs provide a comprehensive assessment that leads to an integrative plan for treatment and the delivery of the treatment in a coordinated and systematic manner that is difficult (if not impossible) to deliver in the primary care setting. These programs commonly emphasize integrating sophisticated medical, rehabilitation, and psychological treatment approaches. Unfortunately, despite widespread recognition of the documented cost-effectiveness of multidisciplinary approaches, their availability is substantially limited to academically affiliated tertiary care settings.

INTEGRATION OF HEALTH PSYCHOLOGY IN THE PRIMARY CARE SETTING: A STEPPED-CARE APPROACH TO PAIN MANAGEMENT

Clinical health psychologists can intervene at several different levels of care to assist primary care providers in treating patients in a primary care setting. An individualized stepped-care approach can be applied to managing pain in primary care in which the level of care is guided by treatment outcome and an individual's readiness to engage in self-care (Von Korff, 1999). Such an approach has been used for a variety of medical conditions and health behaviors, including hypertension (Systolic Hypertension in the Elderly Program [SHEP] Cooperative Research Group, 1991), alcohol use (Sobell & Sobell, 2000; Donovan & Marlatt, 1993), cigarette use (Abrams et al., 1996), and cholesterol reduction (Oster et al., 1995). The approach consists of three successive steps that are guided by the patient's response to treatment in the preceding step.

Step 1 of the stepped-care approach is appropriate for all patients seeking treatment for pain from their primary care provider and involves the provider identifying and addressing specific patient concerns about the patient's pain and enhancing patient readiness for self-care. For example, one common concern of pain patients is that pain is a symptom of some type of underlying pathology. Once this concern is identified, primary care providers can address it by explaining how a medical history and diagnostic examination can exclude conditions such as cancer. A pain patient may also fear that exercise or activity will result in additional injury. This concern can be addressed by explaining the benefits of remaining active and by creating a plan with the patient for returning to a safe level of activity. Techniques based on motivational interviewing (Miller & Rollnick, 1991) can be used by primary care providers to encourage patients' readiness to engage in self-care behaviors. These techniques include addressing a patient's unrealistic expectations of the likelihood of a medical cure for his or her pain, offering support for effective self-care strategies the patient is currently using, and developing a plan for managing pain flare-ups. Clinical health psychologists can facilitate this communication by educating and training primary care providers, medical residents, and interns in motivational interviewing techniques to improve provider–patient communication (Miller & Rollnick, 1991; Rollnick, Heather, & Bell, 1992). Demonstrations of the effectiveness of this approach have been published for such behaviors as alcohol dependence (Ockene, Wheeler, Adams, Hurley, & Hebert, 1997), nicotine dependence (Ockene et al., 1994), and lipid reduction (Ockene et al., 1995).

Step 2 of this approach targets patients who continue to experience pain and disability several weeks after the initial primary care visit. These patients require a more active approach to pain management that may include identifying the specific difficulties a patient is experiencing (e.g., pain when lifting heavy objects at work), developing and implementing a more specific and individually tailored treatment plan, and providing support and follow-up. Given that this intervention likely involves time outside the regular appointment, a consultation with a clinical health psychologist is an important option for a primary care provider. Following a brief screening evaluation, the clinical health psychologist determines if the patient's goals can likely be best achieved through brief individual therapy or a more comprehensive program for pain. Alternatively, the psychologist can encourage the patient's engagement in a group psychoeducational program that requires few health care system resources. Such programs are currently in place at many institutions. For example, at the VA Connecticut Healthcare System (VACHS), the Living with Pain Class is a 6-week-long group that meets for 1 hour each week and is led by several different health care professionals with expertise in the area of pain management (i.e., clinical health psychologist, pharmacist, anesthesiologist, physical therapist, nurse). The group is designed to provide patients with information and support, and also encourages patients to play a more active role in the management of their pain.

In addition to the program conducted at the VACHS, other research studies investigating the efficacy of active interventions for primary care pain patients have also yielded positive results. For example, Von Korff et al. (1998) examined the effects of a brief self-management program for primary patients with chronic back pain. The group was led by a trained layperson with chronic pain and was designed to reduce worry, increase self-care, and increase activity. A group of 255 patients experiencing persistent pain were randomized to either a self-management or a control condition. Participants in the self-management condition attended four group sessions in which they received problem-solving training and educational materials supporting the active management of back pain. Participants in the control condition received usual care and a book on back pain care. The results indicated that participants in the self-management condition reported significantly less worry about back pain and more confidence in self-care. Self-reported disability was also significantly lower among participants in the self-management condition at 6- and 12-month follow-up.

In a related study, Moore and his colleagues (Moore, Von Korff, Cherkin, Saunders, & Lorig, 2000) examined the effects of a brief psychologist-led cognitive–behavioral intervention designed to increase back pain self-care. A total of 226 back pain patients from a primary care setting were randomly assigned to a self-care or usual-care condition. Participants in the self-care condition participated in two sessions of a self-care group, an individual meeting with a therapist, and a telephone call from a psychologist trained in pain management. They also received educational materials endorsing active management of back pain. Participants in the usual-care condition received usual care supplemented by a book on back pain care. The results indicated that participants assigned to the self-care condition showed significantly greater reduction in back-related worry and fear-avoidance beliefs than participants in the usual-care condition. These studies suggest that the involvement of pain patients in brief, low-cost interventions to address pain-related fears and concerns may be beneficial.

Step 3 of the stepped-care approach is designed to target the chronic pain patient who continues to experience a significant level of disability and affective distress despite the efforts of the primary care provider and the availability of brief counseling or psychoeducational programs. Individuals in this stage may present with complex medical and social histories and are often seen as challenging cases to manage within the limitations of the primary care setting. In these cases, more extensive involvement of the clinical health psychologist may be indicated. Psychologists can teach providers to encourage and motivate patients to take a more active role in their self-management approach to pain. In addition, they can teach patients ways of managing their pain, ways of increasing daily activity, and reducing pain-related affective distress. These patients presenting with chronic pain and persistent disability may require more intensive intervention from a variety of health providers and thus are often referred for multidisciplinary treatment.

A MODEL FOR THE MULTIDISCIPLINARY APPROACH TO PAIN MANAGEMENT: THE COMPREHENSIVE PAIN MANAGEMENT CENTER

One model for integrating multidisciplinary pain management into primary care is currently in place at the VACHS. The Comprehensive Pain Management Center (CPMC) is an interdisciplinary clinical, research, and training program for chronic pain that has been in place for more than 20 years. The program emphasizes developing the self-management approach to chronic pain through applying CBT and rehabilitation medicine approaches consistent with this perspective (i.e., education in body mechanics and energy conservation, graded home exercise). The CPMC emphasizes individualized goals and treatment plans designed to promote a problem-solving approach to the management of chronic pain. Such an approach stands in sharp contrast to single or multimodality services that emphasize acute pain relief without addressing the psychosocial factors related to pain.

As part of the CPMC, a clinical health psychologist serves as the case manager for each new patient and has the primary responsibility of providing feedback to the provider who made the original referral. After receiving a consultation request, the psychologist performs a comprehensive review of a patient's medical record, including current medication use and clinical notes from other medical and mental health services, and communicates with the primary care provider (and other key providers) about the specific concerns that prompted the consult. The patient, often along with a family member or significant other, is then engaged in a comprehensive pain assessment with the psychologist. This assessment uses interviewing, standardized self-report questionnaires and inventories, patient and significant other diaries, and occasionally formal behavioral observation methods or psychophysiological assessments and focuses on a comprehensive review of the patient's pain concern and its psychosocial context.

In addition to the psychological evaluation, the patient is commonly evaluated by other members of the team, including an anesthesiology pain management specialist, a neurologist, nurse practitioner, physical therapist, or occupational therapist.

Each specialty represented on the team brings an expertise that is relevant to the assessment and treatment of chronic pain. Anesthesiologists, psychiatrists, neurologists, and advanced practice nurses contribute to discussions on medical diagnosis and physical findings, pain medication alternatives, and the possible merits of additional medical evaluation or procedures. Physical and occupational therapists consider such interventions as body mechanics, posture, activity pacing, and exercise. Although there is diversity among members, there is also overlap with respect to their interests and perspectives. For example, although the anesthesiologist on the team is highly skilled in the use of nerve blocks and other invasive procedures for diagnosis and pain management, this specialist is also aware of the influence of psychological factors on pain perception and treatment outcome.

The results of the evaluation are discussed in an interdisciplinary team meeting. The CPMC director, who is also a psychologist, facilitates an open discussion and integration of assessment data and case conceptualizations, and encourages the development of an integrative and multimodal plan for intervention. Assessment and treatment recommendations resulting from this meeting are communicated verbally and in written form to the primary care provider by the clinical health psychologist and become part of the patient's medical record.

The recommendations of the pain management team are communicated to the patient, and specific efforts are used to engage the patient (and significant others) in developing a treatment plan. Care is taken to foster an active collaborative approach that encourages patient confidence and commitment to the plan. Specific meaningful and measurable behavioral goals for intervention are developed. These may include reducing the use of pain medications, increasing social and recreational activity, increasing exercise, and improving sleep, among others. Once the patient has agreed to a plan and specific goals are established, a time-limited, sequential, graded, and most often multimodal plan for intervention is implemented. This phase of intervention is typically intensive, requiring regular visits of the patient (and significant others) to the health care facility over several weeks. The psychologist maintains overall responsibility for coordinating care and for maintaining close communication among all of the providers involved in the intervention. Progress is monitored over the course of this intervention phase, and at some designated time point, the team participates in a formal reevaluation. Responsibility for continued care is typically then transferred back to the primary care provider with some reduced level of consultation or clinical involvement of the CMPC providers.

Before working in the area of pain management, clinical health psychologists should familiarize themselves with the clinical and research literature in this area and the issues that will be important to assess in a clinical interview. The comprehensive pain assessment interview typically lasts for 45 minutes and may include spouses or other individuals who offer support. However, in circumstances in which first contact is made in the primary care setting following a hand-off by a provider, the amount of time spent with the patient may be far less. In addition to the pain assessment interview, patients may be asked to complete self-report questionnaires to supplement the information obtained in the interview, for treatment goal setting, and to allow for the assessment of treatment outcome. It is important that health psychologists develop a level of expertise in selecting and interpreting the numerous self-report instruments that have been developed specifically for use with chronic pain populations. Standardized questionnaires have been developed to assess various domains, including pain severity, pain behaviors, affective distress, the responses of others to pain behaviors, dependency on others and relevant behavioral and cognitive variables, as well as patients' activity and functional status (see Table 3.1).

COGNITIVE–BEHAVIORAL THERAPY FOR PAIN

Based on the results of the initial evaluation, and in collaboration with the patient and other members of the multidisciplinary treatment team, the clinical health psychologist develops a treatment plan. One particularly effective pain treatment approach is CBT (Turk et al., 1983). CBT uses active, structured techniques aimed at modifying thoughts and behaviors and assisting individuals in developing a perspective of personal control and self-management of their pain. The components of CBT include the (a) identification of idiosyncratic beliefs about pain and pain treatment; (b) reconceptualization of the pain experience as subject to personal control

TABLE 3.1
Assessment Instruments Used in a Cognitive–Behavioral Evaluation
of Chronic Pain

Assessment measures	Domains assessed
Numerical rating scale (0–10)	Pain intensity
McGill Pain Questionnaire (MPQ; Melzack, 1975)	Sensory Affective Evaluative

West Haven–Yale Multidimensional Pain Inventory (WYMPI; Kerns, Turk, & Rudy, 1985)	Pain experience
	  Interference
	  Support
	  Pain severity
	  Self-control
	  Negative mood
	Pain-relevant significant other
	  responses
	  Negative responses
	  Solicitous responses
	  Distracting responses
	Daily activities
	  Household chores
	  Outdoor work
	  Activities away from home
	  Social activities

Beck Depression Inventory (BDI; Beck, Ward, Mendelson, Mock, & Erbaugh, 1961)	Depression
State–Trait Anxiety Inventory (Spielberger, Gorsuch, & Luschene, 1976)	Anxiety
Pain Behavior Checklist (Kerns et al., 1997)	Distorted ambulation Affective distress Facial audible expressions Seeking help
Pain Stages of Change (Kerns, Rosenberg, Jamison, Caudill, & Haythornthwaite, 1997)	Readiness to engage in treatment
Vanderbilt Pain Management Inventory (Brown & Nicassio, 1987)	Active/passive coping style

through the influence of thoughts, feelings, and physical activities; (c) training in a number of cognitive and behavioral coping skills and presentation and discussion of their rationale; and (d) practice and consolidation of these coping skills through imagery, rehearsal, role playing, and contingent reinforcement of their appropriate use.

CBT incorporates a variety of specific cognitive, behavioral, and psychophysiologically based treatment strategies (e.g., diaphragmatic breathing, cognitive restructuring, activity pacing). Proponents of CBT emphasize an inherent flexibility in the approach that encourages choices among multiple possible treatment targets and cognitive and behavioral intervention strategies. Also emphasized is the importance of using a collaborative, problem-solving approach to developing individual treatment goals and an integrative intervention plan. For example, a treatment goal might include a walking or exercise program that complements exercises being taught in physical therapy. Another goal might include developing techniques to adhere to pain medication prescriptions. Significant reductions in pain severity, disability, and affective distress, as well as reductions in health care resource use, have been repeatedly documented (Morley et al., 1999).

A substantial literature exists documenting the efficacy of CBT in a variety of specific chronic pain conditions. For example, CBT has been reported to produce reductions in pain in patients with rheumatoid arthritis (Applebaum, Blanchard, Hickling, & Alfonso, 1988), osteoarthritis (Heinrich, Cohen, Naliboff, Collins, & Bonebakker, 1985) acute back pain (Fordyce, Brockway, Bergman, & Spengler, 1986), chronic back pain (Kerns, Turk, Holzman, & Rudy, 1986; Turner & Jensen, 1993), and tension/migraine headache (Andrasik, 1990; Blanchard, 1992). A recent meta-analysis of 25 published randomized controlled trials of CBT for chronic pain in adults (Morley et al., 1999) concluded that CBT is an effective treatment for chronic pain, relative to waiting list and alternative therapy control conditions, in reducing pain and improving functioning. Thus, studies consistently demonstrate that CBT is a highly effective treatment approach for chronic pain.

RECENT ADVANCES IN PAIN MANAGEMENT IN PRIMARY CARE

Despite the positive outcomes of CBT for chronic pain management, high rates of treatment refusal and dropout continue to be reported in the literature (Turk & Rudy, 1991). Equally problematic are reports that many patients fail to adhere to therapist recommendations related to cognitive–behavioral pain management skill practice (Jensen, 1996; Kerns, Findley, & Bayer, 1998). However, no reliable predictors of engagement in and adherence to CBT have been identified.

Central to the cognitive–behavioral perspective on chronic pain is the observation that the degree of perceived control and responsibility for managing pain varies among individuals (Turk et al., 1983). Similarly, the transtheoretical model of health behavior change hypothesizes that individuals vary in the degree to which they are ready to make targeted behavioral changes (Prochaska & DiClemente, 1984). Informed by these models, Kerns, Rosenberg, Jamison, Caudill, and Haythornthwaite (1997) developed the Pain Stages of Change Questionnaire (PSOCQ), which assesses an individual's stage of readiness to adopt a self-management approach to his or her pain. The four stages described with the PSOCQ include the precontemplation, contemplation, action, and maintenance stages. Initial research data from patients completing CBT show that the extent of improvement in the domains of pain, disability, and distress is related to change in stage (e.g., increases in action and maintenance scores; Kerns & Rosenberg, 2000).

Kerns and colleagues have proposed adopting a patient-centered approach to health behavior change designed to enhance motivation of individuals with chronic pain (Ockene et al., 1995, 1997). This strategy is informed by the transtheoretical model and integrates educational and counseling guidelines based on an individual's stage of change and guidelines for brief practitioner training in motivational interviewing. Recently, Jensen (1996) adapted a motivational interviewing strategy for promoting patient motivation to engage in pain management therapies. Integrating this patient-centered approach with CBT for chronic pain is hypothesized to promote readiness to adopt a self-management approach to chronic pain, adherence to treatment recommendations, and improved outcomes (Kerns et al., 1998).

In an effort to increase patients' engagement in pain management therapy and their readiness to adopt a self-management approach to their pain, Kerns and colleagues are currently involved in research to investigate the utility of a modified CBT approach to chronic pain management influenced by the primary care model of health care delivery, the transtheoretical model of behavior change, and the cognitive–behavioral perspective on chronic pain management. The treatment program, called PRIME-CBT, involves collaborative sessions involving the health psychologist, the primary care provider, and the pain patient. The treatment incorporates specific patient-centered intervention strategies and refinements to therapy sessions designed to promote an individual's readiness to adopt a self-management approach to pain. It is hypothesized that PRIME-CBT will increase successful engagement of a larger proportion of chronic pain patients, improve adherence to therapist treatment recommendations, and ultimately improve outcomes for patients. The study design also calls for comparisons to be made against patients assigned to a CBT condition in which treatment is not provided in the primary care setting and a standard care condition in which participants do not receive CBT for pain.

As part of this research, primary care providers are trained by clinical health psychologists in the delivery of a patient-centered counseling approach developed by Ockene and her colleagues. The goals for the training are to (a) educate practitioners about a multidimensional model of chronic pain and the role of self-management treatment, (b) educate providers about a patient-centered approach to health behavior change and its potential for promoting self-management of chronic pain, and (c) encourage development of patient-centered counseling skills relevant to motivating patients to engage in self-management treatment of chronic pain. Specifically, the physician-delivered patient-centered counseling approach uses nondirective, open-ended questioning to elicit active participation of the patient in decisions about health behavior change. Emphasis is on the importance of tailoring the treatment plan to each patient's specific needs. Primary care providers follow a step-by-step strategy to address a health risk behavior, assess the patient's readiness to change the behavior, advise the patient about the importance of change, assist the patient in developing and implementing a plan for change, and arrange for follow-up. Motivational interviewing techniques are also commonly used. To facilitate training, a video was created with primary care physicians and health psychologists role-playing provider and pain patient interactions. The video and handouts were presented in small groups and individually to attending physicians and residents in primary care.

In PRIME-CBT, treatment by the psychologist takes place in the primary care setting and includes two scheduled meetings between the pain patient, his or her primary care provider, and the psychologist. These meetings occur during sessions 1 and 4 of a 10-session CBT program. It is important to note that given that provider participation in such a pain treatment program will be in addition to their regular patient load, meeting times must remain flexible in an effort to avoid adding an increased burden on the provider. Although the results of this study are currently in the analysis phase, the design of PRIME-CBT intervention could be easily replicated and implemented in other primary care settings. The PRIME-CBT model is unique in that it requires minimal burden on the primary care provider and helps teach patients to take a greater role in the self-management of their pain. As a result, this approach has the potential to decrease overall use of health care resources and decrease patient reliance on providers for medication. Most important, PRIME-CBT has the potential to improve the long-term success of pain treatment and overall quality of life of patients.

THE HEALTH PSYCHOLOGIST AS A PAIN MANAGEMENT SPECIALIST: DEALING WITH BARRIERS TO INTEGRATION IN PRIMARY CARE

The clinical health psychologist's training and expertise in behavior change are of little value if providers are not actively supportive and engaged in the intervention process. At the same time, psychologists should consider that change in any system is frequently met with resistance. Despite the best intentions, suggestions for sweeping changes in primary care or increased responsibility on the part of primary care providers might be rejected or might result in poor adherence. One of the first steps in increasing support for a service is demonstrating its value to providers. In the VACHS, for example, clinical health psychologists have an established presence in the primary care clinics by providing an on-call consultation service, maintaining offices in primary care, and regularly attending primary care clinical rounds and administrative meetings. Over time, the clinical health psychology service has established itself as a valuable resource for assisting primary care providers in treating patients with various maladaptive health behaviors, including tobacco use, weight control, poor medical adherence, as well as chronic pain. Another strategy used to deal with barriers to integration in primary care is to establish positive relationships with primary care physicians and nursing staff by providing in-service presentations about the role of psychological factors in pain and other medical conditions. It has been found to be especially helpful for these presentations to include empirical data from local research programs documenting the effectiveness of psychological interventions for patients with a range of medical difficulties. In addition, at the VA Boston Healthcare System, weekly meetings with primary care providers who have an interest in conducting clinical research have been set up, which has further strengthened collegial relationships and fostered integration of psychology and primary care services.

CONCLUSION

This chapter suggests many future research directions for developing cost-effective early interventions for the large number of individuals seen in the primary care setting who have concerns about pain conditions. Several key parameters of any successful pain intervention have been highlighted, including important provider, patient, and health care system barriers. For example, interventions are likely to be accepted in the primary care setting to the extent that they rely minimally on additional time of the primary care provider, are multidisciplinary and multidimensional, and are population-based and public-health oriented and emphasize secondary prevention rather than being designed to target only individuals with the most complex problems. Although not intended to serve as a comprehensive review of this rapidly evolving field, this chapter provides some detail about a few developing models and the preliminary empirical data that can serve to encourage continued efforts in this promising area.

One particularly promising model for integrating pain management in the primary care setting is the stepped care approach. Continued efforts in this area will likely focus on a determination of the specific format and content for interventions at each level of care to maximize outcomes for the largest proportion of individuals at each level of care. The work accomplished thus far that has been informed by theory and empirical findings regarding pain-related fear, for example, should serve as an important model for continued efforts in this area. Future research is also needed to develop methods for making decisions about when a higher or more intense level of care will need to be required for groups of individuals. Such efforts will have to take in account issues of sensitivity and selectivity in the development of measurement strategies and specific criteria for making these determinations, while also balancing issues of cost-effectiveness.

Consistent with the stepped-care goal of maximizing treatment efficiency and resource allocation, the use of computer or Internet technology to deliver information, provide support, or to assist in providing treatment represents an area with great potential for the future. Given the affordability of computers and widespread use of the Internet by individuals of all age ranges, the use of this type of technology may increase the accessibility of information to a significant number of people. This approach is clearly consistent with efforts to promote the accessibility of care to the larger population (e.g., persons living in rural settings and elderly and disabled individuals who lack mobility). Although preliminary studies in this area have yielded positive results (Lorig et al., 2002; Ström, Pettersson, & Andersson, 2000), continued research in this area is needed.

The PRIME-CBT approach is another area of developing interest. The approach described specifically targets improvements in the process of engagement of patients by promoting the integration of clinical health psychology in the primary care setting. Additional efforts at refining CBT treatment itself, for example, by enhancing the tailoring of individual treatment components, is another alternative worthy of investigation. Increasingly, refinements in these methods that are consistent with early intervention or even primary prevention efforts for at-risk populations are indicated. Preliminary support for the pain stages of change model encourages continued investigation of the relevance of this model in informing these refinements.

It is clear that challenges to our health care system in terms of limitations in resources and the simultaneous desire to promote a public health and population focus of care encourage a commitment to research designed to promote the maximally cost-effective interventions for the largest proportion of individuals with painful conditions. Clinical health psychologists are well positioned to contribute to these efforts. Education and training programs that promote the preparation of psychologists for these specialized professional roles and for conducting the research necessary to advance these efforts are clearly needed.

REFERENCES

Abrams, D. B., Orleans, C. T., Niaura, R. S., Goldstein, M. G., Prochaska, J. O., & Velicer, W. (1996). Integrating individual and public health perspectives for treatment of tobacco dependence under managed health care: A combined stepped-care and matching model. *Annals of Behavioral Medicine, 18,* 290–304.

Andrasik, F. A. (1990). Psychologic and behavioral aspects of chronic headache. *Neurologic Clinics, 8,* 961–976.

Applebaum, K. A., Blanchard, E. B., Hickling, E. J., & Alfonso, M. (1988). Cognitive behavioral treatment of a veteran population with moderate to severe rheumatoid arthritis. *Behavior Therapy, 19,* 489–502.

Beck, A. T., Ward, C. H., Mendelsohn, M., Mock, J., & Erbaugh, J. (1961). An inventory for measuring depression. *Archives of General Psychiatry, 4,* 561–571.

Blanchard, E. B. (1992). Psychological treatment of benign headache disorders. *Journal of Consulting and Clinical Psychology, 60,* 537–551.

Brown, G. K., & Nicassio, P. M. (1987). The development of a questionnaire for the assessment of active and passive coping strategies in chronic pain patients. *Pain, 31,* 53–65.

Donovan, D. M., & Marlatt, G. A. (1993). Recent developments in alcoholism behavioral treatment. *Recent Developments in Alcoholism, 11,* 397–411.

Flor, H., Fydrich, T., & Turk, D. (1992). Efficacy of multidisciplinary pain treatment centers: A meta-analytic review. *Pain, 49,* 221–230.

Fordyce, W. E., Brockway, J. A., Bergman, J. A., & Spengler, D. (1986). Acute back pain: A control group comparison of behavioral versus traditional management methods. *Journal of Behavioral Medicine, 9,* 127–140.

Gureje, O., Von Korff, M., Simon, G. E., & Gater, R. (1998). Persistent pain and well-being. A world health organization study in primary care. *Journal of the American Medical Association, 280,* 147–151.

Heinrich, R. L., Cohen, M. J., Naliboff, B. D., Collins, G. A., & Bonebakker, A. D. (1985). Comparing physical and behavior therapy for chronic low back pain on physical abilities, psychological distress, and patient's perceptions. *Journal of Behavioral Medicine, 8,* 61–78.

Jensen, M. P. (1996). Enhancing motivation to change in pain treatment. In R. J. Gatchel & D. C. Turk (Eds.), *Psychological approaches to pain management: A practitioner's handbook* (pp. 78–111). New York: Guilford Press.

Kerns, R. D., Findley, J. C., & Bayer, L. A. (1998). Motivation and adherence in the management of chronic pain. In A. R. Block, E. F. Kremer, & E. Fernandez (Eds.), *Handbook of pain syndromes: A biopsychosocial perspective* (pp. 99–122). Mahwah, NJ: Erlbaum.

Kerns, R. D., & Rosenberg, R. (2000). Predicting responses to self-management treatment for chronic pain: Application of the pain stages of change model. *Pain, 84,* 49–55.

Kerns, R. D., Haythornthwaite, J., Rosenberg, R., Southwick, S., Giller, E. L., & Jacob, M. C. (1991). The Pain Behavior Check List (PBCL): Factor structure and psychometric properties. *Journal of Behavioral Medicine, 14,* 155–167.

Kerns, R. D., Rosenberg, R., Jamison, R. N., Caudill, M. A. & Haythornthwaite, J. (1997). Readiness to adopt a self-management approach to chronic pain: The Pain Stages of Change Questionnaire (PSOCQ). *Pain, 72,* 227–234.

Kerns, R. D., Turk, D. C., Holzman, A. D. & Rudy, T. E. (1986). Comparison of cognitive–behavioral and behavioral approaches to the outpatient treatment of chronic pain. *Clinical Journal of Pain, 1,* 195–203.

Kerns, R. D., Turk, D. C., & Rudy, T. E. (1985). West Haven–Yale Multidimensional Pain Inventory (WHYMPD). *Pain, 23,* 345–356.

Lorig, K. R., Laurent, D. D., Deyo, R. A., Marnell, M. E., Minor, M. A., & Ritter, P. L. (2002). Can a back pain e-mail discussion group improve health status and lower health care costs? *Archives of Internal Medicine, 162,* 792–796.

Mantyselka, P., Kumpusalo, E., Ahonen, R., Kumpusalo, A., Kauhanen, J., Viina-maki, H., et al. (2001). Pain as a reason to visit the doctor: A study in Finish primary health care. *Pain, 89,* 175–180.

Melzack, R. (1975). The McGill Pain Questionnaire: Major properties and scoring methods. *Pain, 1,* 277–299.

Miller, W. R., & Rollnick, S. (1991). *Motivational interviewing: Preparing people to change addictive behavior.* New York: Guilford Press.

Moore, J. E., Von Korff, M., Cherkin, D., Saunders, K., & Lorig, K. (2000). A randomized trial of a cognitive–behavioral program for enhancing back pain self care in a primary care setting. *Pain, 88,* 145–153.

Morley, S., Eccleston, C., & Williams, A. (1999). Systematic review and meta-analysis of randomized controlled trials of cognitive–behaviour therapy for chronic pain in adults, excluding headache. *Pain, 80,* 1–13.

NIH guide: New directions in pain research. (1998). Washington, DC: U.S. Government Printing Office.

Ockene, J. K., Kristeller, L. P., Hebert, J. R., Luippold, R., Goldberg, R. J., Landon, J., et al. (1994). The physician-delivered smoking intervention project: Can short-term interventions produce long-term effects for a general outpatient population? *Health Psychology, 13,* 278–281.

Ockene, J. K, Ockene, I. S., Quirk, M., Hebert, J. R., Saperia, G. M., Luippold, R. S., et al. (1995). Physician training for patient-centered nutrition counseling in a lipid intervention trial. *Prevention, 24,* 563–570.

Ockene, J. K., Wheeler, E. V., Adams, A., Hurley, T. G., & Hebert, J. R. (1997). Provider training for patient-centered alcohol counseling in a primary care setting. *Archives of Internal Medicine, 157,* 2334–2341.

Oliver, R. L., & Lee, A. T. (2003). Chronic opioid rules. *Practical Pain Management, 3*(2), 30–35.

Oster, G., Borok, G. M., Menzin, J., Heys, J. F., Epstein, R. S., Quinn, V., et al. (1995). A randomized trial to assess effectiveness and cost in clinical practice:

Rationale and design of the Cholesterol Reduction Intervention Study. *Controlled Clinical Trials, 16*, 3–16.

Prochaska, J. O., & DiClemente, C. C. (1984). *The transtheoretical approach: Towards a systematic eclectic framework*. Homewood, IL: Irwin.

Reid, M. C., Engles-Horton, L. L., Weber, M., Kerns, R. D., Rogers, E. L., & O'Connor, P. G. (2002). Long-term opiate use for chronic pain syndromes in primary care. *Journal of General Internal Medicine, 17*, 175–182.

Rollnick, S., Heather, N., & Bell, A. (1992). Negotiating behaviour change in medical settings: The development of brief motivational interviewing. *Journal of Mental Health, 1*, 25–37.

Sobell, M. B., & Sobell, L. C. (2000). Stepped care as a heuristic approach to the treatment of alcohol problems. *Journal of Consulting and Clinical Psychology, 68*, 573–579.

Spielberger, C., Gorsuch, R., & Luschene, N. (1976). *Manual for the State-Trait Anxiety Inventory*. Palo Alto, CA: Consulting Psychologists Press.

Ström, L., Pettersson, R., & Andersson, G. (2000). A controlled trial of self-help treatment of recurrent headache conducted via the Internet. *Journal of Consulting and Clinical Psychology, 68*, 722–727.

Systolic Hypertension in the Elderly Cooperative Research Group. (1991). Prevention of stroke in antihypertensive drug treatment in older persons with isolated hypertension: Final results of the Systolic Hypertension in the Elderly Program. *Journal of the American Medical Association, 265*, 3255–3264.

Turk, D. C. (1996). Efficacy of multidisciplinary pain centers in the treatment of chronic pain. In M. J. M. Campbell & J. N. Campbell (Eds.), *Pain treatment centers at a crossroads: A practical and conceptual reappraisal* (pp. 257–273). Seattle, WA: International Association for the Study of Pain Press.

Turk, D. C., Meichenbaum, D., & Genest, M. (1983). *Pain and behavioral medicine: A cognitive–behavioral perspective*. New York: Guilford Press.

Turk, D. C., & Rudy, T. E. (1991). Neglected topics in the treatment of chronic pain patients—Relapse, noncompliance, adherence enhancement. *Pain, 44*, 5–28.

Turner, J. A., & Jensen, M. P. (1993). Efficacy of cognitive therapy for chronic low back pain. *Pain, 52*, 169–177.

Veterans Health Administration (VHA)/Department of Defense (DoD). (2001). *Clinical practice guideline for the management of opioid therapy for chronic pain*. Retrieved September 30, 2001, from http://www.oqp.med.va.gov/cpg/cpg.htm

Von Korff, M. (1999). Pain management in primary care: An individualized stepped-care approach. In R. Gatchel & D. Turk (Eds.), *Psychosocial factors in pain* (pp. 360–373). New York: Guilford.

Von Korff, M., Moore, J. E. Lorig, K., Cherkin, D. C., Saunders, K., Gonzalez, V., et al. (1998). A randomized trial of a lay person-led self-management group intervention for back pain patients in primary care. *Spine, 23*, 2608–2615.

4

PSYCHOLOGICAL INTERVENTIONS IN PATIENTS WITH CORONARY HEART DISEASE

WILLEM J. KOP

This chapter describes psychological risk factors for onset and progression of coronary artery disease. Psychological risk factors can be grouped into three broad categories, based on their duration and temporal proximity to the occurrence of coronary syndromes: (a) chronic factors promoting gradual coronary disease progression (e.g., hostility); (b) episodic factors (e.g., depression and exhaustion); and (c) acute factors (e.g., anger or mental activity). The stage of coronary disease is a major determinant of the magnitude of risk for coronary syndromes associated with these psychological factors as well as the biobehavioral mechanisms involved. The second section of this chapter addresses psychological interventions aimed at patients with coronary disease or elevated cardiovascular risk factors. This chapter

This chapter was authored or coauthored by an employee of the United States government as part of official duty and is considered to be in the public domain. Any views expressed herein do not necessarily represent the views of the United States government, and the author's participation in the work is not meant to serve as an official endorsement.

Preparation of this chapter was supported in part by grants from the NIH (HL58638, HL66149).

concludes with a proposal for a triage system to optimize treatment allocation in primary care patients at high risk for cardiac events.

PSYCHOSOCIAL RISK FACTORS FOR CORONARY HEART DISEASE

A large body of research suggests that chronic and acute psychological factors are associated with increased risk of coronary artery disease (CAD) and its clinical manifestations as acute coronary syndromes, including myocardial infarction (Kop, 1999; Rozanski, Blumenthal, & Kaplan, 1999; Smith & Ruiz, 2002). Both biological processes as well as health behaviors play a role in the association between psychological factors and cardiovascular disease outcomes (Figure 4.1). The pathophysiological mechanisms accounting for the relationship between psychological factors and CAD progression involve psychophysiological, hemostatic, and immunological processes. This chapter provides a selective review of the interplay between psychological risk factors and biobehavioral mechanisms as related to psychological intervention options at various stages of CAD. Psychological interventions in patients at risk for coronary disease will benefit from an integrative approach, combining pharmacological and health behavior strategies with psychological interventions tailored to patients' specific needs and circumstances.

Psychological risk factors for CAD can be classified into three categories, based on their duration and temporal proximity to coronary syndromes

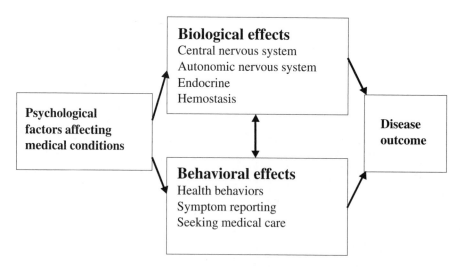

Figure 4.1. Effects of psychological factors on disease risk.

(Kop, 1999): (a) chronic factors, such as negative personality traits (e.g., hostility) and low socioeconomic status; (b) episodic factors, which are transient with a duration of several weeks up to 2 years and recurring, among which are depression and exhaustion; and (c) acute triggers, including mental stress and outbursts of anger.

To understand biobehavioral mechanisms in coronary heart disease (i.e., diseases of the heart muscle resulting from coronary artery disease), it is crucial to consider the basic pathological stages of atherosclerotic coronary disease progression. Blood supply to the heart muscle (myocardium) is provided by three coronary arteries. Coronary artery disease involves the gradual narrowing of one or more of these arteries as a consequence of atherosclerosis. Early stages of coronary atherosclerosis are characterized by deposition of blood particles (monocytes) in the vascular wall. At later stages of CAD, these engulfed monocytes (called macrophages) become lipid-laden. At this point, the lining cells of the coronary artery develop impaired function (called endothelial dysfunction), resulting in attenuated vessel response to increased blood flow or other stimulants that normally increase vessel diameter. Following initial artery damage, cells from the inner layers of the coronary artery (smooth muscle cells) grow and migrate to cover the atherosclerotic plaque. These processes result in a relatively stable layer (fibrous cap) over the atherosclerotic plaque. In the setting of severe CAD, the blood flow through the coronary arteries becomes impaired because the atherosclerosis leads to narrowing (stenosis) of the artery. When the narrowing exceeds 50% of the vessel diameter, blood flow through the artery distal from the stenosis may become impaired. Specifically, when a greater than 50% stenosis exists and an individual engages in activities that increase demand on the heart (e.g., exercise or mental stress), then reduced blood supply to the heart muscle may occur (myocardial ischemia). Exercise- and mental-stress-induced ischemia is generally transient and remits as soon as cardiac demand returns to baseline levels. In addition to stress-induced transient ischemia, several factors may promote plaque activation, leading to plaque instability and thinning of the fibrous cap. Plaque rupture causes more severe ischemia resulting from partial or complete closure of the coronary artery. Plaque rupture is often complicated by blood clot formation as a consequence of plaque content exposure to the blood. Sudden transient obstruction of the coronary artery can cause myocardial ischemia and chest pain (angina), whereas complete sustained occlusion leads to permanent damage of the heart muscle (myocardial infarction). More detailed reviews of this complex process can be found in cardiology textbooks and, for example, Ross (1999). Thus, myocardial infarction and sudden cardiac death are end-points of gradual coronary disease progression and are often the first and dramatic clinical signs of the underlying disease.

Chronic Psychological Risk Factors

Stable characteristics, such as hostile personality, type A behavior pattern, low socioeconomic status, and type D personality are associated with elevated long-term risk of first myocardial infarction (Barefoot, Dahlstrom, & Williams, 1983; Kop, 1999; Marmot, Shipley, & Rose, 1984). Evidence supporting the predictive value of chronic psychological risk factors for recurrent events is less consistent (Ragland & Brand, 1988). There has been substantial controversy about the predictive validity of the type A behavior pattern. Evidence over the past 15 years suggests that hostility is the primary toxic component of type A behavior (Krantz & McCeney, 2002), and meta-analysis indicates that the elevated risk of hostility is significant but not high (Miller, Smith, Turner, Guijarro, & Hallet, 1996).

Job-related stress can be chronic or episodic, depending on the nature of the profession (see later discussion). Working conditions associated with coronary heart disease include an imbalance between effort and reward (Siegrist, Peter, Junge, Cremer, & Seidel, 1990), a combination of low control or low autonomy and high job demand (Reed, La Croix, Karasek, Miller, & MacLean, 1989), and low job satisfaction. Most studies demonstrate significant predictive value of these job characteristics with coronary heart disease and cardiovascular risk factors such as high blood pressure and increased blood clotting measures. Job strain should be considered in the context of family demands as well. For example, working women with children may be at elevated risk of myocardial infarction, whereas working outside the home by itself is not associated with elevated risk of cardiac events (La Croix, 1994). This literature has not fully addressed the variability of job characteristics over time, and cardiovascular research on societal and family demands among retired individuals is generally lacking.

Low socioeconomic status is a powerful predictor of cardiac events. Many factors determine an individual's socioeconomic status, including education, income, occupation, economic resources, and social standing. Evidence indicates a gradient of socioeconomic status and adverse cardiovascular health, suggesting that the increased risk is not limited to the lowest strata only (Marmot et al., 1984; Ruberman, Weinblatt, Goldberg, & Chaudhary, 1984). Many mechanisms may account for this gradient, including access to health care, exposure to environmental risk factors, and elevated distress levels in lower socioeconomic strata (Marmot et al., 1991). Ruberman et al. (1984) noted that social isolation and elevated psychological distress was more prevalent among individuals of low socioeconomic status. Recent investigations have examined the novel construct of the "distressed" personality type, or type D personality. Type D personality has been defined as the tendency to suppress emotional distress (Denollet et al., 1996), which was later refined as a combination of high negative affectivity and high social inhibition (Denollet, 2000). Type D is associated with elevated risk of mortality in patients with documented CAD (OR = 4.1; 95% CI = 1.9–8.8; p = 0.0004), adjusting for traditional risk factors (Denollet et al., 1996).

Social Support

Social support is defined by the availability of social contacts to promote personal goals or needs (Cohen, Underwood, & Gottlieb, 2000). Most aspects of social support can be construed as a chronic psychological risk factor. *Structural social support* refers to the number of available individuals (e.g., marital status, number of friends). *Functional social support* refers to the utility of social support, including instrumental support (actual help in accomplishing tasks) and informational and emotional support (Cohen et al., 2000). Social isolation is an example of lack of structural and functional social support systems. Several studies have documented a greater risk by 1.5 to 2 times of various markers of low social support for first (Orth-Gomer & Johnson, 1987; Vogt, Mullooly, Ernst, Pope, & Hollis, 1992) and recurrent (Berkman, Leo-Summers, & Horwitz, 1992; Ruberman et al., 1984) cardiac events. Evidence also indicates that gender differences exist in the predictive value of marital status for women versus men. The optimal number and quality of social support and roles may also differ between men and women (Hibbard & Pope, 1993; Shumaker & Hill, 1991).

More research is needed to further disentangle the relative predictive value of socioeconomic status, chronic social stresses related to racism or adverse stigmata among individuals with various disadvantages, social isolation, and sustained lack of social support as risk indicators for coronary disease.

Mechanisms

Sympathetic nervous system-mediated proatherogenic processes, including increased lipid deposition and inflammatory processes, are among the pathophysiological pathways accounting for the association between chronic risk factors and early stages of CAD. In addition to the direct pathophysiological pathways, chronic psychological factors also promote development of episodic psychological risk factors (e.g., increased prevalence of exhaustion in type A individuals, elevated distress levels and depression in low socioeconomic status groups) and are associated with increased reactivity to acute stressors (Kop, 1999). As a consequence, the predictive value of chronic psychological risk factors for CAD progression is mediated in part by their association with other (episodic and acute) psychological risk factors for CAD.

The association between low social support and future cardiac events may be mediated via suboptimal coping strategies with daily life challenges. In contrast, the presence of adequate social support may positively affect responses to challenges of daily life, including reduced emotional, neurohormonal, and cardiovascular stress reactivity (Lepore, 1998), supporting what has been referred to as the "buffering" hypothesis. In addition, individuals with good social support tend to have better health behaviors and often adhere better to a medication regimen. Psychological interventions may add the benefits of social support as a treatment component, but the possibility that social contacts can also act as a burden (e.g., demands for assistance, conflict) requires additional research.

Episodic Psychological Risk Factors

Episodic risk factors, such as major depressive disorder and exhaustion, are transient (with a duration ranging from several weeks to two years) and are recurring (Appels, 1997; Kop, 1999; Carney, Freedland, Rich, & Jaffe, 1995). Meta-analysis has indicated elevated risk of first myocardial infarction associated with depression as assessed in apparently healthy individuals (RR = 1.64 [CI = 1.29–2.08]; Rugulies, 2002; Wulsin & Singal, 2003). Depression is an even stronger predictor of recurrent cardiac events and mortality in patients with established coronary disease, with risks ranging from 3.0 to 7.8 (Kop & Ader, 2001). Depression in patients with coronary disease (and other medical conditions) is often atypical (Appels, Kop, & Schouten, 2000; Kop & Ader, 2001). A series of investigations suggests that (vital) exhaustion (extreme fatigue, increased irritability, and feelings of demoralization) is a significant risk factor for incident (Appels & Mulder, 1988) and recurrent cardiac events (Kop, Appels, Mendes de Leon, de Swart, & Bar, 1994). Major life events (e.g., loss of a spouse, unemployment, and financial crisis) often precede the onset of episodic risk factors and will not be discussed in detail in this chapter. It is important to note that the risk of episodic risk factors is primarily observed within the first two years following assessment. For example, in a study of 3,877 male civil servants, Appels and Mulder (1988) demonstrated that the risk of exhaustion for first myocardial infarction is at its peak during the first year (RR = 10.05), tapering off during the subsequent years of follow-up (year 2: RR = 2.23; year 3: RR = 3.04; year 4: RR = 0.68). Similarly, a closer inspection of the results reported by Frasure-Smith and colleagues (1995, 1997, 2002) indicates that the risk of mortality associated with depression in postmyocardial infarction patients is high during the first 6 months (OR = 5.6; CI = 1.4–22.5) and 18 months (OR = 7.8; CI = 2.4–25.2) and declines substantially at 5-year follow-up (OR = 2.3). Some evidence supports a dose–response relationship between depression and risk of cardiac events, but subthreshold levels of depression (depressive symptoms and atypical depression) are associated with a greater than two-fold risk of myocardial infarction. Thus, depression and exhaustion are episodic risk factors with an exposure duration ranging from weeks up until 2 years; the long-term (> 2 years) predictive value of depression for adverse cardiac health outcomes is probably explained by the recurring nature of depression. Because of the transient (i.e., not chronic) nature of episodic risk factors, most studies have not found significant correlations between these psychological factors and CAD severity. Therefore, processes involved in the *transition* from stable to unstable atherosclerotic plaques are probable candidates accounting for the marked predictive value of depression and other episodic factors for acute coronary syndromes (Kop, 1999).

Mechanisms

Increased activation of the corticotropin-releasing hormone (CRH) system has consistently been observed in major (melancholic) depression (Gold, Goodwin, & Chrousos, 1988a). These neurohormonal correlates may affect the immune system component of CAD (Kop & Cohen, 2001). Another correlate of depression and most other episodic risk factors is decreased parasympathetic activity as measured by heart rate variability, which is primarily relevant for increased vulnerability for life-threatening heart rhythm disturbances (e.g., Carney et al., 1995). The neurohormonal correlates of depression and related syndromes may differ depending on the clinical features of the depressive symptoms (i.e., melancholic versus atypical depression). In contrast to major (melancholic) depression, evidence suggests that atypical depression (hyperphagia, hypersomnia, exhaustion) is characterized by reduced CRH activation (Gold et al., 1988a). These changes are similar to the neurohormonal correlates of exhaustion (Nicolson & van Diest, 2000), general distress, and posttraumatic stress disorder (Gold, Goodwin, & Chrousos, 1988b). It is not known whether these neurohormonal differences across various types of depression have consequences for the pathophysiological pathways linking episodic risk factors to acute coronary syndromes.

Acute Psychological Risk Factors

Acute risk factors (i.e., states) such as outbursts of anger can act as triggers of myocardial infarction by inducing myocardial ischemia and promoting plaque rupture in advanced stages of CAD. Epidemiological studies indicate that disasters such as earthquakes and missile attacks increase the risk of cardiac events (for review, see Krantz, Kop, Santiago, & Gottdiener, 1996). Case crossover studies have indicated that acute anger is associated with a greater than twofold risk of myocardial infarction (RR = 2.3; 95% CI = 1.7–3.2; Mittleman et al., 1995). It should be noted that the severity of anger as measured in this study is substantial (i.e., "Furious: almost out of control, very angry, pound table, slam door," "Enraged: Lost control, throwing objects, hurting yourself or others," or "Very angry: body tense, clenching fists or teeth"). Moreover, only 36 of the 1,623 infarctions in this study (2.2%) were triggered by this intense state of anger. Moller et al. have reported similar observations (1999). Therefore, researchers and clinicians have also focused on acute psychological states of milder intensity (e.g., frustration, tension, annoyance) as potential triggers of more common but less severe cardiac events, such as transient myocardial ischemia. Milder types of acute mental or emotional challenges can have adverse effects on the heart. Mental stress in standardized laboratory conditions causes myocardial ischemia in 30% to 60% of patients with CAD (Krantz et al., 1996).

Mechanisms

Pathophysiological mechanisms involved include sympathetic nervous system-mediated increases in catecholamines, cardiac demand (heart rate and blood pressure), as well as stress-induced decreases in plasma volume and coronary constriction (see Krantz et al., 1996 for review).

Summary and Conclusions Regarding Psychological Risk Factors

There are three types of psychological risk factors for coronary artery disease: chronic, episodic, and acute. Chronic psychosocial risk factors are involved in the early stages of CAD and play a role at advanced disease stages primarily because of their association with increased episodic and acute psychological risk factors. Episodic risk factors have a duration of several weeks 2 years (e.g., depression and exhaustion), and play a primary role in the transition from stable coronary disease to clinical manifestations such as myocardial infarction. Acute risk factors such as mental stress and anger are primarily of importance at progressed stages of coronary disease because these factors may cause myocardial ischemia by increasing cardiac demand and decreasing coronary blood supply. Acute risk factors may also promote the risk of life-threatening arrhythmias. Because of the important predictive value of these psychological risk factors for *recurrent* cardiac events, the following section on psychological interventions will primarily focus on treatment options for patients with established coronary disease and those with high levels of cardiovascular risk factors. Health behavior and psychosocial interventions can play an important role in the secondary prevention of high-risk patients attending primary care clinics.

EFFECTS OF PSYCHOLOGICAL INTERVENTIONS ON MORBIDITY AND MORTALITY

The majority of cardiovascular behavioral medicine intervention studies have targeted patients with established coronary disease or individuals with elevated cardiovascular risk factors. Psychological intervention strategies for risk reduction of adverse cardiovascular health outcomes can be grouped into three broad categories: (a) interventions targeting chronic psychological risk factors such as hostility; (b) interventions aimed at improving episodic risk factors such as depression and exhaustion; and (c) interventions addressing health behaviors (e.g., smoking cessation, weight reduction, exercise). The latter category is of utmost importance in primary care but beyond the scope of this chapter.

Interventions Targeting Chronic Psychological Risk Factors

Most interventions aimed at decreasing negative chronic factors address patients' lifestyle and coping with acute stressors. As described earlier, the effects of chronic psychological risk factors in vulnerable patients are primarily medicated by elevated acute stress responses. Therefore, the efficacy of intervention programs on acute and chronic psychological risk factors will be considered together.

The Recurrent Coronary Prevention Project is one of the most convincing investigations in this area (Powell & Thoresen, 1988). The trial randomized 862 postmyocardial infarction patients to group therapy consisting of relaxation, self-monitoring of type A behaviors and stress, and cognitive–behavioral techniques ($N = 592$) or usual care ($N = 270$) (Friedman et al., 1986). The intervention resulted in significant reduction of recurrent events (12.9% versus 21.2%; Friedman et al., 1986) and reduced mortality in patients with less severe coronary disease at study entry (Powell & Thoresen, 1988). It has further been demonstrated that this project not only decreased global type A behavior but also hostility, depression, and anxiety (Mendes de Leon, Powell, & Kaplan, 1991). Ornish and colleagues have successfully applied a combination of stress management (meditation and group support) and lifestyle changes (exercise, low-fat vegetarian diet) in reducing recurrent cardiac events and reversing progressive coronary disease (Gould et al., 1995; Ornish et al., 1990). A more recent study by Blumenthal et al. (1997) revealed that stress management reduced recurrent cardiac events and ischemia in patients with stable coronary disease (Blumenthal et al., 1997). Gidron, Davidson, and Bata (1999) have also demonstrated improved cardiovascular health as a consequence of reducing hostility, but the effects on recurrent events remains to be determined (Gidron et al., 1999). Denollet and colleagues (1996) examined reduction of type D personality in a nonrandomized trial. The program involved a multifactorial rehabilitation using both group and individual sessions for three months. In addition to aerobic exercise training, the program included six psychological sessions focused on how to monitor signs of stress and how to cope with stressful life events and be assertive. Additional individual therapy was provided to 48% of the patients. The intervention reduced negative affect and resulted in a significant reduction in 9-year all-cause mortality (OR 0.2; 95% CI 0.1–0.7; $p = 0.016$; Denollet & Brutsaert, 2001). The nonrandom assignment to the control group in the latter three studies may have introduced a potential bias toward positive results.

Investigations have not consistently confirmed these positive findings. Jones and West (1996) conducted a randomized multicenter intervention trial in 2,328 consecutive and unselected postmyocardial infarction patients and their spouses (Jones & West, 1996). The intervention involved psychotherapy and counseling, relaxation training, and stress management over 7 weeks and was administered in groups of outpatients. The intervention was not successful in reducing anxiety or depression. Although patients in the active treatment condition had a lower frequency of angina, there were no differences in secondary cardiac events or 1-year mortality. Note that the intervention was not targeted at depression and anxiety per se. Lisspers and colleagues (1999) conducted a lifestyle intervention program in coronary angioplasty patients resulting in decreased type A behavior attitudes and decreased chest pain, but the intervention did not decrease most other psychological measures (e.g., trait anger, depression, anxiety), nor did it reduce recurrent cardiac events within 1 year (23% in both groups). It could thus be argued that the failure of this intervention to reduce recurrent cardiac events resulted from its ineffectiveness in reducing psychological risk factors relevant to CAD progression.

Recent investigations have also examined stress management in high risk populations without CAD. For example, one study examined effects of transcendental meditation on carotid artery thickness among 60 Black Americans with high blood pressure (Castillo-Richmond et al., 2000) and reported significant reductions in wall thickness (an index of atherosclerosis). A limitation of this study was the greater than 50% drop-out rate for the major dependent variable.

Interventions Targeting Episodic Psychological Risk Factors

One of the groundbreaking studies in this area was conducted by Frasure-Smith and Prince (1985). Among postmyocardial infarction patients, nurses provided emotional and instrumental support when patients' distress levels increased (the Ischemic Heart Disease Life Stress Monitoring Program). Participants in the active intervention program had a significant reduction in mortality compared to a randomized control group (Frasure-Smith & Prince, 1985). A more recent replication study was not successful in reducing recurrent cardiac events (Frasure-Smith et al., 1997). Post hoc analyses revealed that a repressive coping style may adversely affect this type of intervention (Frasure-Smith et al., 2002).

The recent Enhancing Recovery in Coronary Heart Disease (ENRICHD) trial enrolled 2,481 postmyocardial infarction patients at eight medical centers in the United States (ENRICHD Investigators, 2000, 2003). The patients were recruited within one month of their myocardial infarction and had major or minor depression and/or low social support. The 6 months of active treatment consisted of individual and group cognitive–behavioral therapy sessions targeted at modifying thought patterns and behaviors contributing to depressive symptoms. The comparison group received usual care (ENRICHD Investigators, 2001, 2003). At 6 months, significant reductions were observed in both the treatment group (8.6 scale units reduction in Beck Depression Inventory [BDI; Beck & Steer, 1987], 10.1 units reduction (57%) in Hamilton Depression scale [Hamilton, 1960]) as well as the control group (5.9 units reduction in BDI, 8.4 units reduction (47%) in Hamilton Depression). The reductions in depression were stronger in the active treatment group ($p < 0.001$). Patients with persistently high levels of depression were also referred for additional psychiatric evaluation and prescribed antidepressant medication. It is noteworthy that the use of antidepressants was equally common among active treatment and comparison groups, which may have attenuated group differences. After 3 years, 24.4% of the patients in the treatment group died or had a recurrent myocardial infarction, compared to 24.2% in the control condition (ENRICHD Investigators, 2003). Thus, psychological interventions can significantly reduce (not eliminate) episodic risk factors, but most have not been successful in reducing subsequent cardiac events.

A series of pharmacological trials aimed to reduce depression in patients with coronary artery disease have been conducted. The strongest trial at this point is the double blind, randomized placebo controlled, multinational Sertraline Antidepressant Heart Attack Randomized Trial (SADHART; Glassman et al., 2002). Following a 2-week placebo, 369 patients with myocardial infarction or unstable angina were randomized to 24 weeks of a flexible dose of sertraline (a selective serotonin reuptake inhibitor) or placebo. The active treatment arm resulted in significant improvement in Hamilton Depression scores (8.4 ± 0.4 units reduction), but this decrease was similar in controls (7.8 ± 0.4 units; p [comparison] = 0.14). The active treatment group significantly improved on a clinical rating scale compared with the placebo condition. Additional analyses revealed that the active treatment was also more effective than placebo in improving Hamilton scores among subgroups of severely depressed individuals and those with recurrent depression. The recurrent cardiac event rate during treatment tended to be lower (14.5%) in the treatment than the placebo group (22.4%; RR = 0.77; 95% CI = 0.51–1.16; nonsignificant). The study was primarily designed as a safety study and statistically underpowered to detect differences in clinical outcome. Nonetheless, the effect size is promising, particularly among patients with severe depression.

These intervention studies demonstrate that efforts aimed at reducing depression are difficult enterprises. Residual depression is the main concern and is common in patients with general medical conditions. Approximately 50% of cardiac patients remain depressed after psychological or pharmacological intervention. Similar results are found for exhaustion. In a randomized psychological intervention trial of 710 angioplasty patients, exhaustion remained present in patients with a previous history of CAD. Furthermore, clinical event rates were similar in the active treatment arm (22%) and standard of care control condition (20%; RR = 1.09; 95% CI = 0.79–1.5; Appels et al., 2000). This result is similar to the aforementioned observations in angioplasty patients by Lisspers et al. (1999). In addition to residual depression, another factor contributing to null findings in controlled trials is the high spontaneous recovery rate because initially elevated depression scores after cardiac events often reflect adjustment disorders rather than depression per se. It is well-established that subthreshold depression is a strong predictor of adverse cardiovascular outcomes. Thus, it is not surprising that the suboptimal reduction in episodic risk factors is not paralleled by a subsequent reduction in recurrent cardiac events.

Summary and Conclusions Regarding Psychological Interventions

The initial psychological intervention studies demonstrated beneficial effects on both psychological risk factors as well as recurrent cardiac events. In contrast, more recent studies have failed to support these positive results. A few excellent reviews and meta-analyses have been published on the efficacy of psychological interventions in reducing recurrent cardiac events (Dusseldorp, van Elderen, Maes, Meulman, & Kraaij, 1999; Linden, 2000; Linden, Stossel, & Maurice, 1996; Sebregts, Falger, & Bar, 2000). On average, psychological and educational interventions reduce cardiac mortality by 34% and recurrent myocardial infarction by 29% (Dusseldorp et al., 1999). These effects are at least as strong as those obtained by traditional medical interventions such as beta-adrenergic medication. In addition, improving psychological domains of quality of life could be considered a goal in itself. There is also a strong relationship between psychological measures and perceived symptoms such as shortness of breath and chest pain (Kop et al., 1996). We concur with Dusseldorp and colleagues' conclusion (1999) that psychological interventions are most effective in reducing recurrent cardiac events if they have initial beneficial effects on more proximal medical (e.g., blood pressure, exercise tolerance) and psychological (e.g., depression) measures that are risk factors for these cardiac events. Of note is that most interventions targeting chronic psychological risk factors include management of acute triggers in their treatment. Interventions aimed at episodic risk factors do not appear to fully eradicate these factors, which may interfere with their ability to prevent recurrent cardiac events. It is likely that a combination of pharmacological and psychological intervention is needed to sufficiently reduce and maintain episodic risk factors in patients at high risk of recurrent cardiac events.

CONCLUSION

Several important areas require additional investigation, and this section reviews three areas in cardiovascular behavioral medicine relevant to future clinical intervention efforts: (a) the need to tailor psychological interventions to patient characteristics and allocate patients efficiently to treatments; (b) the relative importance of general versus specific risk factors; and (c) directions for future research and emerging populations at risk for recurrent cardiac events. These issues are of particular importance in patients at risk of cardiovascular events attending primary care settings, because both primary and secondary interventions in patients based on psychological risk factors can have substantial benefits for mental and physical health.

Increasing evidence suggests that it is important to tailor psychological interventions to patient characteristics and needs. One reason why the Jones and West (1996) study was unsuccessful in improving psychological risk factors is that this investigation did not preselect patients for their need for psychological interventions. Based on the literature, we propose a triage system that could facilitate treatment allocation in patients at risk for incident or recurrent cardiac events (Figure 4.2). This triage system stratifies for (a) acute distress disorders, (b) episodic factors such as depression, and (c) chronic factors.

Acute stress disorders occasionally occur in the setting of myocardial infarction. As shown in Figure 4.2, these can include acute emotional reactions to the onset of a life-threatening disease but also major life events such as divorce, decease of a loved one, and job loss. These acutely distressing factors are relatively rare but should be the primary targets of psychological interventions before other approaches are considered. It is also important to differentiate episodic risk factors such as depression and exhaustion from adjustment disorders related to the cardiac event.

As mentioned, episodic risk factors (depression and exhaustion) are crucially important in patients at risk for recurrent cardiac events. Interventions

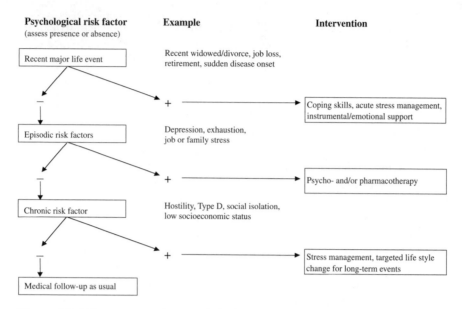

Figure 4.2. Triage system for psychological interventions in patients at risk for recurrent cardiac events.

targeted at these episodic risk factors generally improve patients' quality of life but may also promote cardiovascular health outcomes. The current literature suggests that these factors are unlikely to fully remit by psychological or pharmacological interventions, and a combined approach may prove more successful in eradicating these risk factors.

Chronic psychological risk factors such as hostility can be successfully altered (as described earlier). Treatments generally involve stress management and group support. Anger management has been described by Williams (for review, see Smith & Ruiz, 2002) and is a common feature of hostility interventions. Active conflict reduction may be effective but has not been systematically studied in coronary disease patients. Other chronic factors such as low socioeconomic status and genetic predisposition cannot be addressed through psychosocial interventions. The few options that are open in these circumstances include acquiring coping skills, promoting health behaviors, and minimizing exposure to potential acute triggers of cardiac events. If patients are eligible for interventions targeting chronic risk factors, then it is important to determine that treatment efficacy occurs *within* the high-risk period for recurrent events. Some personality traits are difficult to change rapidly and are thus not optimal targets in the prevention of events occurring in a relatively short time frame.

Psychological risk factors do not exist in a vacuum and often coincide with adverse health behaviors, such as smoking, poor diet, nonadherence to medication regimen, and sedentary life style. Smoking cessation and weight reduction should be primary foci of intervention for patients with these risk factors. Addressing self-efficacy and promoting behavior change are major components of such interventions. Exercise has well-established positive effects on mood (e.g., Blumenthal et al., 1999) and plays an important role in cardiac rehabilitation. It is important to note that lifestyle changes per se do not necessarily improve psychological risk factors (i.e., Lisspers et al., 1999). Furthermore, active lifestyle intervention may decrease rather than improve patient satisfaction with medical care (Meland, Laerum, & Maeland, 1996). Psychological interventions need to be integrated with health behavior interventions.

The relative importance of general versus specific psychological risk factors for coronary heart disease depends on the clinical and research questions under consideration. Psychological risk factors for cardiovascular disease share common variance (Kop, 1999; Rozanski et al., 1999). This common factor has been referred to as *negative affectivity*, among other terms. However, despite these overlapping characteristics, several studies have demonstrated that each of the psychological factors described have unique contributions in the disease process (e.g., Frasure-Smith, Lesperance, & Talajic, 1995; Mendes de Leon, Kop, de Swart, Bar, & Appels, 1996). The advantages of assessing general risk factors include the potential of detecting a wider range of patients at risk for recurrent events and the opportunity to determine common biobehavioral mechanisms. The disadvantages relate to the clinical interpretation (i.e., content validity) and the undetermined treatment options of such general risk factors. Specific risk factors, such as depression, exhaustion, and hostility, have the advantage of being clinically meaningful constructs, with available treatment options. Thus, specific risk factors independently predict outcome and are needed for efficient and targeted clinical interventions, whereas general risk factors are useful in guiding research on biobehavioral mechanisms of coronary artery disease.

Future research and funds are needed to develop and implement common measures of treatment efficacy. Two main sources of variability contribute to this need: (a) the substantial variability in the clinical characteristics of patients referred to (or randomized to) psychological interventions; and (b) the nature of the interventions commonly varies with clinician and investigator experience and theoretical perspective. Outcome evaluations may include common outcome measures such as quality of life, quality-adjusted life years, and health care costs. Such measures will allow comparisons of various psychological interventions and also address the relative importance of psychological versus pharmacological and other interventions targeting traditional cardiovascular risk factors. It will be important to combine these evaluations with cardiac endpoints such as recurrent myocardial infarction and cardiac mortality.

Cardiology and other areas of medicine relevant to cardiovascular disease continue to make substantial improvements in patient care and long-term health outcomes. Hence, the nature of populations at risk for recurrent events is constantly changing. As efficacy of medical interventions increases, there will be less variance left for beneficial effects of psychological interventions on medical outcomes. This may explain the trend toward null findings of psychological interventions as time progresses and medical interventions improve. An important discussion will center on funding and feasibility of the often prohibitively large number of individuals needed to demonstrate clinical effects on reduction of cardiac events (both ENRICHD and SADHART screened over 10,000 potential candidates). However, with increasing efficacy in one domain, other sequelae of cardiovascular disease will emerge. For example, the increased survival after myocardial infarction and the shift in the age distribution of primary care patients have led to a marked increase in the number of patients with congestive heart failure. This development has promoted increased behavioral medicine research in patients with congestive heart failure. It is important for health psychologists and other mental health professionals to monitor these trends in target intervention populations and to develop and evaluate treatment strategies in primary care settings as well as secondary rehabilitation facilities that meet the needs of these patients.

REFERENCES

Appels, A. (1997). Depression and coronary heart disease: Observations and questions [editorial]. *Journal of Psychosomatic Research, 43*, 443–452.

Appels, A., Kop, W. J., & Schouten, E. (2000). The nature of the depressive symptomatology preceding myocardial infarction. *Behavioral Medicine, 26*, 86–89.

Appels, A., & Mulder, P. (1988). Excess fatigue as a precursor of myocardial infarction. *European Heart Journal, 9*, 758–764.

Barefoot, J. C., Dahlstrom, W. G., & Williams, R. B., Jr. (1983). Hostility, CHD incidence, and total mortality: A 25-year follow-up study of 255 physicians. *Psychosomatic Medicine, 45*, 59–63.

Beck, A. T., & Steer, R. A. (1987). *Beck depression inventory manual.* San Antonio, TX: Harcourt Brace Jovanovich.

Berkman, L. F., Leo-Summers, L., & Horwitz, R. I. (1992). Emotional support and survival after myocardial infarction. A prospective, population-based study of the elderly. *Annals of Internal Medicine, 117*, 1003–1009.

Blumenthal, J. A., Babyak, M. A., Moore, K. A., Craighead, W. E., Herman, S., Khatri, P., et al. (1999). Effects of exercise training on older patients with major depression. *Archives of Internal Medicine, 159*, 2349–2356.

Blumenthal, J. A., Jiang, W., Babyak, M. A., Krantz, D. S., Frid, D. J., Coleman, R. E., et al. (1997). Stress management and exercise training in cardiac patients with myocardial ischemia. Effects on prognosis and evaluation of mechanisms. *Archives of Internal Medicine, 157,* 2213–2223.

Carney, R. M., Freedland, K. E., Rich, M. W., & Jaffe, A. S. (1995). Depression as a risk factor for cardiac events in established coronary heart disease: A review of possible mechanisms. *Annals of Behavioral Medicine, 17,* 142–149.

Carney, R. M., Saunders, R. D., Freedland, K. E., Stein, P., Rich, M. W., & Jaffe, A. S. (1995). Association of depression with reduced heart rate variability in coronary artery disease. *American Journal of Cardiology, 76,* 562–564.

Castillo-Richmond, A., Schneider, R. H., Alexander, C. N., Cook, R., Myers, H., Nidich, S., et al. (2000). Effects of stress reduction on carotid atherosclerosis in hypertensive African Americans. *Stroke, 31,* 568–573.

Cohen, S., Underwood, G. L., & Gottlieb, B. H. (2000). *Social support measurement and intervention: A guide for health and social scientists.* New York: Oxford University Press.

Denollet, J. (2000). Type D personality. A potential risk factor refined. *Journal of Psychosomatic Research, 49,* 255–266.

Denollet, J., & Brutsaert, D. L. (2001). Reducing emotional distress improves prognosis in coronary heart disease: 9-year mortality in a clinical trial of rehabilitation. *Circulation, 104,* 2018–2023.

Denollet, J., Sys, S. U., Stroobant, N., Rombouts, H., Gillebert, T. C., & Brutsaert, D. L. (1996). Personality as independent predictor of long-term mortality in patients with coronary heart disease. *Lancet, 347,* 417–421.

Dusseldorp, E., van Elderen, T., Maes, S., Meulman, J., & Kraaij, V. (1999). A meta-analysis of psychoeducational programs for coronary heart disease patients. *Health Psychology, 18,* 506–519.

ENRICHD Investigators. (2000). Enhancing recovery in coronary heart disease patients (ENRICHD): Study design and methods. The ENRICHD investigators. *American Heart Journal, 139,* 1–9.

ENRICHD Investigators. (2003). Effects of treating depression and low perceived social support on clinical events after myocardial infarction: The Enhancing Recovery in Coronary Heart Disease Patients (ENRICHD) Randomized Trial. *Journal of the American Medical Association, 289,* 3106–3116.

Frasure-Smith, N., Lesperance, F., Gravel, G., Masson, A., Juneau, M., & Bourassa, M. G. (2002). Long-term survival differences among low-anxious, high-anxious and repressive copers enrolled in the Montreal heart attack readjustment trial. *Psychosomatic Medicine, 64,* 571–579.

Frasure-Smith, N., Lesperance, F., Prince, R. H., Verrier, P., Garber, R. A., Juneau, M., et al. (1997). Randomised trial of home-based psychosocial nursing intervention for patients recovering from myocardial infarction. *Lancet, 350,* 473–479.

Frasure-Smith, N., Lesperance, F., & Talajic, M. (1995). The impact of negative emotions on prognosis following myocardial infarction: Is it more than depression? *Health Psychology, 14*, 388–398.

Frasure-Smith, N., & Prince, R. (1985). The ischemic heart disease life stress monitoring program: Impact on mortality. *Psychosomatic Medicine, 47*, 431–445.

Friedman, M., Thoresen, C. E., Gill, J. J., Ulmer, D., Powell, L. H., Price, V. A., et al. (1986). Alteration of type A behavior and its effect on cardiac recurrences in post myocardial infarction patients: Summary results of the recurrent coronary prevention project. *American Heart Journal, 112*, 653–665.

Gidron, Y., Davidson, K., & Bata, I. (1999). The short-term effects of a hostility-reduction intervention on male coronary heart disease patients. *Health Psychology, 18*, 416–420.

Glassman, A. H., O'Connor, C. M., Califf, R. M., Swedberg, K., Schwartz, P., Bigger, J. T., et al. (2002). Sertraline treatment of major depression in patients with acute MI or unstable angina. *Journal of the American Medical Association, 288*, 701–709.

Gold, P. W., Goodwin, F. K., & Chrousos, G. P. (1988a). Clinical and biochemical manifestations of depression. Relation to the neurobiology of stress (1). *New England Journal of Medicine, 319*, 348–353.

Gold, P. W., Goodwin, F. K., & Chrousos, G. P. (1988b). Clinical and biochemical manifestations of depression. Relation to the neurobiology of stress (2). *New England Journal of Medicine, 319*, 413–420.

Gould, K. L., Ornish, D., Scherwitz, L., Brown, S., Edens, R. P., Hess, M. J., et al. (1995). Changes in myocardial perfusion abnormalities by positron emission tomography after long-term, intense risk factor modification. *Journal of the American Medical Association, 274*, 894–901.

Hamilton, M. (1960). A rating scale for depression. *Journal of Neurology, Neurosurgery and Psychiatry, 12*, 56–62.

Hibbard, J. H., & Pope, C. R. (1993). The quality of social roles as predictors of morbidity and mortality. *Social Sciences and Medicine, 36*, 217–225.

Jones, D. A., & West, R. R. (1996). Psychological rehabilitation after myocardial infarction: Multicentre randomised controlled trial. *British Medical Journal, 313*, 1517–1521.

Kop, W. J. (1999). Chronic and acute psychological risk factors for clinical manifestations of coronary artery disease. *Psychosomatic Medicine, 61*, 476–487.

Kop, W. J., & Ader, D. N. (2001). Assessment and treatment of depression in coronary artery disease patients. *Italian Heart Journal, 2*, 890–894.

Kop, W. J., Appels, A. P., Mendes de Leon, C. F., de Swart, H. B., & Bar, F. W. (1994). Vital exhaustion predicts new cardiac events after successful coronary angioplasty. *Psychosomatic Medicine, 56*, 281–287.

Kop, W. J., Appels, A., Mendes de Leon, C. F., & Bar, F. W. (1996). The relationship between severity of coronary artery disease and vital exhaustion. *Journal of Psychosomatic Research, 40*, 397–405.

Kop, W. J., & Cohen, N. (2001). Psychological risk factors and immune system involvement in cardiovascular disease. In R. Ader, D. L. Felten, & N. Cohen (Eds.), *Psychoneuroimmunology* (3rd ed., pp. 525–544). San Diego, CA: Academic Press.

Krantz, D. S., Kop, W. J., Santiago, H. T., & Gottdiener, J. S. (1996). Mental stress as a trigger of myocardial ischemia and infarction. *Cardiology Clinics, 14,* 271–287.

Krantz, D. S., & McCeney, M. K. (2002). Effects of psychological and social factors on organic disease: A critical assessment of research on coronary heart disease. *Annual Review of Psychology, 53,* 341–369.

La Croix, A. Z. (1994). Psychosocial factors and risk of coronary heart disease in women: An epidemiologic perspective. *Fertility and Sterility, 62,* 133S–139S.

Lepore, S. J. (1998). Problems and prospects for the social support-reactivity hypothesis. *Annals of Behavioral Medicine, 20,* 257–269.

Linden, W. (2000). Psychological treatments in cardiac rehabilitation: Review of rationales and outcomes. *Journal of Psychosomatic Research, 48,* 443–454.

Linden, W., Stossel, C., & Maurice, J. (1996). Psychosocial interventions for patients with coronary artery disease: A meta-analysis. *Archives of Internal Medicine, 156,* 745–752.

Lisspers, J., Sundin, O., Hofman-Bang, C., Nordlander, R., Nygren, A., Ryden, L., et al. (1999). Behavioral effects of a comprehensive, multifactorial program for lifestyle change after percutaneous transluminal coronary angioplasty: A prospective, randomized controlled study. *Journal of Psychosomatic Research, 46,* 143–154.

Marmot, M. G., Shipley, M. J., & Rose, G. (1984). Inequalities in death—Specific explanations of a general pattern? *Lancet,* 1003–1006.

Marmot, M. G., Smith, G. D., Stansfeld, S., Patel, C., North, F., Head, J., et al. (1991). Health inequalities among British civil servants: The Whitehall II study. *Lancet, 337,* 1387–1393.

Meland, E., Laerum, E., & Maeland, J. G. (1996). Life style intervention in general practice: Effects on psychological well-being and patient satisfaction. *Quality of Life Research, 5,* 348–354.

Mendes de Leon, C. F., Kop, W. J., de Swart, H. B., Bar, F. W., & Appels, A. P. (1996). Psychosocial characteristics and recurrent events after percutaneous transluminal coronary angioplasty. *American Journal of Cardiology, 77,* 252–255.

Mendes de Leon, C. F., Powell, L. H., & Kaplan, B. H. (1991). Change in coronary-prone behaviors in the recurrent coronary prevention project. *Psychosomatic Medicine, 53,* 407–419.

Miller, T. Q., Smith, T. W., Turner, C. W., Guijarro, M. L., & Hallet, A. J. (1996). A meta-analytic review of research on hostility and physical health. *Psychological Bulletin, 119,* 322–348.

Mittleman, M. A., Maclure, M., Sherwood, J. B., Mulry, R. P., Tofler, G. H., Jacobs, S. C., et al. (1995). Triggering of acute myocardial infarction onset by episodes of anger. Determinants of Myocardial Infarction Onset Study Investigators. *Circulation, 92,* 1720–1725.

Moller, J., Hallqvist, J., Diderichsen, F., Theorell, T., Reuterwall, C., & Ahlbom, A. (1999). Do episodes of anger trigger myocardial infarction? A case-crossover analysis in the Stockholm Heart Epidemiology Program (SHEEP). *Psychosomatic Medicine, 61,* 842–849.

Nicolson, N. A., & van Diest, R. (2000). Salivary cortisol patterns in vital exhaustion. *Journal of Psychosomatic Research, 49,* 335–342.

Ornish, D., Brown, S. E., Scherwitz, L. W., Billings, J. H., Armstrong, W. T., Ports, T. A., et al. (1990). Can lifestyle changes reverse coronary heart disease? The Lifestyle Heart Trial. *Lancet, 336,* 129–133.

Orth-Gomer, K., & Johnson, J. V. (1987). Social network interaction and mortality. A six year follow-up study of a random sample of the Swedish population. *Journal of Chronic Diseases, 40,* 949–957.

Powell, L. H., & Thoresen, C. E. (1988). Effects of type A behavioral counseling and severity of prior acute myocardial infarction on survival. *American Journal of Cardiolology, 62,* 1159–1163.

Ragland, D. R., & Brand, R. J. (1988). Type A behavior and mortality from coronary heart disease. *New England Journal of Medicine, 318,* 65–69.

Reed, D. M., La Croix, A. Z., Karasek, R. A., Miller, D., & MacLean, C. A. (1989). Occupational strain and the incidence of coronary heart disease. *American Journal of Epidemiology, 129,* 495–502.

Ross, R. (1999). Atherosclerosis—An inflammatory disease. *New England Journal of Medicine, 340,* 115–126.

Rozanski, A., Blumenthal, J. A., & Kaplan, J. (1999). Impact of psychological factors on the pathogenesis of cardiovascular disease and implications for therapy. *Circulation, 99,* 2192–2217.

Ruberman, W., Weinblatt, E., Goldberg, J. D., & Chaudhary, B. S. (1984). Psychosocial influences on mortality after myocardial infarction. *New England Journal of Medicine, 311,* 552–559.

Rugulies, R. (2002). Depression as a predictor for coronary heart disease. A review and meta-analysis. *American Journal of Preventive Medicine, 23,* 51–61.

Sebregts, E. H., Falger, P. R., & Bar, F. W. (2000). Risk factor modification through nonpharmacological interventions in patients with coronary heart disease. *Journal of Psychosomatic Research, 48,* 425–441.

Shumaker, S. A., & Hill, D. R. (1991). Gender differences in social support and physical health. *Health Psychology, 10,* 102–111.

Siegrist, J., Peter, R., Junge, A., Cremer, P., & Seidel, D. (1990). Low status control, high effort at work and ischemic heart disease: Prospective evidence from blue-collar men. *Social Science Medicine, 31,* 1127–1134.

Smith, T. W., & Ruiz, J. M. (2002). Psychosocial influences on the development and course of coronary heart disease: Current status and implications for research and practice. *Journal of Consulting and Clinical Psychology, 70*, 548–568.

Vogt, T. M., Mullooly, J. P., Ernst, D., Pope, C. R., & Hollis, J. F. (1992). Social networks as predictors of ischemic heart disease, cancer, stroke and hypertension: Incidence, survival and mortality. *Journal of Clinical Epidemiology, 45*, 659–666.

Wulsin, L. H., & Singal, B. M. (2003). Do depressive symptoms increase the risk for the onset of coronary disease? A systematic quantitative review. *Psychosomatic Medicine, 65*, 201–210.

5

MANAGEMENT AND TREATMENT OF HIV/AIDS IN PRIMARY CARE

WENDY A. LAW AND CURT BUERMEYER

As of December 2001, a total of 816,149 cumulative cases of the Acquired Immunodeficiency Syndrome (AIDS) had been reported in the United States. Of these cases, 43,158 were newly reported in 2001 (Centers for Disease Control and Prevention [CDC], 2001). This latter number, although substantial, reflects a slow but steady decrease in the annual rates of new AIDS diagnoses. Similarly, although estimates of new infection rates for the human immunodeficiency virus (HIV; HIV–1) have shown little change in the United States, the duration of pre-AIDS/HIV infection has markedly improved, adding years to the average life expectancy and improving quality of life for infected individuals. These significant improvements in the infection progression can be attributed primarily to the development of aggressive medication treatments and the use of highly active antiretroviral therapies (HAART). Because of these advancements, slowing or halting HIV progression has become the immediate goal of health care providers treating HIV-seropositive patients in primary care settings. Critical to the success of this goal is the patient's willingness and ability to comply with treatment and to adhere to prescribed treatment regimens (Horne & Weinman, 1999; Martin-Fernandez, Escobar-Rodriguez, Campo-Angora, & Rubio-Garcia, 2001).

Problems with behavioral compliance and medication adherence can significantly compromise the course of treatment. Therefore, designing interventions aimed at increasing compliance and improving adherence constitutes an important role for the psychologist working with HIV-infected individuals in primary care settings. The important factors affecting compliance and adherence to treatment in HIV/AIDS can be summarized in terms of three target areas directly related to the role of the psychologist in the medical clinic setting. These target areas are (a) assistance with physician-referred general concerns regarding a specific patient's motivation for medication compliance (general behavioral factors); (b) assessment and intervention regarding psychopathology that can affect medication compliance and quality of life (mood state/psychopathology factors); and (c) evaluation of cognitive features affecting compliance, with recommendations for compensatory strategies to improve medication adherence (neuropsychological factors).

This chapter first provides a brief overview of the history and epidemiology of HIV/AIDS in the United States. The general biopsychosocial aspects of HIV/AIDS are then introduced, with specific emphases on the neurocognitive and psychosocial features. The chapter concludes with a discussion of the role of the psychologist in the outpatient medical clinic setting in relation to the most relevant principles of behavioral medicine and with specific emphasis on adherence.

HIV/AIDS: HISTORY AND BACKGROUND

In 1981, the CDC reported in the *Morbidity and Mortality Weekly Report* (CDC, 1981a, 1981b) isolated cases of diseases commonly associated with marked immunosuppression in otherwise healthy young gay men. By the end of the following year, more than 200 cases had been documented, and a distinct syndrome was identified and characterized as the Acquired Immunodeficiency Syndrome (AIDS; Marx, 1982). At the end of 2001, 20 years after the initial cases of the human immunodeficiency virus (HIV) infection were reported, approximately 450,000 individuals were estimated to be living with HIV/AIDS in the United States (CDC, 2001). Within the United States, the form of HIV with the highest prevalence rates is the type 1 infection (HIV–1; CDC, 1998). Based on an estimated U.S. population of 285 million, approximately 1 out of every 615 individuals is believed to be living with HIV–1 infection. These numbers, combined with the expected rates of very high general patient contact in the average primary care clinic, indicate that practitioners can expect to encounter HIV/AIDS-infected individuals in the clinic. It is essential, therefore, that practitioners become familiar with the unique neurocognitive and psycho-social aspects of the disease and how they contribute to the patient's overall health and well-being. In addition, clinics that specialize in treating and managing HIV/AIDS (i.e., general infectious disease clinics or specific HIV/ AIDS clinics) will need to incorporate knowledge and awareness of contributions from biopsychosocial factors in treating and managing the disease to maximize treatment outcomes. There is clearly a defined role for psychological consultation and intervention within these medical settings.

BIOPSYCHOSOCIAL ASPECTS OF HIV/AIDS

The biopsychosocial model of health outcomes is based on the premise that biological, psychological, and social contributions interactively affect the nature, course, and sequelae of illness conditions (Engel, 1977). When working with individuals who have been diagnosed with HIV/AIDS, psychologists in primary care contexts need not only be familiar with the biological features of the disease related to the progressive immunosuppression that is its hallmark but also should familiarize themselves with its primary neurocognitive features, as well as with the major psychosocial contributions to its course. Impairments in memory and attention, for example, can result in missed visits, inconsistent adherence to medication regimens, or inaccurate reporting of new symptoms. Therefore, the central nervous system (CNS) aspects of HIV–1 infection should be considered when evaluating behavioral difficulties that might affect long-term treatment and management of HIV–1 infection. Psychosocial effects of HIV–1 infection are also common and may significantly contribute to observed behavioral difficulties and provide significant roadblocks in the effective treatment of the infection progression and disease course. Specifically, HIV–1 infection has been associated with high rates of depression, with specific peaks of depression most likely when disease progression has been identified or when treatment resistance develops (Kalichman, Difonzo, Austin, Luke, & Rompa, 2002; Perdices, Dunbar, Grunseit, Hall, & Cooper, 1992). Moreover, characteristics of depression including apathy or loss of energy may reduce motivation for self-care or treatment adherence. Similarly, anxiety can be associated with ruminative worry and distress over potential side effects of treatment, thereby reducing a patient's persistence with the treatment, despite its potential benefits. The role of neurocognitive and psychosocial features of HIV–1 infection must be underscored when designing treatment programs and evaluating compliance problems with behavioral compliance within both primary and specialty care clinic settings.

Neurocognitive Features of HIV/AIDS

The AIDS Dementia Complex (ADC; Navia, Jordan, & Price, 1986; Navia, Cho, Petito, & Price, 1986) is a late-stage condition that has been characterized as a triad of cognitive, motor, and behavioral changes that develops in the presence of significant immunosuppression and progressively worsens over a period of weeks to months, ultimately culminating in death. The cognitive changes involve attention and concentration deficits, memory loss, and psychomotor (cognitive) slowing. Although subjective awareness of cognitive difficulties sometimes may precede any objective assessment findings, perceived difficulties in thinking and processing also can be a result of anxiety and depression without any disruption of neural functions (Mapou et al., 1993). The remaining features of the triad of symptoms include objective motor difficulties (unbalanced gait, motor weakness, and tremor) and behavioral changes that include symptoms of depression with a lack of interest in usual activities and general apathy). Symptoms of mania or psychosis also may occur in some individuals (Navia, Jordan, et al., 1986). The ADC symptom triad and neuropathology (Navia, Cho, et al., 1986) bear striking similarities to well-documented subcortical disorders (e.g., progressive supranuclear palsy, Parkinson's disease, and Huntington's disease), resulting in ADC being classified as a subcortical dementia process.

Although ADC was initially characterized as AIDS because of the evidence of a reduction in immune function combined with HIV seropositivity, over time the accumulating research evidence documented that direct CNS effects from HIV infection could occur well before significant immunocompromise was established (Grant et al., 1987; Hollander & Levy, 1987; McArthur, 1987; Navia & Price, 1987). In addition, dementia in HIV+ individuals independent of documented compromise in immune function was added as an AIDS-defining condition for diagnostic purposes (Centers for Disease Control, 1987). Similar to findings in the early stages of subcortical dementia disorders in general, the neurocognitive features of HIV–1 infection in the earliest stages of infection have been associated with cognitive and motor slowing that can be demonstrated in some individuals who have no objective symptoms of infection (Bornstein et al., 1991, 1992; Grant et al., 1987; A. Martin et al., 1992; E. Martin et al., 1992; Miller, Satz, & Vischer, 1991; Perdices & Cooper, 1989; Wilkie, Eisdorfer, Morgan, Loewenstein, & Szapocznik, 1990; Wilkie et al., 1992). Thus, neurocognitive contributions to behavior are not limited to only those with advanced disease and significant immunosuppression but also can occur and affect behavior in earlier stages.

During the approximately first decade of the HIV pandemic, research on the CNS aspects of this disorder was directed toward understanding the nature and mechanisms of cognitive and motor slowing in HIV–1 infection, with hopes of identifying targets for intervention to reduce the burden of the disease process on infected individuals. This was accomplished by examining neurocognitive changes using more sensitive eletrophysiological measurements (Takakuwa, Callaway, Naylor, Herzig, & Yano, 1993), computerized measurements of performance (Worth, Savage, Baer, Esty, & Navia, 1993), progressively more complex and sensitive measurements of slowing involving complex processing and response time tasks (Dunlop, Bjorklund, Abdelnoor, & Myrvang, 1993; Law et al., 1995), and examination of the independent motor and cognitive features of reaction time slowing (Law et al., 1994; A. Martin, Heyes, Salazar, Law, & Williams, 1993; E. Martin et al., 1993; Sorensen, Martin, & Robertson, 1994). Most recently, examination of the neurocognitive features of HIV–1 infection has focused on the impact of pharmacological treatment effects. Although there continues to be much that is unknown about the mechanisms by which HIV exerts its direct CNS effects, improved (faster) cognitive processing and simple motor reaction times have been demonstrated in patients receiving antiretroviral therapy, regardless of degree of immunosuppression, age, substance use status, and psychiatric symptom status (E. Martin, Pitrak, Novak, Pursell, & Mullane, 1999). Similar improvements also have been evidenced with treatment by methylphenidate, which does not specifically target HIV infection but nonetheless produced faster cognitive processing speeds in an HIV-infected sample (Hinkin et al., 2001). Thus, ongoing medication contributions to the CNS aspects of HIV–1 infection must also be considered when evaluating the HIV+ patient in an outpatient clinic setting.

As may be expected, there is substantial variability in the degree of subjective awareness of cognitive changes and the extent to which subjective perception is accurately related to objective neuropsychological performance measures. Subjective complaints of cognitive changes in HIV–1 infection have been found in some instances to be related to psychiatric symptoms (e.g., van Gorp et al., 1991; Wilkins et al., 1991) and in others to be highly associated with cognitive and motor slowing independent of mood-related psychiatric symptoms (Beason-Hazen, Nasrallah, & Bornstein, 1994; Mapou et al., 1993). In addition, there has been evidence of variability in the relationship between neuropsychological performance weaknesses and psychiatric symptoms across progressive stages of disease severity. Thus, although complaints of neurocognitive changes in the early stages of infection or disease progression often will reflect mood-state factors (Maj et al., 1994), such complaints also can represent early indications of actual neurocognitive changes that are not attributable solely to psychiatric symptoms (Marsh & McCall, 1994).

Finally, the development of effective medication interventions and pharmacological treatment regimens has substantially improved the longevity and quality of life for individuals infected with HIV–1. In addition, medication effects in some instances have been associated with improvement of the behavioral manifestations of cognitive and motor slowing. Nonetheless, side effects of medications also can cause adverse sequelae that include neurological damage and cognitive interference. Although these side effects are generally temporary when medications are discontinued, discontinuation of medication may in turn eliminate the beneficial impact of the medications on disease progression and may even contribute further to the development of CNS-related symptoms and conditions. Thus, the impact of such medications and pharmacological treatments over longer durations is as yet undetermined.

Psychosocial Features of HIV/AIDS

In addition to the neurocognitive aspects of HIV–1 infection, the unique psychological and psychosocial effects of infection must be underscored when working with HIV–1 infected individuals in a primary care clinic. Although the rates and degree of major depression are generally comparable to rates in other chronic health conditions, individuals with HIV–1 infection are susceptible to higher rates of major depression and anxiety disorders after receiving information that their condition has progressed or after learning that they have developed a resistance to previously beneficial medication treatments (Perdices, Dunbar, Grunseit, Hall, & Cooper, 1992). Psychosocial effects also are unique to HIV/AIDS in association with the identified "high risk" groups in which the majority of cases fall and the related stigma often associated with these risk groups (Herek, Capitanio, & Widaman, 2003). Thus, HIV–1-infected individuals may find that their usual support group is no longer available once their serostatus becomes known. Ironically, the clinical experience of one author (WAL) included working with a newly infected gay male who reported that he had "confessed" to his 11-year-old daughter that he had become infected because he experimented with an injection drug in an unsafe condition, whereas an addicted injecting drug user (IDU) "confessed" to his family that he had become infected after a brief sexual experience with another man. In both instances, the individuals felt that they needed to keep their specific behavioral causes of infection from their family members, because the family members would be unable to accept the converse reality. All professionals who have worked closely with these groups can provide similar revealing incidents of the profound psychosocial impact of the individual's perceived sense of stigma and the interaction with that individual's psychosocial network (e.g., what is the more "acceptable" explanation for becoming infected in that person's world).

Additional psychosocial features of HIV–1 infection that can affect the psychologist's role in medical clinic settings include its rapidly and broadly changing demographic makeup. Initially, HIV–1 infection in the United States was evidenced primarily in white gay males, with IDUs representing the second highest infection rates of all reported cases. Although blood transfusion rates were somewhat high early in the history of the infection, these rates have decreased substantially as a result of the initiation of blood screening programs. Over the past decade, there has been a steady and notable change in the demographic features associated with the highest rates of new infection. Specifically, from 1996 to 2001, minority females showed the highest new rates across successive years, and general heterosexual rates of new infection steadily increased at rapid rates. The changing demographics of new incident cases indicate that the psychosocial features of HIV–1 infection also are likely to change and can be expected to present a new and varied profile in the clinic. Psychologists must be prepared to consider how these changing demographics might affect treatment response and how best to respond to the specific needs of individual patient populations.

HIV/AIDS AND OUTPATIENT CLINIC CARE

Outpatient clinical care of individuals with HIV/AIDS may occur in the general primary care setting in which the presenting problem may or may not be directly related to factors associated with the disease process. Alternatively, outpatient clinical care may be provided in more specialized clinics that emphasize treatment of infectious diseases in general or HIV/AIDS in particular. In either context, it is important for psychologists consulting with outpatient care of HIV/AIDS patients to maintain awareness of the complex biopsychosocial interactions that can directly affect medical treatment for individuals who struggle with this disease process.

Treatment Effectiveness

The effectiveness of potentially beneficial medication interventions is necessarily contingent on the individual patients' adherence to recommended treatments, including maintaining the strictly regimented schedule of multiple medications and multiple treatment episodes per day. Strategies to improve the outcome of HIV–1 infection can be viewed as falling into two basic domains: interventions that provide effective medication combinations ("cocktails": to reduce viral load; increase CD4 cells; reduce opportunistic infections) and interventions that improve the adherence to these medication regimens. Neurocognitive, behavioral, and psychosocial features of HIV/AIDS all have direct implications and effects on medication adherence. The various factors that can affect patient adherence and alter disease course can be illustrated via three cyclical patterns that have been developed for the purposes of this chapter, involving neurocognitive (Cycle 1), psycho-pathological–behavioral (Cycle 2), or psychosocial (Cycle 3) contributions of HIV. Each of these cycles represents a point of intervention for psychologists working with HIV-infected patients in the medical care setting.

Cycle 1: Neurocognitive Factors Affecting Adherence

In the first cycle (Cycle 1), CNS involvement associated with the general process of HIV–1 disease progression can have important neurocognitive effects that affect adherence. HIV infection has a direct effect on physical health, depleting the immune cells that defend the physical system against diseases and infections. The impact of viral infection is demonstrated in a cyclical, progressive pattern. As the depletion of healthy immune cells increases, the physical system becomes vulnerable to developing diseases that commonly are held at bay by normal immune function. Such developing diseases are referred to as *opportunistic infections*. When opportunistic infections develop, defensive immune cell functioning is activated, causing more immune cell targets to be available for infection and destruction by HIV–1 (Gougeon & Montagnier, 1999; Mosier, 2000). These systemic effects continue to deplete the available cellular immune system defenses, leading to the generation of higher HIV–1 serologic loads with a corresponding increase in the availability of HIV to enter the CNS.

CNS invasion occurs when HIV crosses the blood–brain barrier (BBB), either through direct macrophage transport mechanisms (Lane et al., 1996; Ross et al., 2001) or through disruption of the usual CNS protective mechanisms afforded by the barrier (Moses & Nelson, 1994). Once HIV has entered the CNS, damaging neuronal effects characterized by decreased concentration and attention, impaired memory, and reaction time can result from CNS opportunistic infections or from the direct effects of the virus itself. The development and increased use of HAART has improved many HIV-related CNS diseases and effects. However, because there are several different mechanisms by which HIV is believed to act on the CNS, some of the HIV-related neurocognitive effects do not respond to HAART (Dore et al., 1999; Von Giesen, Hefter, Jablonowski, & Arendt, 2000). This lack of response can affect adherence, interfering with a patient's ability to remember complicated medication regimens, follow through with dosing recommendations, or plan in advance to carry needed medications when traveling outside of the home (prospective memory). This inconsistent adherence, including reduced medication intake, may lead to the production of treatment-resistant strains of HIV, advancing the HIV infection and reinitiating the cycle. Thus, neurocognitive disruption in patients treated with available antiretroviral therapies may have a substantial impact on adherence to treatment and eventual treatment outcome. (See Exhibit 5.1.)

EXHIBIT 5.1
Cycle 1: HIV Effects on CNS

HIV infection and progression
HIV and BBB
HIV and neural deterioration
HIV, HAART, and BBB, side effects of medications
HIV reservoirs
Neurocognitive impairment
Adherence/nonadherence, treatment resistant strains of HIV

Cycle 2: Psychopathological–Behavioral Factors Affecting Adherence

A second adherence-related cycle has to do with the psychological and emotional reactions of individuals who carry a diagnosis of HIV–1 infection. Personality, coping style, and past and current vulnerabilities to psychopathology have general treatment adherence effects, including HAART treatment adherence in HIV/AIDS infected individuals (Demas, Schoenbaum, Wills, Dolls, & Klein, 1995). For example, to cope with emotional distress, individuals may abuse nonprescribed mind-altering medications or illicit drugs, further disrupting their clarity of thinking and memory for taking prescribed treatments. Alternatively, characteristics such as pessimism may interfere with an individual's belief that medication is effective, leading to a worsening of symptoms and ultimately perpetuating the belief that there is no hope. Patients also may try to prevent themselves from experiencing emotional distress by avoiding stimuli that are associated with being ill (e.g., HIV clinics, HIV medications, HIV treatment material). Finally, preexisting or new onset mood disorders and anxiety have well-established impact on attention and concentration (Lezak, 1995), which again may negatively affect treatment adherence. In terms of HIV/AIDS, symptoms of depression and anxiety initially occur following diagnosis or when the patient has been informed that the virus has progressed to a more advanced stage (Chandra, Ravi, Desai, Subbakrishna, 1998; Kalichman et al., 2002; Kaplan, Marks, & Mertens, 1997). These and other psychological reactions to the diagnosis and symptoms of HIV infection all can be expected to adversely affect adherence as a result of motivational and cognitive disruption and lead to detrimental health consequences that perpetuate the cycle. (See Exhibit 5.2.)

Cycle 3: Psychosocial Factors Affecting Adherence

The third cycle of adherence is associated with the psychosocial sequelae of HIV infection. Despite improvements in accuracy of information available to the public regarding the HIV transmission and risk-relevant behaviors, there continues to be a heavy social stigma associated with an

EXHIBIT 5.2
Cycle 2: HIV Effects on Psychological Functioning

HIV infection and progression
Preexisting psychological vulnerabilities and conditions
Personality, coping style (avoidance)
Drug use, promiscuity, high-risk/parasuicidal behaviors
Depression, anxiety, adjustment disorder
Loss of concentration, pessimism
Adherence/nonadherence, treatment resistant strains of HIV

HIV diagnosis. This stigma can lead to a thinning of pre-HIV social support networks, job loss, financial problems, health insurance difficulties, housing problems, and the loss of tangible resources that are needed for obtaining and adhering to HIV medications (e.g., transportation). For instance, individuals who suffer from financially taxing medical illnesses often turn to family and friends for assistance with transportation for getting to medical appointments or to pharmacies to acquire necessary medications. However, many family and presumed close friends summarily reject affected individuals who have been diagnosed with HIV/AIDS, eliminating this important pyschological resource for maintaining continuity of care and treatment. In addition, ethnocultural social support networks may have biases and beliefs based on previous experiences that have direct impact on treatment adherence because of a lack of trust (e.g., knowledge of the Tuskegee study in which Black men with syphilis were studied without treatment: Shavers, Lynch, & Burmeister, 2000). Finally, the loss of usual support networks may contribute to greater involvement in alternative social support networks (e.g., drug use networks: Suh, Mandell, Latkin, & Kim, 1997) that can further increase the risks of engaging in behaviors that promote or increase the likelihood of nonadherence. (See Exhibit 5.3.)

Treatment Effectiveness Summary

In all three of these cycles, the potential for improving treatment outcome through effective assessment and intervention by psychologists

EXHIBIT 5.3
Cycle 3: HIV Effects on Psychosocial Functioning

HIV infection and progression
Social stigma of HIV/AIDS
Loss of social support/pursuit of maladaptive social support
Job loss, financial problems, health insurance
Housing problems, loss of tangible resources
Sociocultural views re: HIV treatment (e.g., Tuskegee syphilis experiment)
Adherence/nonadherence, treatment-resistant strains of HIV

exists on multiple levels and offers a critical role for providing needed services in the clinical setting. Additional targets include consultation with the clinical staff who provide and monitor the direct medical contact with patients, as well as direct patient care management by the psychologist, addressing patients' clinical psychological issues and mental health conditions or concerns.

ASSESSMENT AND INTERVENTION: TARGETS AND METHODS

Psychologists have the potential to affect treatment outcome through a variety of mechanisms, including continuously educating staff and professional care providers on the nature and importance of psychosocial contributions to adherence and by facilitating team-based approaches to patient care. Also important are psychologists' direct contributions to patient care management and treatment in outpatient medical clinic settings, which can include several stages of client contact. First, a patient may be referred for a one-time consult for evaluation of an acute emotional or behavioral crisis. Such an acute emergency consult may occur in relationship to HIV/AIDS, such as when clinic patients are first diagnosed with HIV/AIDS, when medical findings indicate a change toward greater illness severity, or when everyday life events coincide with the patients' scheduled clinic visit (e.g., recent death of a loved one). Similarly, patients may be referred for intervention of an acute exacerbation of preexisting mental health conditions (e.g., Axis I or II condition; generalized anxiety disorder) that could undermine patients' adherence to treatment. Intervention in the context of a one-time consultation may involve implementing cognitive–behavioral techniques for reframing the acute trigger or assessing for Axis I pathology requiring more extensive intervention and referral for medication evaluation (e.g., major depression). These and other services may be provided through a variety of roles within medical clinic settings, each of which has its own unique contribution to the assessment or intervention of HIV management in outpatient clinic settings.

Psychologist as Educator

The most broad and enduring contribution of the psychologist in a primary care setting involves staff education. The psychologist can provide valuable contributions on mind–body issues through informal interactions with staff members, scheduled in-service trainings, or formal continuing education instruction. Topics may include the nature and importance of various psychological factors on adherence and health outcomes, including neuropsychological factors, behavioral health principles, psychopathology, and psychosocial stressors.

Multidisciplinary treatment teams also provide an excellent format for informal staff education. Psychologists may facilitate team effectiveness by extending the conceptualization of nonadherence risk to include various behavioral, emotional, and environmental factors. Although many treatment teams comprise diverse and highly competent health professionals, including infectious disease physicians, clinical social workers, nurses, and technicians, all of whom have a basic understanding of psychological factors, the psychologist can help to integrate perspectives and see "the whole person" in his or her psychosocial context. During team meetings, when difficult or nonadherent patients are discussed, the psychologist can help reduce the tendency to "blame the victim." Rather, potential sources of nonadherence (e.g., pessimism, neurocognitive impairments, learning disability, poor coping skills, limited social support, psychopathology) may be given greater importance.

Psychologist as Consultation–Liaison

In addition to educating clinic staff on factors that can affect treatment outcome in HIV/AIDS, psychologists also may have direct contact with patients for assessment of factors affecting medical care and patient well-being. This contact may occur at various points in the patient's outpatient clinical care and may offer opportunities for proactive contributions to treatment effectiveness, as well as for more traditional referral-driven consultations that can affect treatment and care.

Proactive Assessment for Nonadherence Risk

Medical facilities that are committed to a biopsychosocial philosophy may include psychologists in the routine assessment of patients at intake. This proactive approach may include assessment of a patient's general psychological well-being or risk for nonadherence. When conducting a proactive assessment of patients' psychological well-being, psychologists may gather important data related to nonadherence risk. This may include screening for memory disturbance, depression, anxiety, and comprehension of health status.

Reactive Assessment for Nonadherence Risk

In the course of a patient's medical visit, information may be obtained that indicates a strong likelihood of medication nonadherence (e.g., no change in viral load or CD4 count). Although it is possible that a patient has a treatment-resistant strain of HIV, psychologists may be consulted to assess patterns of treatment adherence/nonadherence. This assessment may focus on gathering self-report data regarding the patient's memory of taking medications (e.g., time of day, dosage, conjunction with meals) and reasons for missing doses (e.g., "just forgot to take them," incorrect memory of when or how to take them). Following this assessment, the psychologist may immediately consult with the primary health provider to provide feedback and help design a course of action.

Reactive Assessment for Acute Psychopathology–Endangerment

Acute psychological reactions to HIV-related information may prompt psychological consultation. Evidence of suicidal or homicidal ideation or intent or impairment in judgment and reasoning that may result in harm to self, others, or property are examples of acute reactions that warrant psychological intervention.

Reactive Extensive Psychological–Neuropsychological Assessment for Decline in Function

Should there be evidence that a patient may be unable to adhere to a medication regimen, despite apparent motivation, a psychologist may conduct a comprehensive assessment. Because important information concerning a patient's medication regimen may only be given verbally, patients with learning disabilities, receptive language impairments, or central auditory processing difficulties may miss important information. In addition, patients with impaired long-term memory may process the information accurately but have difficulty remembering the information when taking their medication weeks after their medical appointment. These and many other neuropsychological problems may be assessed during the course of a comprehensive psychological assessment.

Psychologist as Treatment Provider

Direct patient intervention for treating mental health concerns offers another potential contribution for psychologists working in outpatient medical clinic settings. When working with individuals who have been diagnosed with HIV/AIDS, the nature of the treatment can be expected to depend on contributions from the medical condition itself as well as from its associated complexities.

Emotional Supporter, Stabilizer

Patients who are suicidal, delusional, or who are otherwise acutely in danger of causing harm to their self, others, or property may be referred to the psychologist. After the assessment, psychologists may attempt to stabilize a patient using interventions that include calming, refocusing, reducing cognitive distortions, building optimism, reducing anger, or assessing reasons for living.

Adherence Training

Because HIV medication treatment requires a high level of adherence (80% to 95% of doses accurately), the psychologist can provide an indispensable component of the treatment strategy. Specifically, psychologists may assess unique sources of adherence risk and develop or tailor adherence training packages for each patient. Customized adherence training may begin with retention of information about the medication regimen. Subsequently, behavioral strategies to remind patients to take their medication at specified times could be developed. These interventions might include the use of pillboxes, timers, sticky notes, and significant others to remind patients when take scheduled medications. Although it is often assumed that patients will develop their own system for taking their medications as prescribed, it is typically helpful to work out the specific details with patients so that medications are taken at the appropriate time of day, with the correct type of food, and in the correct dosages.

Psychoeducational Resource

Being diagnosed with HIV/AIDS is overwhelming, both emotionally and intellectually. Although the amount of information needed subsequent to diagnosis varies, most patients need some amount of education about HIV, medication, biological indexes of health (e.g., CD4 count, viral load), medication, and the prognosis. Misinformation about the virus, methods of transmission, opportunistic infections, alternative–herbal remedies, effective medications, and treatment resistance necessitates that educational–psychoeducational interventions be included in the treatment plan. Nurses and physicians often provide basic information about HIV progression, but patients may need more information, or repeated information, before more fully understanding their illness. Psychologists who possess a basic understanding of the biological mechanisms involved in viral replication and immune suppression may be able to tailor explanations for individual patients in a manner that maximizes understanding and facilitates learning.

Psychotherapist

Although many primary care clinics may not have the resources and space for psychologists to provide traditional psychotherapy, there is an increasing trend for psychologists to conduct therapy in, or in affiliation with, the primary care clinic. Psychologists may be able to schedule weekly psychotherapy appointments to be conducted in consultation or treatment rooms, depending on the resources provided. Conditions such as depression, anxiety, adjustment disorder, and personality disorders may be effectively treated before patients can be expected to adhere to complex treatment regimens that require a desire to live, motivation for a better life, or general desire for self-improvement. Additional targets for intervention are associated with psychosocial factors that are more specific to being infected with HIV. These include forgiveness, self-esteem/worth, anger at the person who may have transmitted the virus (primary transmission), guilt at transmitting the virus (secondary transmission), outcome pessimism, perceptions of HIV as a terminal illness, and couples therapy either within a discordant (one partner seropositive and the other seronegative) or coinfected (both partners seropositive) relationship.

Behavioral Health

Another aspect of behavior modification involves helping patients develop healthier lifestyles. Weight management, smoking cessation, and exercise training are examples of interventions psychologists may use when working in primary care. Although many patients already understand the importance of living healthier lifestyles, psychologists can serve to intensify patients' aspiration for change. Helping clients take small, measurable, and achievable steps to change poor health habits can lead to a greater commitment to health and health self-efficacy. A second area of behavioral health interventions includes the modification of sexual practices. To reduce secondary transmission risk and infection with other strains of HIV, psychologists may help patients to understand the importance of changing sexual habits. In addition, they may inform patients how to disclose HIV status to their partners and how to practice safe sex.

Assessor and Referral Agent

Because psychologists in primary care may be unable to provide the services needed by every client, an important role for psychologists is the ability to assess treatment needs and make appropriate referral for more specialized assessment or intervention. Evidence of cognitive deterioration may be suggestive of CNS effects. In such cases, mental status screening assessment and review of basic patient complaints involving memory, attention, and psychomotor slowing may be warranted. Psychologists should be familiar with local practitioners who are able to provide neuropsychological assessments, individual and group therapy, alcohol and substance abuse treatment, in-patient and out-patient treatment, and other needed services.

Scientist–Practitioner

Finally, the role of the psychologist in care and management of individuals infected with HIV/AIDS can include the opportunity to contribute to effectiveness literature by applying scientist–practitioner methods for systematically testing and examining the impact of various factors on outcome (e.g., disease-specific, psychosocial, neurocognitive, and psychiatric factors on disease progression, quality of life, and treatment adherence). As one example, disease-specific factors represent the potential effects associated with different opportunistic infections. Thus, diagnosis with Kaposi's sarcoma (KS) has a relatively more positive prognosis than diagnosis with progressive multifocal leukoencephalopathy (PML). As a result, the behavioral, neurocognitive, and psychiatric impact from each diagnosis will differ, and the intervention that may be of greatest benefit to improve outcome associated with each diagnosis may have different targets (e.g., impact of HAART on improved outcome with KS may suggest specific focus on adherence, whereas improved treatment for PML with HAART but continued worst outcome of the HIV/AIDS-related CNS disorders may indicate a greater emphasis on referral for end-of-life issues). Similarly, psychosocial, neurocognitive, and psychiatric factors all can and will affect the progression of illness, patient's quality of life, and adherence to treatment. However, systematic scientific explorations of the interactions among these factors have not been implemented to determine the effectiveness of available treatments in the patients' actual lives and day-to-day hurdles. Thus, social support networks may be critically important for those patients who have available resources for meeting basic living needs but may be irrelevant for those patients who are without access to consistent food or shelter. The increasing nondiscriminatory infectiousness of HIV/AIDS will continue to bring additional challenges to notions of identifying the evidence-based interventions that are best suited for obtaining the maximal outcome. This also does not address how a decision is made or who makes it with regard to what is the "best" outcome to strive toward. Therefore, scientific exploration by a psychologist should help to drive recognition of the importance in characterizing the sample and identifying key biopsychosocial differences across studies that may contribute to apparently conflicting outcomes.

CONCLUSION

Treatments for and outcomes of infection with HIV/AIDS have improved significantly since its original manifestations in the United States during the late 1970s and early 1980s, leading to the change in characterization of this disease process in terms of a long-term survival rather than a terminal illness emphasis. Nonetheless, a "cure" has yet to be identified, and recent evidence of changes in behavioral risk factors toward increased risk-taking (Stolte & Coutinho, 2002) indicate that HIV/AIDS is not likely to become less prevalent in our health care systems in the near future.

Because infection, transmission, and treatment adherence for improving outcome of HIV/AIDS all are contingent on an individual's behaviors, psychologists have a unique opportunity for providing an important contribution in the prevention and treatment of this disease process. This opportunity can best be manifested within the primary care clinic in either general medicine or specialized HIV/AIDS treatment settings in which large rates of patients infected with HIV/AIDS can be expected to continue to be seen for outpatient care and management.

Compliance with treatment and adherence to proscribed medication regimens are critical features in the efforts of health care providers to slow or halt HIV disease progression in infected individuals. Problems with compliance and medication adherence occur for a variety of reasons and can significantly compromise the course of treatment. Designing interventions aimed at increasing compliance and improving adherence constitutes an important role for the psychologist working with HIV-infected individuals in primary care settings. When designing these interventions, psychologists should remain cognizant of the changing demographics of the patient and the varied needs of the infected patient population. Factors such as cultural biases, educational status, occupational status, support network, religious beliefs, sexual orientation, and cognitive and emotional resources may separately or together affect how an individual manages his or her illness status and responds to treatment. Additional important contributions may be related to consultation services to clinic health providers, involving education of behavioral and cognitive factors affecting patient treatment and assessment services to identify neurocognitive or behavioral considerations for patient treatment. The health professional involved in treating HIV/AIDS infected individuals in outpatient medical clinic settings should become informed about the specific needs of the individual patient and the treating clinic, and make efforts to be flexible with regard to the use of assessments and interventions to maximize treatment efficacy and outcome.

REFERENCES

Beason-Hazen, S., Nasrallah, H. A., & Bornstein, R. A. (1994). Self-report of symptoms and neuropsychological performance in asymptomatic HIV-positive individuals. *Journal of Neuropsychiatry and Clinical Neurosciences, 6*, 43–49.

Bornstein, R. A., Nasrallah, H. A., Para, M. F., Fass, R. J., Whitacre, C. C., & Rice, R. R. (1991). Rate of CD4 decline and neuropsychological performance in HIV infection. *Archives of Neurology, 48*, 704–707.

Bornstein, R. A., Nasrallah, H. A., Para, M. F., Whitacre, C. C., Rosenberger, P., Fass, R. J., et al. (1992). Neuropsychological performance in asymptomatic HIV infection. *Journal of Neuropsychiatry and Clinical Neurosciences, 4*, 386–394.

Centers for Disease Control. (1981a). Kaposi's sarcoma and pneumocystis pneumonia among homosexual men—New York City and California. *Morbidity and Mortality Weekly Report, 30,* 305–308.

Centers for Disease Control. (1981b). Pneumocystis pneumonia—Los Angeles. *Morbidity and Mortality Weekly Report, 30,* 25–252.

Centers for Disease Control. (1987). Revision of the CDC surveillance case definition acquired immunodeficiency syndrome. *Morbidity and Mortality Weekly Report, 35,* 334–339.

Centers for Disease Control and Prevention. (1998). *Human Immunodeficiency Virus Type 2.* Retrieved 2001 from http://www.cdc.gov/hiv/pubs/facts/hiv2.htm

Centers for Disease Control and Prevention. (2001). *HIV/AIDS Surveillance Report, 13*(2), 1–48.

Chandra, P. S., Ravi, V., Desai, A., & Subbakrishna, D. K. (1998). Anxiety and depression among HIV-infected heterosexuals—A report from India. *Journal of Psychosomatic Research, 45,* 401–409.

Demas, P., Schoenbaum, E. E., Wills, T. A., Dolls, L. S., & Klien, R. S. (1995). Stress, coping, and attitudes toward HIV treatment in injecting drug users: A qualitative study. *AIDS Education and Prevention, 7,* 429–442.

Dore, G. J., Correll, P. K., Li, Y., Kaldor, J. M., Cooper, D. A., & Brew, B. J. (1999). Changes to AIDS dementia complex in the era of highly active antiretroviral therapy. *AIDS, 13,* 1249–1253.

Dunlop, O., Bjorklund, R., Abdelnoor, M., & Myrvang, B. (1993). Total reaction time: A new approach in early HIV encephalopathy. *Acta Neurologica Scandinavica, 88,* 344–348.

Engel, G. (1977). The need for a new medical model: A challenge for biomedicine. *Science, 196,* 129–136.

Gougeon, M. L., & Montagnier, L. (1999). Programmed cell death as a mechanism of CD4 and CD8 T cell deletion in AIDS. Molecular control and effect of highly active anti-retroviral therapy. *Annals of the New York Academy of Science, 887,* 199–212.

Grant, I., Atkinson, J. H., Hesselink, J. R., Kennedy, C. J., Richman, D. D., Spector, S. A., et al. (1987). Evidence for early central nervous system involvement in the acquired immunodeficiency syndrome (AIDS) and other human immunodeficiency virus (HIV) infections. *Annals of Internal Medicine, 107,* 828–836.

Herek, G. M., Capitanio, J. P., & Widaman, K. F. (2003). Stigma, social risk, and health policy: Public attitudes toward HIV surveillance policies and the social construction of illness. *Health Psychology, 22,* 533–540.

Hinkin, C. H., Castellon, S. A., Hardy, D. J., Farinpour, R., Newton, T., & Singer, E. (2001). Methylphenidate improves HIV–1-associated cognitive slowing. *Journal of Neuropsychiatry and Clinical Neurosciences, 13,* 248–254.

Hollander, H., & Levy, J. A. (1987). Neurologic abnormalities and recovery of human immunodeficiency virus from cerebrospinal fluid. *Annals of Internal Medicine, 106,* 692–695.

Horne, R., & Weinman, J. (1999). Patient's beliefs about prescribed medicines and their role in adherence to treatment in chronic physical illness. *Journal of Psychosomatic Research, 47,* 555–567.

Kalichman, S. C., Difonzo, K., Austin, J., Luke, W., & Rompa, D. (2002). Prospective study of emotional reactions to changes in HIV viral load. *AIDS Patient Care STDS, 16,* 113–120.

Kaplan, M. S., Marks, G., & Mertens, S. B. (1997). Distress and coping among women with HIV infection: Preliminary findings from a multiethnic sample. *American Journal of Orthopsychiatry, 67,* 80–91.

Lane, J. H., Sasseville, V. G., Smith, M. O., Vogel, P., Pauley, D. R., Heyes, M. P., et al. (1996). Neuroinvasion by simian immunodeficiency virus coincides with increased numbers of perivascular macrophages/microglia and intrathecal immune activation. *Journal of Neurovirology, 2,* 423–432.

Law, W. A., Martin, A., Mapou, R. L., Roller, T. L., Salazar, A. M., Temoshok, L. R., et al. (1994). Working memory in individuals with HIV infection. *Journal of Clinical and Experimental Neuropsychology, 16,* 173–182.

Law, W. A., Mapou, R. L., Roller, T. L., Martin, A., Nannis, E. D., & Temoshok, L. R. (1995). Reaction time slowing in HIV–1-infected individuals: Role of the preparatory interval. *Journal of Clinical and Experimental Neuropsychology, 17,* 122–133.

Lezak, M. D. (1995). *Neuropsychological assessment* (3rd ed.). London: Oxford University Press.

Maj, M., Satz, P., Janssen, R., Zaudig, M., Starace, F., D'Elia, L., et al. (1994). WHO neuropsychiatric AIDS study, cross-sectional phase II. *Archives of General Psychiatry, 51,* 51–61.

Mapou, R. L., Law, W. A., Martin, A., Kampen, D., Salazar, A. M., & Rundell, J. R. (1993). Neuropsychological performance, mood, and complaints of cognitive and motor difficulties in individuals infected with the human immunodeficiency virus. *Journal of Neuropsychiatry and Clinical Neurosciences, 5,* 86–93.

Marsh, N. V., & McCall, D. W. (1994). Early neuropsychological change in HIV infection. *Neuropsychology, 8,* 44–48.

Martin, A., Heyes, M. P., Salazar, A. M., Kampen, D. L., Williams, J., Law, W. A., et al. (1992). Progressive slowing of reaction time and increasing cerebrospinal fluid concentrations of quinolinic acid in HIV-infected individuals. *Journal of Neuropsychiatry and Clinical Neurosciences, 4,* 270–279.

Martin, A., Heyes, M. P., Salazar, A. M., Law, W. A., & Williams, J. (1993). Impaired motor-skill learning, slowed reaction time, and elevated cerebrospinal fluid quinolinic acid in a subgroup of HIV-infected individuals. *Neuropsychology, 7,* 149–157.

Martin, E. M., Pitrak, D. L., Novak, R. M., Pursell, K. J., & Mullane, K. M. (1999). Reaction times are faster in HIV-seropositive patients on antiretroviral therapy: A preliminary report. *Journal of Clinical and Experimental Neuropsychology, 21,* 730–735.

Martin, E. M., Robertson, L. C., Edelstein, H. E., Jagust, W. J., Sorenson, D. J., San Giovanni, D., et al. (1992). Performance of patients with early HIV–1 infection on the Stroop task. *Journal of Clinical and Experimental Neuropsychology, 14*, 857–868.

Martin, E. M., Robertson, L. C., Sorensen, D. J., Jagust, W. J., Mallon, K. F., & Chirurgi, V. A. (1993). Speed of memory scanning is not affected in early HIV–1 infection. *Journal of Clinical and Experimental Neuropsychology, 15*, 311–320.

Martin-Fernandez, J., Escobar-Rodriguez, I., Campo-Angora, M., & Rubio-Garcia, R. (2001). Evaluation of adherence to highly active antiretroviral therapy. *Archives of Internal Medicine, 161*, 2739–4270.

Marx, J. L. (1982). New disease baffles medical community. *Science, 217*, 618–621.

McArthur, J. C. (1987). Neurologic manifestations of AIDS. *Medicine, 66*, 407–433.

Miller, E. N., Satz, P., & Vischer, B. (1991). Computerized and conventional neuropsychological assessment of HIV–1-infected homosexual men. *Neurology, 41*, 1608–1616.

Moses, A. V., & Nelson, J. A. (1994). HIV infection of human brain capillary endothelial cells—Implications for AIDS dementia. *Advances in Neuroimmunology, 4*, 239–247.

Mosier, D. E. (2000). Virus and target cell evolution in human immunodeficiency virus type 1 infection. *Immunology Research, 21*, 253–258.

Navia, B. A., Jordan, B. D., & Price, R. W. (1986). The AIDS dementia complex I: Clinical features. *Annuals of Neurology, 19*, 517–524.

Navia, B. A., Cho, E. S., Petito, C. K., & Price, R. W. (1986). The AIDS dementia complex: II: Neuropathology. *Annuals of Neurology, 19*, 525–535.

Navia, B. A., & Price, R. W. (1987). The Acquired Immunodeficiency Syndrome dementia complex as the presenting or sole manifestation of Human Immunodeficiency Virus infection. *Archives of Neurology, 44*, 65–69.

Perdices, M., & Cooper, D. A. (1989). Simple and choice reaction time in patients with human immunodeficiency virus. *Annals of Neurology, 25*, 260–267.

Perdices, M., Dunbar, N., Grunseit, A., Hall, W., & Cooper, D. A. (1992). Anxiety, depression, and HIV related symptomatology across the spectrum of HIV disease. *Australian New Zealand Journal of Psychiatry, 24*, 560–566.

Ross, H. L., Gartner, S., McArthur, J. C., Corboy, J. R., McAllister, J. J., Milhouse, S., et al. (2001). HIV–1 LTR C/EBP binding site sequence configurations preferentially encountered in brain lead to enhanced C/EBP factor binding and increased LTR-specific activity. *Journal of Neuroviology, 7*, 235–249.

Shavers, V. L., Lynch, C. F., & Burmeister, L. F. (2000). Knowledge of the Tuskegee study and its impact on the willingness to participate in medical research studies. *Journal of the National Medical Association, 92*, 563–572.

Sorensen, D. J., Martin, E. M., & Robertson, L. C. (1994). Visual attention in HIV–1 infection. *Neuropsychology, 8*, 1–9.

Stolte, I. G., & Coutinho, R. A. (2002). Risk behaviour and sexually transmitted diseases are on the rise in gay men, but what is happening with HIV? *Current Opinion in Infectious Diseases, 15,* 37–41.

Suh, T., Mandell, W., Latkin, C., & Kim, J. (1997). Social network characteristics and injecting HIV-risk behaviors among street injection drug users. *Drug and Alcohol Dependence, 47,* 137–143.

Takakuwa, K. M., Callaway, E., Naylor, H., Herzig, K. E., & Yano, L. M. (1993). The effects of the human immunodeficiency virus on visual information processing. *Biological Psychiatry, 34,* 194–197.

van Gorp, W. G., Satz, P., Hinkin, C., Selnes, O., Miller, E. N., McArthur, J., et al. (1991). Metacognition in HIV–1 seropositive asymptomatic individuals: Self-ratings versus objective neuropsychological performance. *Journal of Clinical and Experimental Neuropsychology, 13,* 812–819.

Von Giesen, H. J., Hefter, H., Jablonowski, H., & Arendt, G. (2000). HAART is neuroprophylactic in HIV–1 infection. *Journal of the Acquired Immunodeficiency Syndrome, 23,* 380–385.

Wilkie, F. L., Eisdorfer, C., Morgan, R., Loewenstein, D. A., & Szapocznik, J. (1990). Cognition in early human immunodeficiency virus infection. *Archives of Neurology, 47,* 433–440.

Wilkie, F. L., Morgan, R., Fletcher, M. A., Blaney, N., Baum, M., Komaroff, E., et al. (1992). Cognition and immune function in HIV–1 infection. *AIDS, 6,* 977–981.

Wilkins, J. W., Robertson, K. R., Snyder, C. R., Robertson, W. K., van der Horst, C., & Hall, C. D. (1991). Implications of self-reported cognitive and motor dysfunction in HIV-positive patients. *American Journal of Psychiatry, 148,* 641–643.

Worth, J. L., Savage, C. R., Baer, L., Esty, E. K., & Navia, B. A. (1993). Computer-based neuropsychological screening for AIDS dementia complex. *AIDS, 7,* 677–681.

6

INNOVATIVE STRATEGIES FOR TREATING DIABETES MELLITUS

JAY E. EARLES

Diabetes mellitus is a chronic and progressive disease that affects 16.5 million Americans, many of whom are unaware of their hyperglycemia. Given that obesity is a major risk factor for the development of diabetes and that obesity rates are increasing dramatically in the United States, it is likely that the number of Americans with diabetes will continue to increase (Chan, Rimm, Colditz, Stampfer, & Willett, 1994). As the prevalence of diabetes rises, there are subsequent increased demands for medical care and diabetes-related health care costs (Caro, Ward, & O'Brien, 2002). Direct care for diabetes and its complications in America were estimated at $44 billion dollars in 1997, with additional significant indirect costs such as disability claims and decreased work productivity (Ramsey et al., 2002).

Diabetes is a disease of carbohydrate metabolism in which one of two processes occurs. Either the body's immune system is destroying the insulin-producing cells (type 1 diabetes) or the body is producing insulin but its

This chapter was authored or coauthored by an employee of the United States government as part of official duty and is considered to be in the public domain. Any views expressed herein do not necessarily represent the views of the United States government, and the author's participation in the work is not meant to serve as an official endorsement.

cells have developed resistance to the insulin (type 2). Although a chronic and progressive disease, diabetes and its complications are manageable with proper metabolic control (American Diabetes Association [ADA], 2004). Maintaining metabolic control is dependent on individuals managing several disease-related behaviors (ADA, 2004). Fortunately, during the current information age and technological revolution, great progress is being made to implement innovative approaches to improve diabetes care. Many of these strategies involve new medications and self-monitoring equipment for blood glucose levels that directly affect the treatment regimen of people with diabetes. However, comprehensive and optimal diabetes care is complex and involves more than glycemic control or medication regimens. There is an increasing emphasis on patient empowerment among diabetes care providers, with a corresponding expectation for people with diabetes to increase their diabetes-specific knowledge and self-care behaviors (Anderson et al., 1995). Because even the most basic aspect of diabetes care, medication regimen adherence, is a behavior, psychologists are well positioned to participate in the cutting edge of innovative diabetes care.

Psychologists add a unique perspective to treating diabetes and are increasingly part of innovative strategies for improved diabetes care. The strategies discussed in this chapter involve psychologists directly addressing diabetes, its course and consequences, via health behavior change of individuals with diabetes versus a more traditional focus on coexisting mental health complaints such as depression. Although depression among people with diabetes is more prevalent than among the general population and leads to poorer outcomes and increased health care costs, there are broader aspects of diabetes care that psychologists can address (Egede, Zheng, & Simpson, 2002; Lustman, Griffith, Gavard, & Clouse, 1992). Many psychologists writing about diabetes operate with a psychosocial or mental health filter and seek to assess or treat people's attitude toward the disease (denial or acceptance), their anxiety or mood state. Psychologists can successfully address mood states and attitudes, but they can also participate directly in diabetes care. The specific strategies involving psychologists that are discussed in this chapter are multidisciplinary treatment teams, behavioral telehealth solutions, physiological arousal, and group medical appointments. A case example is included to highlight a psychological intervention with someone with diabetes.

MULTIDISCIPLINARY TREATMENT TEAMS

As demonstrated in the Diabetes Control and Complications Trial, people with diabetes who received intensive and frequent treatment from a multidisciplinary team of health care providers tend to maintain metabolic control better than those who have infrequent contact with a health care team (Diabetes Control and Complications Trial Research Group, 1993). Effective diabetes treatment also requires long-term involvement from a multidisciplinary health care team. The American Diabetes Association's (ADA) Standard of Medical Care recommends that diabetes treatment include a health care team minimally consisting of a physician, nurse, dietician, and mental health professional (ADA, 2004).

Although health care professionals may interact regarding certain diabetes patients, this interaction may not necessarily constitute an integrated team approach. Health psychologists at Tripler Army Medical Center (TAMC) in Hawaii are involved in a multidisciplinary program that is an aggressive, biopsychosocial diabetes immersion program called *Holopono*. *Holopono*, which is Hawaiian for success, is a replication of the Joslin Diabetes Center's Diabetes Outpatient Intensive Treatment (DOIT) program. DOIT is a 3-day diabetes treatment and education program combined with a year of Internet-assisted case management. The diabetes treatment involves medical evaluation and subsequent regimen changes when indicated. The training consists of diabetes education classes and real-time observation and demonstration of diabetes self-care skills. The goal of the program is to develop a comprehensive, individual diabetes self-management plan for each patient that will result in lower glycosylated hemoglobin and blood glucose levels. The *Holopono* team consists of an endocrinologist, nurse, dietitian, clinical health psychologist, and pharmacist.

The first day of the program consists of individual assessments by the diabetes nurse practitioner and pharmacist and team rounds. During rounds, team members provide feedback on each participant and assist in creating a treatment plan and focus of intervention for each individual patient. The other 2 days of the program begin with team rounds to update the progress and status of each participant. After rounds, team members alternate presenting diabetes education and self-management classes within their specialty. The overall treatment philosophy of the team members emphasizes the participants' confidence, hope, empowerment, clarity of self-care plan, and diabetes knowledge.

At the conclusion of the program, a treatment summary letter is sent to the participant's primary care manager based on each team members' final recommendation. A nurse case manager maintains contact with the participants for a year to assist with adherence to their self-management plan. The case manager, a nurse practitioner, also coordinates with the endocrinologist and primary care managers when alterations in diabetes medication regimens are made.

Psychologists are an integral part of the diabetes treatment team. The role of the psychologists in diabetes management has grown in conjunction with mounting evidence of the importance of behavioral and psychosocial aspects of the disease (Anderson & Rubin, 1996; Gonder-Fredrick, Cox, & Ritterband, 2002). The clinical health psychologist's role in *Holopono* is to assist patients with self-management plans, reinforce and foster social support among participants, and build the cohesion of group and team members. The overall goal of the health psychologist's intervention is to improve patient self-management and to decrease barriers to self-care.

The psychologist leads the first group meeting that allows the participants to interact with one another and develop rapport. The multidisciplinary philosophy of the program is instilled and reinforced during this 45- to 60-minute session. Relevant information that is gathered during this initial meeting includes the participant's struggles with diabetes, his or her overall mood, coping strategies, and potential psychosocial barriers to self-care. The psychologist also teaches the last class of the program, which is focused on setting specific, realistic plans for self-monitoring of blood glucose levels (SMBG), physical activity, and food choices. The content of the discussion includes establishing realistic, sustainable goals for patients' self-care plan, overcoming barriers to their plan, and formulating strategies for applying their plan to everyday life.

Individual consultation is provided as needed by the psychologist for particular behavior changes relating to participants' self-management plans and for more traditional mental health concerns such as depression. Specific issues related to diabetes that affect patients' self-care include fear of hypoglycemia, diabetes-related distress, weight management, disordered eating, and needle phobias.

The psychologist also provides consultation to the team to improve patient–provider relationships. This consultation consists of providing input on the content and style of recommendations for regimen changes and feedback to patients, making suggestions for increasing patient participation, and working with the participants to alter their lifestyles. The clinical health psychologist also teaches the other team members about helping people change their diabetes self-care behaviors without becoming authoritarian or overbearing.

One important aspect of the *Holopono* approach and other integrated diabetes teams is the focus on empowering people with diabetes in their treatment. *Holopono* participants are active participants in medical and behavioral treatment planning. To improve their health behaviors, changes that they are willing and able to make are emphasized. Participants contribute information regarding their present lifestyle and areas of their self-care regimen about which they feel confident and interested in changing. Team members can then make realistic recommendations for future self-care behaviors with options on how patients may incorporate them into their daily living. Participants also assist with assessing the success of medication and lifestyle changes by completing food intake and blood glucose logs. Using a group format provides vital social support among the participants while they socialize during breaks and meals.

Holopono is dependent on team participation and commitment, participants faithfully doing their part, and a well-designed program. The results of *Holopono* and the success of treatments like it have been documented and demonstrate that people with diabetes who experience a brief, intensive medical management and diabetes education program can lower their HbA1c levels significantly more than participants who received treatment as usual (Earles et al., 2001; Jackson, Ovalle, & Quickel, 1998; Polonsky et al., 2003).

Psychologists have also been involved in multidisciplinary teams trying to prevent diabetes. A large multisite clinical study comparing placebo, an oral diabetes medication, and an intensive lifestyle-modification program found that the lifestyle change intervention most effectively prevented diabetes in a nationwide sample of 3,234 people over 2.8 years (Diabetes Prevention Program Research Group, 2002). Psychologists were instrumental in conceptualizing and designing the lifestyle program and in training the case managers who delivered the intervention. Multidisciplinary programs can be personnel-intensive but are also instrumental in significantly affecting people with diabetes as they manage their lives and disease. Psychologists are an indispensable part of these diabetes teams.

PSYCHOPHYSIOLOGICAL TREATMENT

The role of perceived stress in blood glucose changes and diabetes self-care behavioral disruption has been well established (Frenzel, McCaul, Glasgow, & Schafer, 1988; Lloyd et al., 1999; McCowen, Malhotra, & Bistrian, 2001; Surwit, Schneider, & Feinglos, 1992). At least two possibilities for this relationship are discussed in the literature (Peyrot & McMurray, 1992; Surwit et al., 1992). First, perceived stress tends to alter the individual's established diabetes self-care routine, which often results in hyperglycemia. Second, perceived stress increases sympathetic arousal, during which counterregulatory hormones (glucocorticoids, catecholamines, etc.) are secreted, thereby increasing blood glucose levels. Several studies have looked at improving glycemic control with interventions designed to decrease levels of perceived stress. These interventions are typically termed *stress management*, a rather broad term encompassing a multitude of skills that include various types of relaxation training, with or without biofeedback, meditation, time management, and visualization among others. The techniques generally involve self-regulation of sympathetic nervous system arousal, potentially affecting both the behavioral and physiological aspects of the stress and hyperglycemia theory.

One of the most promising of these studies used relaxation training to demonstrate the effect of psychophysiological training on glycemic control and physiological arousal (Surwit et al., 2002). Researchers at Duke University, building on several pilot studies (Lane, McCaskill, Ross, Feinglos, & Surwit, 1993; McGrady, Bailey, & Good, 1991), randomized 108 people with type 2 diabetes to a short-term group-based diabetes education program with or without stress management training to assess the impact of stress management training on glucose levels. The stress management training consisted of five group sessions, during which participants were taught progressive muscle relaxation, diaphragmatic breathing, mental imagery, and cognitive–behavioral techniques to increase both the awareness and regulation of physiological arousal. Participants were given an audiotape of the relaxation skill to practice over the year of follow-up. At one year there was a significant decrease in HbA1c among the stress management group, and a third of that group had lowered their HbA1c by 1%, compared to only 12% of the diabetes education-only group. Baseline trait anxiety was not a predictive factor of who improved, and there were no differences in body mass index, diet, or exercise between the two groups during the year of follow-up.

Teaching people to self-regulate physiological arousal was beneficial to people with diabetes regardless of their perceived arousal or stress level. Relaxation training is often characterized as simply decreasing mental and behavioral stress, but it is also quite possible that during treatment and subsequent practice that baseline arousal levels were decreased or managed so as to not engage sympathetic arousal and the subsequent counterregulatory hormones that raise glucose levels.

DIABETES CARE VIA TELEHEALTH

A key aspect of the information age has been the advent of telecommunications. The use of communications technology in the delivery of health care over distance is called *telehealth*. Although the term is fairly recent, its actual practice is as old as the telephone. The technology now incorporated in telehealth is increasingly diverse and ubiquitous. Beyond the telephone, the Internet has been in widespread use for almost a decade, and newer technologies such as personal digital assistants (PDAs) are becoming commonplace.

Diabetes care, like other medical interventions, has been and will likely continue to be greatly influenced by the continuing evolution of communications technology in health care. Current telehealth diabetes care applications involve the Internet, PDAs, and the telephone. As part of the health care team, psychologists play an integral role in patient management.

This is no less true in the integration of the previously noted areas of technological expansion.

The Internet is a ready-made supplier of health care information and support. Interest in online health care information has burgeoned, with an estimated 110 million Americans searching for health information online (Harris Poll, 2002). There is a vast amount of medical information already available on the Internet. Unfortunately, accurate and appropriate information may be difficult to identify or simply may not meet the specific needs of a given patient (Graber, Roller, & Kaeble, 1999; Pinker, 1999; Woodall, 1998). Partly as a result of the sheer number of health-related Web sites and their questionable quality and reliability, many people would like access to a Web site operated by their physician's office. Incorporating diabetes self-management education and resources via the Internet improves the availability of information and accessibility of the health care team to patients without necessitating trips to a medical facility. This approach is more reliable, efficient, quicker, and potentially more cost-effective than mailing information to patients and has the additional advantage of being able to serve patients over a greater geographical distance with almost instantaneous contact and two-way interaction.

Numerous Internet applications are now available to help providers and patients manage diabetes. Internet-based blood glucose monitoring systems that provide immediate feedback and communication between patient and provider have demonstrated efficacy in lowering HbA1c (Kwon et al., 2004). As a telemedicine initiative at TAMC, *Holopono* uses a secure, interactive Web site with a relational database. The *Holopono* Diabetes Project Web site was designed to aid the ongoing case management of participants by the team's diabetes nurse educator and provide computer-assisted learning via diabetes education modules. The Web site adds another means of communication between the diabetes team and patients because it is secure behind TAMC's firewall and requires a user name and password for access. Participants can e-mail team members their questions and concerns regarding their health status, meal plan, exercise, or any other diabetes-related issues. *Holopono* participants also provide recent blood glucose results via the Internet to the nurse case manager, who is able to reply with recommendations for changes in medications, food, and activity behaviors or make requests for follow-up labs.

By allowing patients to input and track their blood glucose data and access their lab results, patients receive some physiological feedback on the lifestyle choices they are making. Overall diabetes care is improved as the nurse educator, physicians, and other team members can conveniently access patient laboratory data to help them make treatment recommendations. This use of telemedicine enables the chronic follow-up necessary in diabetes care to take place easily over wide geographical areas, saving participants unnecessary visits to the hospital or a trading of telephone messages. The participants also have access to four interactive diabetes self-management education modules. The online educational modules reinforce the clinical and lifestyle information that is provided in the Holopono experience at TAMC.

Internet-based interventions greatly expand the accessibility of the health care team in an increasingly popular and familiar format for patients. These interventions also improve the patient-to-patient support as demonstrated in a prototype of an Internet-based peer support program (McKay, Feil, Glasgow, & Brown, 1997). Other telehealth strategies currently being developed involve ecological monitoring using PDAs and biomedical equipment in patients' homes that monitor blood sugar, blood pressure, and HbA1c. Biomedical results gathered by the patients can be entered into a PDA and then sent to a secure Web site monitored by a provider or automatically sent by the monitoring equipment itself (Gomez, del Pozo, & Hernando, 1996; Mease et al., 2000). The information the diabetes team needs to suggest regimen changes is collected and forwarded in real time, thus decreasing the feedback cycle for regimen changes. Personalized behavioral and medical recommendations consistent with previously negotiated goals can also be sent to the patients electronically. Access to the entire health care team is thus improved. Pilot studies have noted the acceptability, feasibility, and effectiveness of these approaches in improving metabolic control (Edmonds et al., 1998; Tsang et al., 2001; Wojcicki et al., 2001). Psychologists have participated in these interventions by helping create the style and substance of feedback, biomedical data presentation, tailored behavioral strategies, and educating the health care team on assisting patients with their progress.

GROUP MEDICAL APPOINTMENTS

It has been clearly and repeatedly demonstrated that good metabolic control reduces the risk of diabetes-related complications. Optimizing this control requires multidisciplinary efforts focused on lifestyle choices and medical status. However, the majority of type 2 diabetes interventions are a combination of individual treatment and formal but infrequent diabetes education efforts, which are not truly multidisciplinary interventions. There are two primary disadvantages of diabetes care as currently practiced. First, diabetes education as traditionally delivered in a didactic setting with an emphasis on imparting knowledge is not effective for individual behavior change and does not improve metabolic control (Norris, Engelgau, & Narayan, 2001). Second, individual treatment is frequently not efficient, as the health care provider may repeat him- or herself several times a day to various patients. One strategy developed in various primary care clinics is the group medical appointment.

Group medical appointments are collaborative, comprehensive medical management programs involving a team of health care providers and a group of patients with homogeneous medical complaints. Group medical appointments are more interactive and personable than the traditional didactic group education model and can be more efficient. A two-hour group appointment with 20 patients involves medical management, education, and social support that cannot be achieved in a 15-minute individual appointment. Even though it is a group visit, individuals may be seen at the end of the session to manage urgent complaints. Masley, Sokoloff, and Hawes (2000) suggested that highly prevalent medical problems that are costly and responsive to lifestyle changes, such as diabetes, are best suited to group appointments. In a pilot study using group appointments in the treatment of type 2 diabetes, Masley et al. (2000) noted improved total cholesterol/HDL ratios, HbA1c, and health care use. Besides diabetes, other medical conditions that have benefited from group appointments include high health care utilizers, asthma, and chronic pain (Kent & Gordon, 1997; Weinger, 2003).

Trento et al. (2001) completed a two-year follow-up of group appointments supplanting routine diabetes care in people with type 2 diabetes. People with non-insulin-treated type 2 diabetes (n = 112) were randomized into care as usual or received diabetes medical management with diabetes education in a group setting. Participants attended four group sessions over the course of one year. During the group visit the members met with their physician and a multidisciplinary health care team that included a psychologist.

The four sessions focused on meal planning, weight management, SMBG and improving metabolic control, and preventing complications from diabetes. Patients set individualized behavioral and educational objectives at the start of the program. Two years after the start of the program, group participants had lower triglycerides and had maintained their HbA1c levels, whereas the control participants' levels had increased. The group appointment participants were also choosing more appropriate health behaviors. The group appointment intervention saved physicians 30 to 80 minutes per 10 patients compared to individual consultation, even when preparation and postgroup consultation time was included. The authors of the study also concluded that participants benefited from the cohesion and social support of other people with diabetes.

Sadur et al. (1999) had previously demonstrated the benefits of group medical appointments in the Kaiser Permanente Medical Care Program, Northern California. They also randomized patients to the group appointment model or care as usual. One-year outcomes of the 6-month group intervention showed lower HbA1c levels, increased self-efficacy and patient satisfaction, and reduced health care use among the group care patients. A psychologist was involved in the monthly groups and provided some individual consultation during the program. The psychologist also worked with the nurse case manager to help patients transition to their primary care managers at the end of the program. Plans for maintaining lifestyle and medication changes were formulated at this time.

Primary care clinics have been the target of group appointments to date. The primary care setting is ideal for group appointments because that is where the individual's overall health care is managed, the individual is comfortable with the provider, and a model for comprehensive care is already established. As psychologists are becoming more active in primary care and early group appointment interventions have included them, this may be a good opportunity. The group appointment is an evolving strategy that provides a continuous process for managing a chronic disease by a multidisciplinary team in an accessible health care setting, all factors that are key to proper diabetes care.

CASE EXAMPLE

M. M. was a 59-year-old married White woman who attended the *Holopono* program. She was well-educated, having earned a master's degree in education, and worked as a substitute teacher in a local junior high school. She was seen in the *Holopono* program to improve her diabetes self-management behaviors and to address her needle phobia. She had had diabetes mellitus type 2 for 10 years and was a breast cancer survivor. Her hemoglobin A1c (HbA1c) was 10.3%, her systolic blood pressure was elevated (147/88), and her low- and high-density lipoprotein and triglycerides were within normal limits. Her medication regimen included insulin, two classes of oral diabetes (a thiazolidinedione and alpha-glucosidase blocker), and simvastatin to maintain her cholesterol levels. She was 66 inches tall and weighed 190 pounds, with a Body Mass Index of 30.7. She did not use tobacco or alcohol.

In the *Holopono* program her diabetes self-management was discussed, and targets for intervention were negotiated with her. Based on her blood sugar monitoring and lab results, it was recommended she increase insulin administration to three shots per day. Unfortunately, her needle phobia resulted in skipping a postlunch insulin shot. Her husband administered all her insulin shots, so her insulin dosing was limited to before and after work. During day 1 of *Holopono* her needle phobia history, experience with medical procedures regarding needles was gathered, and her morning insulin shot was observed. Her needle phobia predated her cancer treatment. She had tried relaxation strategy and hypnosis when receiving her chemotherapy without relief. The author talked with an oncology nurse who verified the patient's experience and stated that at least four people were required to hold her still when administering IV drugs or gathering blood tests. She claimed her main problems were feeling her skin being pierced, having the needle in her body, and feeling out of control of her physical sensations. When her husband administered the shot, she displayed obvious signs of arousal and discomfort, flinching at the moment of injection and the sound of the autoinjector.

On day 2 the *Holopono* psychologist used a cognitive–behavioral approach, with the goal of her giving her own shots by the end of the program. M. M.'s fear and quaking over needles was contrasted with her incredible physical and mental strength in needing four people to restrain her, dealing with new junior high students on a daily basis, and not succumbing to cancer. Her ability to rise to a challenge and exude confidence and power when she desired was established. The desire to improve her health was also discussed. Employing questions used in motivational interviewing she established that it was important to have lower blood sugar and to feel in control of diabetes, she was confident she could do it, and now was a good time to alter her regimen (Rollnick, Mason, & Butler, 1999). However, the *Holopono* team's recommendation was an added insulin shot in the afternoon, which only she could administer because she was at work. Therefore, insulin shots were reframed as helpful and necessary to her stated goal. Giving herself insulin became something she wanted to do to feel healthier, not a completely aversive event. She was using her strength to help herself, to be more self-supportive and in control. During her afternoon shot she repeated this rationale with the psychologist while her husband held the autoinjector and she released the needle.

On day 3 of the program she administered the morning shot herself and expressed great relief afterward. The *Holopono* psychologist was present and repeated brief themes of self-control and her stated desire to help herself. After the shot she was reinforced for her tremendous and quick learning. Any arousal she experienced was normalized as part of the learning process and suggested that it would likely lessen as she practiced more. The self-talk themes were reviewed, and she was encouraged to practice them before and during each self-insulin administration. She maintained contact with the program nurse practitioner and psychologist throughout the year of follow-up. She reported administering all other insulin shots during the year and denied any arousal or avoidance symptoms. The *Holopono* staff was able to recommend a much more flexible insulin regimen for her, which she adopted and was able to maintain. After one year in the program and receiving follow-up care from the nurse practitioner, her blood pressure was normotensive at 132/76, her HbA1c had decreased to 7.2%, and her lipids remained within normal limits. She maintained her oral medication regimen and slightly altered her diet with positive results.

CONCLUSION

As the prevalence of diabetes grows, there will be a commensurate increased demand for comprehensive diabetes care. Technological advances and new scientific discoveries are making it easier for people with diabetes to access multidisciplinary health care and improve their self-care behaviors. In response, diabetes care is steadily improving and is embracing the skills clinical health psychologists have to offer. As more research is published about the importance of behavior change in altering the course of diabetes, the role of clinical health psychologists should continue to expand. Psychologists are well trained in assisting behavior change, mood complaints, and interpersonal interactions, three areas of vital importance in helping people with diabetes and their providers in efforts to manage diabetes.

REFERENCES

American Diabetes Association. (2004). Standards of medical care for patients with diabetes mellitus. *Diabetes Care, 27*(Suppl. 1), S15–S35.

Anderson, B. J., & Rubin, R. R. (1996). (Eds.). *Practical psychology for diabetes clinicians*. Alexandria, VA: American Diabetes Association.

Anderson, R. A., Funnell, M. M., Butler, P. M., Arnold, M. S., Fitzgerald, J. T., & Feste, C. C. (1995). Patient empowerment: Results of a randomized controlled trial. *Diabetes Care, 18*, 943–949.

Caro, J. J., Ward, A. J., & O'Brien, J. A. (2002). Lifetime costs of complications resulting from type 2 diabetes in the U.S. *Diabetes Care, 25*, 476–481.

Chan, J. M., Rimm, E. B., Colditz, G. A., Stampfer, M. J., & Willett, W. C. (1994). Obesity, fat distribution, and weight gain as risk factors for clinical diabetes in men. *Diabetes Care, 17*, 961–969.

Diabetes Control and Complications Trial Research Group. (1993). The effect of intensive treatment of diabetes on the development and progression of long-term complications in insulin dependent diabetes mellitus. *New England Journal of Medicine, 329*, 977–986.

Diabetes Prevention Program Research Group. (2002). Reduction in the incidence of type 2 diabetes with lifestyle intervention or metformin. *New England Journal of Medicine, 346*, 393–403.

Earles, J. E., Hartung, G. H., Moriyama, H. H., Dickert, J. D., Coll, K. J., Aiello, L., et al. (2001). Interdisciplinary treatment of diabetes mellitus in a military treatment facility. *Military Medicine, 166*, 848–852.

Edmonds, M., Bauer, M., Osborn, S., Lutfiyya, H., Mahon, J., Doig, G., et al. (1998). Using the Vista 350 telephone to communicate the results of home monitoring of diabetes mellitus to a central database and to provide feedback. *International Journal of Medical Informatics, 51*, 117–125.

Egede, L. E., Zheng, D., & Simpson, K. (2002). Comorbid depression is associated with increased health care use and expenditures in individuals with diabetes. *Diabetes Care, 25*, 464–470.

Frenzel, M. P., McCaul, K. D., Glasgow, R. E., & Schafer, L. C. (1988). The relationship of stress and coping to regimen adherence and glycemic control of diabetes. *Journal of Social and Clinical Psychology, 6*, 77–87.

Gonder-Fredrick, L. A., Cox, D. J., & Ritterband, L. M. (2002). Diabetes and behavioral medicine: The second decade. *Journal of Consulting and Clinical Psychology, 70*, 611–625.

Gomez, E. J., del Pozo, F., & Hernando, M. E. (1996). Telemedicine for diabetes care: The DIABTel approach towards diabetes telecare. *Medical Informatics, 21*, 283–295.

Graber, M. A., Roller, C. M., & Kaeble, B. (1999). Readability levels of patient education materials on the World Wide Web. *Journal of Family Practice, 48*, 58–61.

Harris Poll. (2002). Retrieved June 26, 2002, from http://www.harrisinteractive.com/harris_poll/index.asp

Jackson, R. A., Ovalle, K., & Quickel, K. (1998). Diabetes immersion: The Joslin Diabetes Outpatient Intensive Treatment (DOIT) Program. *Diabetes, 47*(Suppl. 1), A422.

Kent, J., & Gordon, M. (1997). Integration: A case for putting humpty and dumpty together again. In N. A. Cummings, J. L. Cummings, & J. N. Johnson (Eds.), *Behavioral health in primary care: A guide for clinical integration* (pp. 103–120). Madison, CT: Psychosocial Press.

Kwon, H., Cho, J., Kim, H., Song, B., Ko, S., Lee, J., et al. (2004). Establishment of blood glucose monitoring system using the Internet. *Diabetes Care, 27*, 478–483.

Lane, J. D., McCaskill, C. C., Ross, S. L., Feinglos, M. N., & Surwit, R. (1993). Relaxation training for NIDDM: Predicting who may benefit. *Diabetes Care, 16*, 1087–1094.

Lloyd, C. E., Dyer, P. H., Lancashire, R. J., Harris, T., Daniels, J. E., & Barnett, A. H. (1999). Association between stress and glycemic control in adults with type 1 diabetes. *Diabetes Care, 22*, 1278–1283.

Lustman, P. J., Griffith, L. S., Gavard, J. A., & Clouse, R. E. (1992). Depression in adults with diabetes. *Diabetes Care, 15*, 1631–1639.

Masley, S., Sokoloff, J., & Hawes, C. (2000). Planning group visits for high-risk patients. *Family Practice Management, 7*, 33–37.

McCowen, K. C., Malhotra, A., & Bistrian, B. R. (2001). Stress-induced hyperglycemia. *Critical Care Clinics, 17*, 107–124.

McGrady, A., Bailey, B. K., & Good, M. P. (1991). Controlled study of biofeedback-assisted relaxation in type 1 diabetes. *Diabetes Care, 14,* 360–365.

McKay, H. G., Feil, E. G., Glasgow, R. E., & Brown, J. E. (1997). Feasibility and use of an Internet support service for diabetes self-management. *Diabetes Education, 24,* 174–179.

Mease, A., Whitlock, W. L., Brown, A., Moore, K., Pavliscsak, H., Dingbaum, A., et al. (2000). Telemedicine improved diabetic management. *Military Medicine, 165,* 579–584.

Norris, S. L., Engelgau, M. M., & Narayan, K. M. V. (2001). Effectiveness of self-management training in type 2 diabetes. *Diabetes Care, 24,* 561–587.

Peyrot, M. F., & McMurray, J. F. (1992). Stress buffering and glycemic control. *Diabetes Care, 15,* 842–846.

Piette, J. D., & Mah, C. A. (1997). The feasibility of automated voice messaging as an adjunct to diabetes outpatient care. *Diabetes Care, 20,* 15–21.

Pinker, S. (1999). Breast cancer online: Helping patients navigate the Web. *Canadian Medical Association Journal, 160,* 239.

Polonsky, W. H., Earles, J., Smith, S., Pease, D. J., Macmillan, M., Christensen, R., et al. (2003). Integrating medical management with diabetes self-management training: A randomized control trial of the Diabetes Outpatient Intensive Treatment (DOIT) program. *Diabetes Care, 26,* 3048–3053.

Ramsey, S., Summers, K. H., Leong, S. A., Birnbaum, H. G., Kemner, J. E., & Greenberg, P. (2002). Productivity and medical costs of diabetes in a large employer population. *Diabetes Care, 25,* 23–29.

Rollnick, S., Mason, P., & Butler, C. (1999). *Health behavior change: A guide for practitioners.* Edinburgh, Scotland: Churchill Livingstone.

Sadur, C. N., Moline, N., Costa, M., Michalik, D., Mendlowitz, D., Roller, S., et al. (1999). Diabetes management in a health maintenance organization: Efficacy of care management using cluster visits. *Diabetes Care, 22,* 2011–2017.

Surwit, R. S., Schneider, M. S., & Feinglos, M. N. (1992). Stress and diabetes mellitus. *Diabetes Care, 15,* 1413–1422.

Surwit, R. S., van Tilburg, M. A. L., Zucker, N., McCaskill, C. C., Parekh, P., & Feinglos, M. N., (2002). Stress management improves long-term glycemic control in type 2 diabetes. *Diabetes Care, 25,* 30–34.

Trento, M., Passera, P., Tomalino, M., Bajardi, M., Pomero, F., Allione, A., et al. (2001). Group visits improve metabolic control in type 2 diabetes. *Diabetes Care, 24,* 995–1000.

Tsang, M. W., Mok, M., Kam, G., Jung, M., Tang, A., Chan, U., et al. (2001). Improvement in diabetes control with a monitoring system based on a hand-held, touch-screen electronic diary. *Journal of Telemedicine and Telecare, 7,* 47–50.

Weinger, K. (2003). Group medical appointments in diabetes care: Is there a future? *DiabetesSpectrum, 16,* 104–107.

Wojcicki, J. M., Ladyzynski, P., Krzymien, J., Jozwicka, E., Blachowicz, J., Janczewska, E., et al. (2001). What we can really expect from telemedicine in intensive diabetes treatment: Results from 3-year study on type 1 pregnant diabetic women. *Diabetes Technology and Therapeutics, 3,* 581–589.

Woodall, S. C. (1998). In search of literature on cancer on the Internet. *American Journal of Health-Systems Pharmaceuticals, 55,* 2429–2431.

7

BEHAVIORAL TREATMENT OF INSOMNIA IN PRIMARY CARE SETTINGS

WILLIAM C. ISLER III, ALAN L. PETERSON, AND DIANE E. ISLER

Although rarely the chief reason for a medical visit, insomnia is one of the most common clinical symptoms in primary care settings (National Heart, Lung, and Blood Institute Working Group on Insomnia, 1999). Insomnia is associated with increased health care utilization (Kapur et al., 2002) and decreased health-related quality of life (Katz & McHorney, 2002; Zammit, Weiner, Damato, Sillup, & McMillan, 1999). Insomnia may be seen in primary care clinics as an acute or chronic primary disorder or as a condition secondary to another clinical condition. Whereas pharmacological treatments for insomnia are the most commonly used approaches in primary care settings (Chesson et al., 1999; Morin, Colecchi, Stone, Stood, & Brink, 1999; Morin & Wooten, 1996), drug treatments are most helpful with acute insomnia (Smith et al., 2002). Nonpharmacological behavioral treatments for insomnia have been demonstrated to be both efficacious (Lichstein &

The views expressed in this article are those of the authors and are not the official policy of the Department of Defense or the United States Air Force. The authors would like to acknowledge Dr. Charles M. Morin for his support over the years in the development of the Wilford Hall Insomnia Program.

Riedel, 1994; Morin, Colecchi, et al., 1999; Morin, Hauri, et al., 1999; Murtagh & Greenwood, 1995; Smith et al., 2002) and clinically effective, (Hryshko-Mullen, Broeckl, Haddock, & Peterson, 2000; Morin, Stone, Mc-Donald, & Jones, 1994) and therefore are recommended as the first-line intervention for insomnia of all types (Morin, Colecchi, et al., 1999; Smith et al., 2002). However, implementing behavioral treatments in primary care settings may pose some challenges because of the heavy reliance on medication treatments, the limited knowledge of many primary care providers of evidenced-based behavioral treatment approaches, and the time limitations associated with treatment in these settings (Richardson, 2000). In addition, controlled research of insomnia conducted specifically in primary care settings is limited. This chapter reviews the use of evidenced-based behavioral treatments for insomnia in primary care settings.

PREVALENCE OF INSOMNIA

The prevalence of insomnia in a primary care setting has been estimated at 32% for chronic insomnia (Kushida et al., 2000). Other research has indicated that up to 69% of primary care patients report a history of insomnia, including 50% with occasional insomnia and 19% with chronic sleep problems (Schochat, Umphress, Israel, & Ancoli-Israel, 1999). Although information about the prevalence of insomnia in the general population is limited, it has been estimated that 30% to 40% of adults report some level of insomnia within any given year, and as many as 10% indicate chronic to severe problems (Mellinger, Balter, & Uhlenhuth, 1985). Most primary care settings do not have an established means to effectively identify and treat such a large population of individuals with insomnia.

CONSEQUENCES OF INSOMNIA

A growing body of research has established that untreated insomnia has significant negative consequences. People with insomnia tend to report more health concerns, less physical activity, less vitality, and more emotional problems (Zammit et al., 1999). Sleep problems may actually increase the severity of daytime symptoms of chronic diseases such as arthritis or fibromyalgia (Walsh, Muehlback, Lauter, Hilliker, & Schweitzer, 1996). Another consequence of chronic insomnia is decreased quality of life. Although controlled research of chronic insomniacs suggests that they do not have impaired alertness during the day (Chambers & Keller, 1993; Regestein, Dambrosia, Hallett, Murawski, & Paine, 1993), they do frequently complain of an overall decrease in quality of life, and in one study were found to miss 10 times more days from work than those without insomnia (Zammit et al., 1999). Severe insomniacs have been shown to have lower scores than mild insomniacs on all dimensions of the Short-Form 36 (SF–36; Ware, Snow, Kosinski, & Gandek, 1997), an objective measure of quality of life (Leger, Scheuermaier, Philip, Paillard, & Guilleminault, 2001; Zammit et al., 1999), and overall quality of life scores are correlated with the severity of insomnia (Leger et al., 2001).

The high prevalence of insomnia with the accompanying impact on health care utilization and quality of life result in a significant economic consequence. The direct cost of insomnia in 1995 in the United States was estimated to be $13.93 billion (Walsh & Engelhardt, 1999). These costs included $1.97 billion to treat insomnia, less than half of which was for prescription medication. Other costs included $11.96 billion for health care services for insomnia. These staggering economic costs highlight the importance of evidenced-based assessment and treatment programs for insomnia in primary care settings.

THE ETIOLOGY OF INSOMNIA

Insomnia can result from a variety of physical, emotional, cognitive, behavioral, or environmental factors. Spielman (1986) proposed that insomnia is the result of predisposing, precipitating, and perpetuating factors. Predisposing factors, or conditions that set the stage for insomnia, include a preference for staying up late or sleeping in, history of recurrent depression, heightened psychophysiological arousal, and family history of sleep disturbances (Spielman & Glovinsky, 1991). Precipitating factors are associated with the initiation of insomnia and can include acutely stressful situations, changes in work schedule, or physical discomfort such as a pain condition. Perpetuating factors include both mental states and behavioral practices that are not present at the initiation of the insomnia but develop as compensatory strategies. Spending more time in bed in an attempt to get sleep, inconsistent bedtimes and awakening times, and worry or rumination over consequences of perceived lack of sleep can all serve as perpetuating factors. Identification of the predisposing, precipitating, and perpetuating factors involved in the development of insomnia can help guide the choice of behavioral strategies.[1]

---

[1] It may be helpful to address acute insomnia with behavioral approaches in the primary care setting to try to prevent compensatory behaviors that may lead to the onset and maintenance of chronic insomnia.

DIAGNOSIS OF INSOMNIA

In the simplest terms, insomnia is a disorder of initiating and maintaining sleep. Insomnia can include difficulties falling asleep, frequent awakenings during the night, or early-morning awakenings. The diagnosis of insomnia is accomplished through interview of the patient, matching symptoms to diagnostic criteria while ruling out other sleep disorders and accounting for medical and psychological conditions that contribute to the initiation and maintenance of insomnia.

Classification Systems

Several formal diagnostic systems have been developed for the diagnosis of insomnia, including the International Classification of Sleep Disorders (ICSD; American Sleep Disorders Association [ASDA], 1990), the *Diagnostic and Statistical Manual of Mental Disorders* (DSM–IV–TR; American Psychiatric Association, 2000), and the *ICD–10 Classification of Mental and Behavioral Disorders* (World Health Organization, 1993). The ICSD is the most widely used classification system for sleep disorders and contains approximately 80 different sleep disorder diagnoses, 12 of which involve insomnia or symptoms of insomnia, including psychophysiological insomnia, idiopathic insomnia, sleep state misperception, inadequate sleep hygiene, and insufficient sleep syndrome (ASDA, 1990). Research comparing the *DSM–IV* and ICSD diagnostic criteria suggests that the *DSM–IV* diagnosis of primary insomnia tends to be a broader definition of insomnia that encompasses several of the ICSD categories of insomnia (Ohayon & Roberts, 2001). However, the value of the ICSD in everyday practice is probably limited (Morgan, 2000). All three diagnostic systems characterize insomnia as difficulty initiating or maintaining sleep or not feeling rested on wakening for at least 1 month and report of some type of daytime impairments (Morin, 1993). For the average clinician, the *DSM–IV* diagnostic criteria of primary insomnia are more user friendly for diagnosing insomnia in primary care settings. The *DSM–IV* criteria are included in Exhibit 7.1.

Insomnia is also often classified according to its duration (ASDA, 1990). Transient insomnia occurs intermittently in most people and may last for only a few nights. It may be associated with illness, hospitalization, or jet lag. Short-term insomnia may last up to three or four weeks and is often associated with situational stress or a serious illness. Long-term insomnia lasts for more than a month and may be related to psychological disorders, medical conditions, or another sleep disorder (ASDA, 1990).

EXHIBIT 7.1
The *Diagnostic and Statistical Manual for Mental Disorders* Diagnostic Criteria for Primary Insomnia

1. Difficulty in initiating or maintaining sleep or nonrestorative sleep.
2. Sleep difficulties persist for at least 1 month.
3. Significant distress or impairment in social or occupational functioning reported as a consequence of the sleep disturbance.
4. The sleep disturbance does not occur exclusively during the course of another mental disorder or narcolepsy, breathing-related sleep disorder, circadian rhythm sleep disorder, or a parasomnia.
5. The sleep disturbance is not a result of substance use or abuse or a general medical condition.

Note. From *Diagnostic and Statistical Manual of Mental Disorders,* 4th ed., Text Revision, 2000, p. 604, by American Psychiatric Association, Washington, DC: American Psychiatric Association. Reprinted with permission from the *Diagnostic and Statistical Manual of Mental Disorders, Text Revision,* Copyright 2000 American Psychiatric Association.

Differential Diagnosis

Familiarity with other sleep disorders is important in making differential diagnoses between insomnia and other disorders or to determine if another sleep disorder is present in addition to insomnia. Several excellent textbooks are available for detailed descriptions of sleep disorders (e.g., ASDA, 1990; Lichstein & Morin, 2000; Morin, 1993; Pressman & Orr, 1997). Refer to Exhibit 7.2 for questions to ask when making a differential diagnosis with other sleep-related disorders.

Three of the most common sleep disorders that may be related to insomnia include restless legs syndrome (RLS), periodic limb movements (PLM), and obstructive sleep apnea (OSA; ASDA, 1990). RLS is characterized by unpleasant sensations in the legs that are temporarily relieved by moving them. These sensations increase during the evening and seem particularly disturbing when the person is lying down. Symptoms of RLS are frequently accompanied by PLM and as a result contribute to difficulty falling and staying asleep. PLM disorder is characterized by repeated rhythmic jerking or twitching movements in the lower extremities. These movements lead to arousals and can occur every 20 to 90 seconds. Although PLMs do not typically cause awakenings, they do cause a reduction in deep sleep, with the side effect of excessive daytime sleepiness. The patient's bed partner may be able to detect the movement problem and the bed partner's sleep may also be disrupted. Overall, PLM is more common in older adults (Ancoli-Israel et al., 1991; Fichten, Libman, Bailes, & Alapin, 2000). OSA is associated with snoring, excessive daytime sleepiness, obesity, and hypertension. Patients with sleep apnea typically self-report and demonstrate more

EXHIBIT 7.2
Useful Questions for the Differential Diagnosis of Sleep Disorders in Primary Care Settings

Interview question	Rule out sleep disorder
Do you feel the need to sleep at a different time than most people?	Circadian rhythm disorder
Do you snore? If yes: Do you have a dry mouth when awaking? Do you experience excessive daytime sleepiness? Do you have morning headaches? Does your sleeping partner ever complain that you stop breathing during the night?	Sleep-related breathing disorders (apnea)
(If the patient reports awakenings during the night)	Gastroesophargeal reflux disorder (GERD)
Do you awaken with a bad taste in your mouth?	GERD
Do you ever notice that your legs are moving during the night or does your sleeping partner complain that your legs move during the night?	Periodic limb movements
Does any feeling in your legs ever keep you from going to sleep or sleeping well during the night? If yes, ask qualitative questions. Patients may give descriptors such as "It feels like I just have to move my legs," or "It feels like something is crawling in my legs."	Restless legs syndrome
Do you ever have strange things happen to you at night? If yes, please describe.	Parasomnias such as REM behavior disorder and sleep paralysis
Do you fall asleep at inappropriate times? Do your muscles ever feel like they just give way (cataplexy)? Do you ever have a difficult time moving when you are waking up or falling asleep?	Narcolepsy

Note. From *Treatment of Late-Life Insomnia* (p. 83), by K. L. Lichstein and C. M. Morin (Eds.), 2000. Thousand Oaks, CA: Sage. Copyright 2000 by Sage Publications, Inc. Reprinted with permission.

excessive daytime sleepiness than those experiencing only primary insomnia. The treatment for apnea often involves surgery or nasal administered continuous positive airway pressure (CPAP), a device worn while sleeping that keeps the airway open for the exchange of air.

The report of the patient's sleeping partner can be helpful when making a differential diagnosis, especially in cases of OSA or PLM when the patient may not be aware of experiencing difficulty breathing or movement problems at night. Often the sleeping partner is awakened by these symptoms even if the patient is not. In addition, sleeping partners may be able to provide collateral information on the impact of sleep problems for daily functioning, fatigue, mood, and excessive daytime sleepiness.

Polysomnograph

A polysomnograph (PSG) is a sleep study in which multiple recordings including brain waves, eye movements, muscle tension, and so forth are taken during a night's sleep. A PSG is not required for the diagnosis of insomnia and is usually not performed unless there is another suspected sleep disorder in addition to insomnia, such as OSA or PLM (Eddy & Walbroehl, 1999; Rajput & Bromley, 1999). When patients present with complaints of apneas or awakenings with gasping for air, they should be referred for a PSG (Pallesen, Nordhus, Havik, & Nielsen, 2001). A referral for a PSG should also be made when the symptoms of cataplexy and sleep attacks are present and a diagnosis of narcolepsy is strongly suspected (Pallesen et al., 2001). The comorbidity of PLM and RLS is high, and patients strongly suspected to have these disorders should also be referred for a PSG; the treatment typically is pharmacological.[2]

Medical Conditions Associated With Insomnia

Perhaps the most common medical conditions associated with insomnia are those that include chronic pain such as musculoskeletal pain disorders, fibromyalgia, arthritis, and complex regional pain syndrome (Currie, Wilson, & Curran, 2002; Currie, Wilson, Pontefract, & deLaplante, 2000; Smith, Perlis, Carmody, Smith, & Giles, 2001; Walsh et al., 1996; Wilson, Eriksson, D'Eon, Mikail, & Emery, 2002). Fragmented sleep is one of the main complaints from those in pain, and sleep disturbances may even increase the severity of pain (Affleck, Urrows, Tennen, Higgins, & Abeles, 1996; Wilson et al., 2002). Research with patients experiencing rheumatoid arthritis suggested that pain exacerbated problems with sleeping and that both pain and sleep problems appeared to contribute to depression over time (Walsh et al., 1996). Smith et al. (2001) examined how cognitions affect sleep with patients experiencing pain and found that among the most frequently reported presleep cognitions were general pain-related thoughts (36%). Morin, Kowatch, and Wade (1989) also found that patients with chronic pain who were instructed in stimulus control (Bootzin & Epstein, 2000) and sleep restriction techniques (Speilman, Saskin, & Thorpy, 1987) made significant improvement in sleep quality and mood. Behavioral interventions used in the treatment of insomnia secondary to medical conditions

---

[2]For a more detailed discussion of sleep disorders and when to refer to a sleep lab, see Pallesen et al., 2001.

are based on the assumption that the sleep disruption may have begun in response to the pain, but the maintenance and exacerbation of the problem involve compensatory behaviors and cognitions that can be moderated to manage sleep better.

Psychological Conditions Associated With Insomnia

Affective disorders (Wilson et al., 2002) and anxiety disorders (Bourdet & Goldenberg, 1994; Lepola, Koponen, & Leinonen, 1994) are among the most typical psychological diagnoses associated with insomnia, although psychological disorders may account for less than 50% of insomnia cases (Ford & Kamerow, 1989). Although insomnia is often considered to occur secondary to psychological disorders, chronic insomnia is actually a risk factor for the development of anxiety, depressive, and addictive disorders (Gillin, 1998). In addition, early detection and treatment of insomnia may prevent the later development of depression (Ford & Kamerow, 1989).

Secondary Insomnia

Insomnia is often referred to as secondary insomnia if it is secondary to other sleep, medical, or psychological disorders. However, determining the causal relationship between insomnia and other conditions is not always easy. The common lore is that if the primary condition is successfully treated, then the insomnia will be similarly improved. However, there is a dearth of research on changes in secondary insomnia as related to the treatment of the primary medical or psychological disorder. In addition, recent research has suggested that although insomnia may be precipitated by another disorder, over time the insomnia may become self-sustaining. Lichstein, Wilson, and Johnson (2000) conducted a randomized trial of the treatment of secondary insomnia with a standard behavioral treatment program consisting of sleep hygiene, stimulus control, and relaxation. The results indicated that secondary insomnia improved to about the same degree as is ordinarily seen in studies of the behavioral treatment of primary insomnia. This finding suggests that both primary and secondary insomnia are likely to respond in a similar fashion when treated with behavioral approaches in primary care settings.

Behaviors That Exacerbate Insomnia

In many cases, regardless of the cause or whether it is primary or secondary, insomnia is exacerbated by voluntary and often addictive behaviors. The most frequently assessed in the primary case setting include, but are not limited to, the consumption of alcohol, tobacco, and caffeine.

Frequently, these substances are used to compensate for existing sleep problems, but instead they contribute to the maintenance or intensification of insomnia.

Alcohol Use

Insomnia has been found to be significantly related to alcohol consumption (Brower, Aldrich, Robinson, Zucker, & Greden, 2001; Janson, Lindberg, Gislason, Elmasry, & Boman, 2001). Alcohol consumption is a common method used by individuals with insomnia to try to help them relax and sleep. Unfortunately, consumption of alcohol has an iatrogenic effect on sleep. Alcohol is known to decrease sleep onset but lead to sleep fragmentation, nightmares, and early morning awakenings (Zarcone, 1994). A study of individuals with alcohol dependence indicated that 61% had a history of insomnia, and insomnia was also a significant factor related to relapse to drinking after successful abstinence (Brower et al., 2001).

Tobacco Use

Smoking is associated with difficulty in initiating sleep and other symptoms suggestive of sleep fragmentation (Wetter & Young, 1994). Insomnia is included as a nicotine withdrawal sign in the *DSM–IV* (American Psychiatric Association, 1994). Among dependent smokers assessed with polysomnographs, tobacco withdrawal was found to increase sleep disturbances (sleep fragmentation), and nicotine replacement (patches) actually resulted in some postcessation improvements (Wetter, Fiore, Baker, & Young, 1995). Zyban has been frequently associated with an increase in difficulty falling and staying asleep, whereas the patches are known to increase the vividness of dreams (Imperial Cancer Research Fund General Practice Research Group, 1993; Wetter et al., 1995; Wolter et al., 1996). Although overall there may be few long-term effects to sleep from smoking cessation therapies, their association with accompanying sleep disturbance may contribute to patients stopping the medications sooner than is recommended. Cigarette smoking may also be an exacerbating factor in some sleep behaviors such as RLS and bruxism (Lavigne, Lobbezoo, Rompre, Nielsen, & Montplaisir, 1997).[3]

Caffeine Consumption

Caffeine consumption is also known to disrupt sleep (Bonnet & Arand, 1992; Levy & Zylber-Katz, 1983). Coffee, tea, and soda are widely recognized

---

[3] Patients undergoing smoking cessation treatment and using Zyban or nicotine replacement therapy should be warned in advance of the possible sleep disruption and informed that their symptoms usually diminish when the medications are discontinued.

as sources of caffeine. Lesser known sources include pain medications, weight loss pills, various exercise-enhancing supplements, and some cold and allergy medications. Reduction of caffeine consumption, especially in the evening, is a relatively simple behavioral approach to help reduce insomnia and improve sleep. Patients should be educated about the unsuspected sources of caffeine to optimize treatment effect.

ASSESSMENT OF INSOMNIA

Although a thorough assessment of insomnia is critical for effective treatment planning, the authors have found that sufficient information can be gathered within 20 to 30 minutes to formulate and initiate behavioral treatment within the primary care setting. Some of the common terms used in the assessment of insomnia are included in Exhibit 7.3. The assessment of insomnia can be accomplished through the use of clinical interviews, sleep diaries, or sleep questionnaires (Sateia, Doghramji, Hauri, & Morin, 2000). Mahowald (2002) recommended the integration of a three-question sleep history in every primary care patient encounter:

1. How is your sleep at night?
2. Are you too sleepy during the day?
3. Does anything unusual happen to you in your sleep?

Spielman and Anderson (1999) presented an interview that provides structure and allows for a rating of symptoms in relation to the ICSD categories. Whichever assessment tools the clinician chooses, certain information must be gathered. Exhibit 7.4 includes a list of pertinent questions for interviewing patients in a time-limited primary care interview along with the rationale for the questions.

Sleep Diaries

The use of a sleep diary is the gold standard for the objective assessment of insomnia on an outpatient basis, and it is the most frequently used outcome measure in insomnia research (Mimeault & Morin, 1999). Although people with insomnia often overreport sleep problems, they tend to do so consistently within themselves (Espie, Lindsay, & Espie, 1989); sleep diaries provide a relatively reliable picture of the patient's sleep patterns. Reliable and valid estimates of sleep parameters have been recorded when using the sleep diary, although they are not considered to reflect the absolute values obtained from polysomnography (Coates et al., 1982). Morin's (1993) daily sleep diary provides a good example and includes entries for bedtime, arising time, naps, sleep onset latency, wake after sleep onset, early morning awakening,

EXHIBIT 7.3
Terms Commonly Used in the Assessment and Treatment of Insomnia

Term	Definition
Sleep onset latency (SOL)	The amount of time required to initially fall asleep after going to bed with the intention of sleeping
Frequency of nighttime awakenings (FNA)	The number of awakenings after the initial onset of sleep
Wake after sleep onset (WASO)	The duration of awake time after sleep onset, including early awakening before getting out of bed in the morning
Time in bed (TIB)	The total amount of time spent in bed from bedtime to getting out of bed in the morning
Total sleep time (TST)	The total amount of time asleep during the TIB[a]
Sleep efficiency (SE)	The percentage of time spent asleep as compared to the TIB[b]

[a]TST = TIB − (SOL + WASO).
[b]SE = TST/TIB.

frequency of night awakenings, medication intake, and two measures of sleep quality (scored on a 5-point scale). Entries allow for the calculation of total sleep time, sleep-onset latency, number of night-time awakenings, sleep efficiency score, and so forth. Sleep efficiency (the percentage of time spent asleep compared to the total time in bed) of less than 85% of people who are measured is generally considered to reflect poor sleep efficiency.

Spielman and Glovinsky (1997) have devised a version of the sleep diary that is less complex and much easier to visually scan for important sleep information. Whereas some information such as sleep quality is sacrificed, it is considered user friendly for both the patient and clinician. The patient uses symbols instead of exact times to fill in a 7-day × 24-hour grid sheet. Sleep is depicted by drawing a horizontal line anchored on both ends by a vertical line depicting sleep onset and awakening. Length of awakenings during the night are identified by the gaps between the sleep marks. Overall, the authors believe that this sleep diary provides more benefits for the rapid assessment and brief interventions in primary care.

Standardized Sleep Questionnaires

Standardized questionnaire measures of sleep and insomnia with potential usefulness in primary care settings include the Athens Insomnia Scale (Soldatos, Dikeos, Paparrigopoulos, 2000), the Pittsburgh Sleep Quality

EXHIBIT 7.4
Useful Questions for the Assessment of Insomnia in Primary Care Settings

Interview question	Interviewer's rationale
When did your sleep problems start?	Determine onset and differentiate acute versus chronic insomnia.
What do you think started these sleep problems?	Assess initiating factors.
How many hours do you typically sleep?	Estimate of total sleep time.
How much sleep do you think you need each night?	Find out patient's expectations for treatment. Are they realistic?
What time do you go to bed?	Some people may be staying up late by choice or going to bed early to try to "catch up on sleep."
How long does it take you to fall asleep?	Estimate of average sleep onset latency.
How many awakenings do you have each night and for what length of time?	Estimate of frequency of nighttime awakenings and duration of wake after sleep onset.
What do you do during the night when awake?	Look for cognitions or racing thoughts that may be affecting sleep onset latency or return to sleep. If present, intervene with training in relaxation techniques.
When do you typically awaken for the last time?	Terminal insomnia could be an indication of depression.
How do these sleep problems affect you during the day?	Look for complaints of fatigue, mood disturbance, poor concentration, or limiting activities.
What is your sleep like on the weekends?	Some people sleep in on the weekends, not realizing that this compensatory behavior is affecting them during the week.
How much nicotine, caffeine, and alcohol do you use?	These can significantly fragment sleep although use does not always result in awakenings.
What are you doing now to help yourself sleep better?	Assess possible over-the-counter medications or other compensatory behaviors that may be compounding the sleep problem.

Index (Buysse, Reynolds, Monk, Berman, & Kupfer, 1989), the Insomnia Severity Index, and the Epworth Sleepiness Scale (Johns, 1991, 1992, 1993). Morin and Espie's book *Insomnia: A Clinical Guide to Assessment and Treatment* (2003) includes several additional measurement devices that could be helpful in assessing insomnia.

Athens Insomnia Scale

From a population health perspective, one of the newest and most potentially applicable measures is the Athens Insomnia Scale (AIS; Soldatos, Dikeos, & Paparrigopoulos, 2000). A self-administered brief measure, the AIS is based on ICD–10 criteria for insomnia. It can be administered in either an eight- or five-question variation. The first five items measure sleep induction, awakenings during the night, terminal awakening, total sleep duration, and sleep quality. The last three questions assess well-being, daily functioning, and daytime sleepiness. Each item of the AIS can be rated from 0 to 3 (0 = no problem at all and 3 = very serious problem) for a total possible score of 40. The initial validation of the AIS was based on a sample of 299 participants: 105 primary insomniacs, 144 psychiatric patients, and 50 nonpatient controls. The internal consistency for both versions was .90, and a factor analysis of the scale produced a single component. The test–retest reliability correlation coefficient during a 1-week interval was reported at .90.

Pittsburgh Sleep Quality Index

The Pittsburgh Sleep Quality Index (PSQI; Buysse, Reynolds, Monk, Berman, & Kupfer, 1989) is a 19-item self-administered questionnaire that assesses sleep quality and disturbances over a 1-month time frame). The PSQI was originally validated on a sample of 52 healthy participants, 54 depressed patients, and 62 patients with sleep disorders. The scoring process is laborious: The 19-items generate 7 component scores that are then summed to provide a global score. A global score greater than 5 indicates moderate to severe difficulties with sleep (Buysse et al., 1989). The PSQI is primarily intended to measure sleep quality or to identify good and bad sleepers. It can be used to measure outcome, but its relatively complex calculations limit its potential usefulness in primary care settings (Soldatos et al., 2000).

Although the PSQI and the AIS both have applications to clinical and research settings, the AIS is briefer and much easier to score. Therefore, the AIS appears to provide the best global measure of sleep for use in a primary care setting. Nevertheless, the PSQI provides more breadth of information and may be more applicable for primary care research, single case studies, or measuring change during an individual intervention in primary care.

Insomnia Severity Index

The Insomnia Severity Index (ISI; Bastien, Vallières, & Morin, 2001) is a 7-item questionnaire that yields a quantitative index of sleep impairment and can be used to gauge treatment outcome. Patients are asked to rate the following components on a 5-point Likert scale (ranging from 0 = not at all to 4 = extremely): (a) severity of sleep onset, sleep maintenance, and early morning awakening problems; (b) satisfaction with current sleep patterns; (c) interference with daily functioning; (d) impairment attributed to the sleep problems; and (e) level of distress caused by the sleep problems. The ISI has been demonstrated to show adequate psychometric properties and has been verified in previous insomnia treatment studies as sensitive to changes (Bastien et al., 2001).

Epworth Sleepiness Scale

The Epworth Sleepiness Scale (ESS; Johns, 1991, 1992, 1993) is an 8-item questionnaire designed to assess level of daytime sleepiness. Patients rate the likelihood that they would doze off or fall asleep in eight different situations commonly encountered in daily life, such as watching TV, riding in a car, and so forth.

Compensatory Behaviors

An important component of assessing for insomnia is questioning patients on their use of behaviors to compensate for the unwanted effects of sleeping disorders. For example, patients may try to counter excessive daytime sleepiness, which frequently accompanies OSA, PLM, and RLS, by napping, sleeping later into the day, or taking over-the-counter medications that contain ephedrine or caffeine. Many individuals with excessive daytime sleepiness may also increase their use of stimulants by consuming more caffeinated drinks (sodas, coffee) or using more tobacco products.[4]

In addition, over-the-counter medications and herbal supplements have become common self-management approaches for patients with insomnia. In two studies with college students, more women than men (11.4% vs. 6.4%) who reported sleep problems at least 1 day a month used some type of over-the-counter sleep aid, whereas more men than women used alcohol to induce sleep (23.4% vs. 10.9%; Pillitteri, Kozlowski, Person, & Spear, 1994). Research with an elderly sample of 176 individuals found that 50% had used one or more nonprescription products to promote sleep, including dimenhydrinate (21%), acetaminophen (19%), diphenhydramine (15%), alcohol (13%), and herbal products (11%; Sproule, Busto, Buckle, Herrmann, & Bowles, 1999).

---

[4]Young males who are lifting weights regularly or those on shift work are specific populations that should be screened for use of supplements containing stimulants.

CULTURE OF PRIMARY CARE

In spite of the growing demand for sleep services, most physicians appear to have limited training in sleep disorders (Richardson, 2000). A 1993 national survey of medical schools indicated that fewer than 2 hours of total teaching time was allotted to sleep and sleep disorders, and 37 out of the 126 accredited medical schools completing the survey reported no structured teaching on the subject whatsoever (Rosen, Rosekind, Rosevear, Cole, & Dement, 1993).

Primary care providers (PCPs) may find it difficult to apply behavioral treatments because of training in the medical model, lack of knowledge of behavioral treatment approaches, limited appointment time, and expectations of patients. The medical model promotes the idea that if the underlying problem is treated (e.g., chronic pain), the accompanying symptoms will remit. However, learned compensatory behaviors often maintain or increase insomnia over time. The volume of information that PCPs must manage is enormous, and they have limited time to remain current on behavioral treatments for the myriad disorders they treat. Appointment times are typically 10 to 20 minutes, which leaves little time to explore more than one to two major complaints in any one clinical appointment. Finally, the expectations of some patients can certainly influence the outcome of a primary care visit, and many patients seek medications for their complaints. Morin, Colecchi, et al. (1999) point out a hidden problem with the administration of hypnotic medications, even in combination with behavioral treatments: Patients may attribute initial gains exclusively to their medications. This may place the patient at increased vulnerability to relapse when the medication is discontinued. Overall, the PCP has limited time, and behavioral interventions have traditionally been presented to them as lengthy, involved, and specialized.

TREATMENT OF INSOMNIA

Although the treatment for insomnia most commonly initiated in the primary care setting is pharmacological (Kupfer & Reynolds, 1997; Morin & Wooten, 1996), behavioral treatments have been shown to be just as effective and longer lasting (Morin, Colecchi, et al., 1999). Several excellent reviews of pharmacological treatment of insomnia have been published (Buysse & Reynolds, 2000; Eddy & Walbroehl, 1999; Rajput & Bromley, 1999). Two large-scale meta-analyses (Morin, Culbert, & Schwartz, 1994; Murtagh & Greenwood, 1995) and a recent American Academy of Sleep Medicine Review (Morin, Hauri, et al., 1999) have provided strong scientific evidence that behavioral treatments for insomnia produce significant and long-lasting results. A recent comparative meta-analysis of pharmacotherapy and behavior therapy including four studies of insomnia concluded that there were no differences in magnitude of effect sizes between pharmacological and behavioral treatments except for sleep onset latency (Smith et al., 2002). Smith and colleagues (2002) also pointed out that there is an absence of data concerning the long-term efficacy of pharmacotherapy for insomnia and that the information available only supports the short-term (2 to 4 weeks) effectiveness of medications. In addition, no studies exist to suggest that there are any sustained improvements when medication is withdrawn (Smith et al., 2002). Evidence of long-term benefits of the use of behavioral interventions with sustained and even increasing improvements is demonstrated in some outcome measures of sleep (e.g., Espie, Inglis, Tessier, & Harvey, 2001).

In perhaps the best randomized placebo-controlled trial to date, Morin, Colecchi, et al. (1999) evaluated the clinical efficacy of pharmacological treatment using tamazepam (Restoril), behavioral treatment, a combined treatment, and placebo for the treatment of late-life insomnia in 78 adults. Each of the three treatments was more effective than placebo at posttreatment assessment. However, long-term outcome measures (12 and 24 months) showed that participants receiving the behavioral treatment sustained clinical gains, whereas those treated with the drug alone did not. Behavioral treatment was rated by participants, significant others, and clinicians as more effective than drug therapy alone, and participants were most satisfied with the behavioral approach overall.

Behavioral Treatment of Insomnia

Behavior therapy for insomnia meets the American Psychological Association's criteria for an empirically supported psychological treatment (Morin, Hauri, et al., 1999). The behavior therapy treatments that are most commonly cited in research include sleep hygiene, stimulus control, sleep restriction, relaxation training, biofeedback, and paradoxical intention (Chesson et al., 1999; Hryshko-Mullen et al., 2000; Morin, Hauri, et al., 1999).

Before the initiation of treatment for insomnia, specific and realistic goals for treatment should be established. Goals are generated during the assessment and often include decreasing sleep onset latency, reducing the frequency or duration of nighttime awakenings, and improving sleep efficiency. Patients should be educated so they understand the nature of normal sleep and the changes in sleep associated with aging, including increased fragmentation, decreased deep sleep, and increased nighttime awakenings. It is important to remember that the average increase in total sleep time after behavioral treatment for insomnia is only about 30 minutes (e.g., Hrysko-Mullen et al., 2000; Mimeault & Morin, 1999; Morin, Colecchi, et al., 1999) and that improved sleep does not necessarily lead to meaningful changes in daytime well-being or performance (Morin, Hauri, et al., 1999). It is also important to help patients distinguish between daytime fatigue, tiredness, and "sleepiness." Other behavioral approaches (e.g., cognitive therapy, increased physical exercise, improved nutrition) may be necessary to increase energy and vigor during the day. Many patients using behavioral techniques are able to reduce their level of frustration, leading to significant improvement in their qualitative measures of sleep. Therefore, improvement in qualitative measures is often a realistic goal for insomnia treatment.

Sleep Hygiene

Sleep hygiene education involves providing the patient with instructions that typically emphasize five behaviors affecting sleep: (a) caffeine consumption, (b) smoking, (c) alcohol use, (d) exercise, and (e) napping (Riedel, 2000). Exhibit 7.5 includes a list of recommendations for proper sleep hygiene. Although sleep hygiene education alone does not often lead to significant improvements in insomnia (Morin, Hauri, et al., 1999), poor sleep hygiene can aggravate insomnia (Mimeault & Morin, 1999; Reynolds, Kupfer, Buysse, Coble, & Yeager, 1991).[5]

Stimulus Control

Stimulus control is the behavioral treatment approach with the strongest scientific evidence for its efficacy (Chesson et al., 1999). Stimulus control procedures (Bootzin & Nicassio, 1978) were designed to break the cycle of spending too much time in bed awake and the accompanying negative associations with the bed that often develop. For people with insomnia, the bed, which was previously associated with the onset and maintenance of sleep, has lost its discriminative property and no longer serves as a cue for sleep (Bootzin & Nicassio, 1978). Approximately 30 controlled studies have evaluated the efficacy of stimulus control treatment of insomnia (Morin, Hauri, et al., 1999). The guidelines listed in Exhibit 7.6 describe the initial recommendations for stimulus control and the rationale behind them. Stimulus control guidelines should be described to the patient as a powerful tool for breaking the cycle of staying awake in bed and for reestablishing the positive associations with the bed as a place for peaceful rest. This approach

---

[5]Although sleep hygiene is not typically offered as a stand-alone treatment, it is usually a good idea to start by asking about these areas or having a brief checklist that patients can complete themselves.

EXHIBIT 7.5
Guidelines for Sleep Hygiene

Caffeine: Avoid Caffeine 4–6 Hours Before Bedtime. Caffeine disturbs sleep, even in people who do not subjectively experience such an effect. Individuals with insomnia are often more sensitive to mild stimulants than are normal sleepers. Caffeine is found in items such as coffee, tea, soda, chocolate, and many over-the-counter medications (e.g., Excedrin).

Nicotine: Avoid Nicotine Before Bedtime. Although some smokers claim that smoking helps them relax, nicotine is a stimulant. Thus, smoking, dipping, or chewing tobacco should be avoided near bedtime and during the night.

Alcohol: Avoid Alcohol After Dinner. A small amount of alcohol often promotes the onset of sleep, but as alcohol is metabolized sleep becomes disturbed and fragmented. Thus, alcohol is a poor sleep aid.

Sleeping Pills: Sleep Medications Are Effective Only Temporarily. Scientists have shown that sleep medications lose their effectiveness in about 2–4 weeks when taken regularly. Despite advertisements to the contrary, over-the-counter sleeping aids have little impact on sleep beyond the placebo effect. Over time, sleeping pills actually can make sleep problems worse. When sleeping pills have been used for a long period, withdrawal from the medication can lead to an insomnia rebound. Thus, after long-term use, many individuals incorrectly conclude that they "need" sleeping pills in order to sleep normally.

Exercise: Avoid Vigorous Exercise Within 2 Hours of Bedtime. Regular exercise in the late afternoon or early evening seems to aid sleep, although the positive effect often takes several weeks to become noticeable. However, exercise within 2 hours of bedtime may elevate nervous system activity and interfere with sleep onset.

Hot Bath: A Hot Bath May Promote Sleep. Spending 20 minutes in a tub of hot water an hour or two prior to bedtime may promote sleep.

Bedroom Environment: Moderate Temperature, Quiet, and Dark. Extremes of heat or cold can disrupt sleep. A quiet environment is more sleep promoting than a noisy one. Noises can be masked with background white noise (such as the noise of a fan) or with earplugs. Bedrooms may be darkened with blackout shades or sleep masks can be worn. Position clocks out-of-sight since clock-watching can increase anxiety about the lack of sleep.

Eating: A Light Snack at Bedtime May Promote Sleep. A light bedtime snack, such a glass of warm milk, cheese, or a bowl of cereal can promote sleep. You should avoid the following foods at bedtime: any caffeinated foods (e.g., chocolate), peanuts, beans, most raw fruits and vegetables (since they may cause gas), and high-fat foods such as potato chips or corn chips. Avoid snacks in the middle of the night since awakening may become conditioned to hunger.

Note. From "Behavioral Treatment of Insomnia: The Wilford Hall Insomnia Program," by A. S. Hryshko-Mullen, L. S. Broeckl, C. K. Haddock, and A. L. Peterson, 2000, *Military Medicine, 165,* pp. 202–203. Copyright 2000 by Association of Military Surgeons of U.S. Reprinted with permission.

EXHIBIT 7.6
Guidelines for Stimulus Control

Set a Reasonable Bedtime and Arising Time and Stick to Them. Spending excessive time in bed has two unfortunate consequences: (1) you begin to associate your bedroom with arousal and frustration and (2) your sleep actually becomes more shallow. Set the alarm clock and get out of bed at the same time each morning, weekdays and weekends, regardless of your bedtime or the amount of sleep you obtained on the previous night. You probably will be tempted to stay in bed in the morning if you did not sleep well, but try to maintain your new schedule. This guideline is designed to regulate your internal biological clock and reset your sleep-wake rhythm.

Go to Bed Only When You Are Sleepy. There is no reason to go to bed if you are not sleepy. When you go to bed too early, it only gives you more time to become frustrated with your inability to sleep. Individuals often ponder the events of the day, plan the next day's schedule, or worry about their inability to fall asleep. You should therefore delay your bedtime until you are sleepy. This may mean that you go to bed even later than your scheduled bedtime. Remember to stick to your scheduled arising time regardless of the time you go to bed.

Get Out of Bed When You Can't Fall Asleep or Go Back to Sleep in About 15 Minutes. Return to Bed Only When You Are Sleepy. Repeat This Step as Often as Necessary. Although we don't want you to be a clock-watcher, get out of bed if you don't fall asleep fairly soon. Remember, the goal is for you to fall asleep quickly. Return to bed only when you are sleepy. The object is for you to reconnect your bed with sleeping rather than frustration. It will be demanding to follow this instruction, but many people have found ways to adhere to this guideline.

Use the Bed or Bedroom for Sleep and Sex Only; Do Not Watch TV, Listen to the Radio, Eat, or Read in Your Bedroom. The purpose of this guideline is to associate your bedroom with sleep rather than wakefulness. Just as you may associate the kitchen with hunger, this guideline will help you associate sleep with your bedroom. Follow this rule both during the day and at night. You may have to temporarily move the TV or radio from your bedroom to help you during treatment.

Do Not Nap During the Day. Most sleep experts agree that daytime napping almost always disrupts sleep rhythm, making it harder to go to sleep at night. This guideline will help your body to acquire a consistent sleep rhythm so that you feel drowsy and ready to sleep at about the same time each night.

Allow Yourself at Least an Hour Before Bedtime to Unwind. The brain is not a light switch that you can instantly cut on and off. Most of us cannot expect to go full speed till 2000 then fall peacefully to sleep at 2015. Take a hot bath, read a novel, watch some TV, or have a pleasant talk with your spouse or kids. Find what works for you. Be sure not to struggle with a problem, get into an argument before bed, or anything else that might increase your arousal.

Note. From "Behavioral Treatment of Insomnia: The Wilford Hall Insomnia Program," by A. S. Hryshko-Mullen, L. S. Broeckl, C. K. Haddock, and A. L. Peterson, 2000, *Military Medicine, 165,* pp. 202–203. Copyright 2000 by Association of Military Surgeons of U.S. Reprinted with permission.

is often misunderstood by patients initially and seen as counterintuitive to their goal of improving their sleep.[6]

Sleep Restriction (Or Sleep Compression)

Approximately 10 controlled studies have evaluated the efficacy of sleep restriction for treating insomnia (Morin, Hauri, et al., 1999). Sleep restriction involves limiting or restricting the sleep window (established bedtime and awakening time) to the estimated total sleep time (Spielman et al., 1987). The goal of sleep restriction is to decrease sleep onset latency, decrease wake after sleep onset, and improve sleep efficiency ($\geq 85\%$). The use of a sleep diary or careful clinical assessment to determine sleep parameters is necessary to implement sleep restriction. For example, suppose on average a patient goes to bed at 10:00 p.m., takes 120 minutes to fall asleep, awakens three times during the night, remains awake in bed for 40 minutes each awakening, and then gets out of bed at 8:00 a.m. immediately after awakening. Thus the time in bed equals 10 hours, total sleep time equals 6 hours, and sleep efficiency is 60%. In this case, a sleep window of 6 hours (equal to the total sleep time) might be recommended. The provider would then collaborate with the patient to establish the sleep window (set bedtime and awakening time; e.g., midnight to 6:00 a.m.) and the importance of using the stimulus control procedures. This sleep restriction procedure usually results in decreased sleep onset latency, decreased wake after sleep onset, and improved sleep efficiency. It typically requires that a patient stay up significantly later than his or her usual bedtime, which is often perceived as an impossible or at least counterintuitive task. Asking the patient, "Which do you think would be more difficult to do, force yourself to stay awake or force yourself to fall asleep?" often helps the patient understand the rationale behind sleep restriction. When sleep efficiency remains consistently above 85% for at least a week, the duration of the sleep window can be increased by 20 to 30 minutes, and the procedure can be repeated until sleep disruption occurs (i.e., sleep efficiency falls below 85%), at which point the patient has reached the optimum sleep window (Morin, 1993).

Relaxation Training

Approximately 50 studies have evaluated the efficacy of relaxation training for treating insomnia (Morin, Hauri, et al., 1999). Numerous relaxation-training approaches have been evaluated, including progressive

---

[6]Stimulus control procedures are difficult for some patients to understand (e.g., How can getting up after 15 to 20 minutes help me sleep better?). Careful discussion of the rationale of the procedure and its relationship to their overall established sleep goals is often important for patients to be willing to implement stimulus control procedures.

muscle relaxation, imagery training, meditation, and autogenic training. The specific details for relaxation training have been previously outlined (Benson, 1975; Bernstein & Borkovec, 1973; Schultz & Luthe, 1969). Some studies have shown that relaxation training is less effective with insomnia than stimulus control or sleep restriction (Morin, Hauri, et al., 1999).

Biofeedback

Biofeedback treatment for insomnia has been evaluated in about 10 controlled studies as reviewed by Morin and colleagues (Morin, Hauri, et al., 1999), with outcomes generally similar to those for relaxation training. However, biofeedback should only be administered by those trained and certified to do so. Therefore, relaxation training in lieu of biofeedback is ideal in primary care settings because no certification is needed and because of the ease of its instruction and implementation.

Paradoxical Intention

Paradoxical intention involves suggesting that patients engage in behaviors that are opposite to their desired effect. For example, individuals having trouble falling asleep are encouraged to stay awake as long as possible. One reason this approach works is that it indirectly promotes improved sleep hygiene and stimulus control. About six studies have demonstrated the efficacy of this treatment approach (Morin, Hauri, et al., 1999). However, establishing appropriate paradoxical intention interventions requires considerable clinical time and clinician training. Therefore, paradoxical intention is not recommended as a first-line behavioral intervention in primary care settings.

Cognitive Therapy

Cognitive therapy helps patients challenge their unrealistic or irrational beliefs about their sleep and insomnia (e.g., I must get 8 hours of sleep every night or I cannot function during the day). At least six studies have evaluated cognitive therapy of insomnia and shown it to be an effective treatment (Morin, Hauri, et al., 1999). However, similar to biofeedback and paradoxical intention, the time requirements for becoming proficient in and implementing cognitive therapy limit its applicability in primary care settings.

Behavioral Group Treatment of Insomnia

Behavioral group treatments for insomnia have been shown to be about as effective as behavioral treatments implemented on an individual basis (Hryshko-Mullen et al., 2000). One of the most relevant and well-controlled

EXHIBIT 7.7
Resources for Patients and Clinician

Self-help manuals
—*No More Sleepless Nights Workbook* (Hauri, Jarman, & Linde, 2001)
—*Say Goodnight to Insomnia* (Jacobs, 1998)
—*Good Nights* (Zammit, 1997)

Resources for clinicians
—*Treatment for Late-Life Insomnia* (Lichstein & Morin, 2000)
—*Assessment and Management of Sleep Disorders in Primary Care Practice* (Mahowald, 2002)
—*Insomnia: Psychological Assessment and Management* (Morin, 1993)
—*Understanding Sleep: The Evaluation and Treatment of Sleep Disorders* (Pressman & Orr, 1997)

studies to date of the application of behavioral principles to groups in the primary care setting provided strong support for their clinical effectiveness (Espie et al., 2001). This study randomized 139 participants with insomnia to a cognitive–behavioral therapy (CBT) or self-monitoring control condition. The CBT was delivered by primary care nurses in a six-session format in groups of 4 to 6 patients. Significantly reduced sleep latency and wakefulness during the night was maintained at a 1-year follow-up. There was also evidence that the total amount of sleep significantly increased during the follow-up period. Group behavioral treatments for insomnia in primary care settings hold great promise because of the ability to treat multiple patients with significantly reduced provider time commitments.

Self-Administered and Minimal-Contact Behavioral Treatments

Several studies have demonstrated that insomnia can be treated effectively with minimal-contact interventions (Hauri, 1993), phone consultations (Mimeault & Morin, 1999), bibliotherapy (Alperson & Biglan, 1979; Mimeault & Morin, 1999), audiotapes (Morawetz, 1989), and videotapes (Riedel, Lichstein, & Dwyer, 1995). These techniques have shown great promise and are applicable to the primary care setting because of their brevity, affordability, and ease of administration to a large patient population. Exhibit 7.7 lists books that are recommended for patient use, as well as resources for clinicians.

INITIATING A BEHAVIORAL TREATMENT PROGRAM FOR INSOMNIA

Because patients respond well to behavioral intervention and because objective measures of improved sleep can easily be shown to PCPs, behavioral treatment of insomnia provides an excellent avenue for psychologists to become involved in primary care settings. Whether or not the psychologist is currently practicing in that setting, he or she should educate him- or herself about sleep and assess clinic population needs. In addition, psychologists are advised to design a clinical pathway and devise a stepped-care approach to treating insomnia.

Educate Yourself

As a provider in the primary care setting, you should start by educating yourself on normal sleep, sleep disorders, and effective behavioral treatments for insomnia (Lichstein & Morin, 2000; Mahowald, 2002; Morin, 1993; Morin, Hauri, et al., 1999; Pressman & Orr, 1997). A total knowledge of all aspects of sleep is not necessary to successfully implement a behavioral treatment program for insomnia. A thorough understanding of the behavioral concepts, the rationale behind their implementation, and confidence in the techniques tend to increase the likelihood of patients' adherence and treatment results. Recommended books for further reading and information beyond the scope of this chapter are listed in Exhibit 7.7.

Assess Population Needs

Next, it is important to assess needs of your specific primary care population regarding sleep. The primary care providers should be questioned regarding their perception of sleep problems and the need for additional treatments. Because the referrals are likely to be from PCPs, it is important to assess their likelihood of using such a service. One way of gathering information to present to primary care providers on the prevalence of sleep problems would be to survey a portion of their patient population and present this data to them during a staff meeting. You should also assess who in the clinic will be providing the insomnia treatment. The clinician should think creatively regarding the format (individual, group, telephone consultations, etc.) and who will be responsible for teaching the behavioral principles (e.g., nurses, primary care providers, psychologist, etc.).

Design a Clinical Pathway

After you have educated yourself, assessed the need for treatment, and decided who will be providing the treatment, we suggest that you design a clinical pathway for the treatment of insomnia. The clinical pathway would typically begin with a flow chart of two or three assessment questions with an accompanying decision tree on how to treat and when or where to refer patients for additional assessment or treatment. The threshold for some primary care providers on when to refer for a sleep study may be low, resulting in unnecessary evaluation of patients without significant sleep disorders. The provider of behavioral treatment for insomnia has the potential to save the medical system and patients from nonessential medical tests that are often uncomfortable, time-consuming, and expensive (Sateia et al., 2000).

Stepped-Care

Stepped-care is one way to approach insomnia treatment in the primary care setting. Minimal interventions may include using pamphlets or presenting sleep information during health education or prevention classes (e.g., prelabor classes or diabetes management). Other levels may include a self-referral prevention class in which information is presented on normal sleep and the self-administration of behavioral principles for improving sleep. The highest level might be a specific treatment class or an individual assessment on referral from a primary care provider.

A significant portion of setting up a behavioral treatment program in primary care that demands attention and planning includes educating the primary care provider and staff on assessment, behavioral intervention, and when to refer. The authors have found that providers may be unwilling to thoroughly assess their patients' sleep unless the steps listed in the preceding paragraphs are already well established. Primary care providers need to know that there is a support system available to provide the appropriate level of care for potentially identified needs. We have found that once the primary care providers have been assured that a behavioral treatment program is available to refer patients to and that they can confidently assess, make a clinical decision regarding care, and refer to the appropriate level of intervention, the referrals will come.

CONCLUSION

This chapter has outlined the behavioral treatment of insomnia in the primary care setting with the intention of encouraging individual providers to initiate new programs. Information was reviewed on the available types and modalities (individual, groups, self-help) of treatments of insomnia in the primary care setting. Significant positive results to the medical system, providers of care, and patients were shown. Although treatment techniques have been described separately, clinicians should not restrict themselves to just one; most of the insomnia treatment programs evaluated to date are multicomponent treatments (i.e., various combinations of stimulus control, modified sleep restriction, sleep hygiene, etc.). We have found the behavioral treatment of insomnia to be both clinically efficacious for patients and personally rewarding for providers. Because many people with insomnia are seen in the primary care setting and because clinical psychologists and health psychologists are in short supply, it will be important to increase training for PCPs on the behavioral management of sleep problems. Espie and colleagues (2001) have provided evidence that nurses with no previous experience were able to learn and provide effective group interventions.

Improved sleep through the widespread use of brief behavioral interventions in primary care settings will likely lead to medical system improvements, such as reductions in medical complaints, prescription medication costs, and the number of primary care visits. Individual patients who sleep better may also experience fewer accidents while increasing overall productivity and quality of life. The continued dissemination of behavioral treatments for insomnia in primary care settings has the potential to significantly improve population health

Additional research is needed to evaluate the use of innovative behavioral treatment approaches in primary care settings. For example, self-management intervention programs such as CD-ROMs (Espie et al., 2001), Web-based interventions (e.g., weight management: Tate, Wing, & Winett, 2001; headaches: Ström, Pettersson, & Andersson, 2000; sleep: Strom, Pettersson, & Andersson, 2004) or self-help manuals may prove to be effective.

REFERENCES

Affleck, G., Urrows, S., Tennen, H., Higgins, P., & Abeles, M. (1996). Sequential daily relations of sleep, pain intensity, and attention to pain among women with fibromyalgia. *Pain, 68,* 363–368.

Alperson, J., & Biglan, A. (1979). Self-administered treatment of sleep onset insomnia and the importance of age. *Behavior Therapy, 10,* 347–356.

American Psychiatric Association. (2000). *Diagnostic and statistical manual of mental disorders* (4th ed., text rev.). Washington, DC: Author.

American Sleep Disorders Association. (1990). *The international classification of sleep disorders: Diagnostic and coding manual.* Rochester, MN: Author.

Ancoli-Israel, S., Kripke, D. F., Klauber, M. R., Mason, W. J., Fell, R., & Kaplan, O. (1991). Periodic limb movements in sleep in community dwelling elderly. *Sleep, 14,* 496–500.

Bastien, C., Vallières, A., & Morin, C. M. (2001). Validation of the Insomnia Severity Index as a clinical outcome measure for insomnia research. *Sleep Medicine, 2,* 297–307.

Benson, H. (1975). *The relaxation response.* New York: Avon Books.

Bernstein, D. S., & Borkovec, T. D. (1973). *Progressive relaxation training.* Champaign, IL: Research Press.

Bonnet, M. H., & Arand, D. L. (1992). Caffeine use as a model of acute and chronic insomnia. *Sleep, 15,* 526–536.

Bootzin, R. R., & Epstein, D. R. (2000). Stimulus control. In K. L. Lichstein & C. M. Morin (Eds.), *Treatment of late-life insomnia* (pp. 167–184). Thousand Oaks, CA: Sage.

Bootzin, R. R., & Nicassio, P. M. (1978). Behavioral treatments for insomnia. In M. Hersen, R. M. Eisler, & P. M. Miller (Eds.), *Progress in behavior modification* (Vol. 6, pp. 1–45). New York: Academic Press.

Bourdet, C., & Goldenberg, F. (1994). Insomnia in anxiety: Sleep EEG changes. *Journal of Psychosomatic Research, 38,* 93–104.

Brower, K. J., Aldrich, M. S., Robinson, E. A., Zucker, R. A., & Greden, J. F. (2001). Insomnia, self-medication, and relapse to alcoholism. *American Journal of Psychiatry, 158,* 399–404.

Buysse, D. J., & Reynolds, C. F. (2000). Pharmacological treatment. In K. L. Lichstein & C. M. Morin (Eds.), *Treatment of late-life insomnia* (pp. 231–267). Thousand Oaks, CA: Sage.

Buysse, D. J., Reynolds, C. F., Monk, T. H., Berman, S. R., & Kupfer, D. J. (1989). The Pittsburgh Sleep Quality Index: A new instrument for psychiatric practice and research. *Psychiatry Research, 28,* 193–213.

Chambers, M. J., & Keller, B. (1993). Alert insomniacs: Are they really sleep deprived? *Clinical Psychology Review, 13,* 649–666.

Chesson, A. L., Anderson, W. M., Littner, M., Davila, D., Hartse, K., Johnson, S., et al. (1999). Practice parameters for the nonpharmacologic treatment of insomnia. *Sleep, 22,* 1128–1133.

Coates, T. J., Killen, J. D., George, J., Marchine, E., Silverman, S., & Thoresen, C. (1982). Estimating sleep parameters: A multitrait multimethod analysis. *Journal of Consulting and Clinical Psychology, 50,* 345–352.

Currie, S. R., Wilson, K. G., & Curran, D. (2002). Clinical significance and predictors of treatment response to cognitive–behavior therapy for insomnia secondary to chronic pain. *Journal of Behavioral Medicine, 25,* 135–153.

Currie, S. R., Wilson, K. G., Pontefract, A. J., & deLaplante, L., (2000). Cognitive–behavioral treatment of insomnia secondary to chronic pain. *Journal of Consulting and Clinical Psychology, 68,* 407–416.

Eddy, M., & Walbroehl, G. S. (1999). Insomnia. *American Family Physician, 59,* 1911–1917.

Espie, C. A. (2000). Assessment and differential diagnosis. In K. L. Lichstein & C. M. Morin (Eds.), *Treatment of late-life insomnia* (pp. 81–108). Thousand Oaks, CA: Sage.

Espie, C. A, Inglis, S. J., Tessier, S., & Harvey, L. (2001). The clinical effectiveness of cognitive behaviour therapy for chronic insomnia: Implementation and evaluation of a sleep clinic in general medical practice. *Behaviour Research and Therapy, 39,* 45–60.

Espie, C. A., Lindsay, W. R., & Espie, L. C. (1989). Use of the Sleep Assessment Device (Kelley and Lichstein, 1980) to validate insomniacs' self-report of sleep pattern. *Journal of Psychopathology and Behavioral Assessment, 11,* 71–79.

Fichten, C. S., Libman, E., Bailes, S., & Alapin, I. (2000). Characteristics of older adults with insomnia. In K. L. Lichstein & C. M. Morin (Eds.), *Treatment of late-life insomnia* (pp. 37–79). Thousand Oaks, CA: Sage.

Ford, D. E., & Kamerow, D. B. (1989). Epidemiological study of sleep disturbances and psychiatric disorders: An opportunity for prevention? *Journal of the American Medical Association, 262,* 1479–1484.

Gillin, J. C. (1998). Are sleep disturbances risk factors for anxiety, depressive and addictive disorders? *Acta Psychiatrica Scandinavica, 393,* 39–43.

Hauri, P. J. (1993). Consulting about insomnia: A method and some preliminary data. *Sleep, 16,* 344–350.

Hauri, P., Jarman, M., & Linde, S. (2001). *No more sleepless nights workbook: Tracking your progress toward a great night's sleep.* New York: Wiley.

Hryshko-Mullen, A. S., Broeckl, L. S., Haddock, C. K., & Peterson, A. L. (2000). Behavioral treatment of insomnia: The Wilford Hall insomnia program. *Military Medicine, 165,* 200–207.

Imperial Cancer Research Fund General Practice Research Group. (1993). Effectiveness of a nicotine patch in helping people stop smoking: Results of a randomized trial in general practice. *British Medical Journal, 306,* 1304–1308.

Jacobs, G. D. (1998). *Say good night to insomnia: The 6-week solution.* New York: Henry Holt.

Janson, C., Lindberg, E., Gislason, T., Elmasry, A., & Boman, G. (2001). Insomnia in men—A 10-year prospective population based study. *Sleep, 24,* 425–430.

Johns, M. W. (1991). A new method for measuring daytime sleepiness: The Epworth Sleepiness scale. *Sleep, 14,* 540–545.

Johns, M. W. (1992). Reliability and factor analysis of the Epworth Sleepiness scale. *Sleep, 15,* 376–381.

Johns, M. W. (1993). Daytime sleepiness, snoring and obstructive sleep apnea: The Epworth Sleepiness scale. *Chest, 103,* 30–36.

Kapur, V. K., Redline, S., Nieto, F. J., Young, T. B., Newman, A. B., & Henderson, J. A. (2002). The relationship between chronically disrupted sleep and health-care use. *Sleep, 25,* 289–296.

Katz, D. A., & McHorney, C. A. (2002). The relationship between insomnia and health-related quality of life in patients with chronic illness. *Journal of Family Practice, 51,* 229–235.

Kupfer, D. J., & Reynolds, C. F. (1997). Management of insomnia. *New England Journal of Medicine, 336,* 341–346.

Kushida, C. A., Nichols, D. A., Simon, R. D., Young, T., Grauke, J. H., Britzmann, J. B., et al. (2000). Symptom-based prevalence of sleep disorders in an adult primary care population. *Sleep and Breathing, 4,* 9–14.

Lavigne, G. J., Lobbezoo, F., Rompre, P. H., Nielsen, T. A., & Montplaisir, J. (1997). Cigarette smoking as a risk factor or an exacerbating factor for restless legs syndrome and sleep bruxism. *American Sleep Disorders Association and Sleep Research Society, 20,* 290–293.

Leger, D., Scheuermaier, K., Philip, P., Paillard, M., & Guilleminault, C. (2001). SF–36: Evaluation of quality of life in severe and mild insomniacs compared with good sleepers. *Psychosomatic Medicine, 63,* 49–55.

Lepola, U., Koponen, H. J., & Leinonen, E. (1994). Sleep in panic disorder. *Journal of Psychosomatic Research, 38*(1), 105–111.

Levy, M., & Zylber-Katz, E. (1983). Caffeine metabolism and coffee-attributed sleep disturbances. *Clinical Pharmacological Therapy, 33,* 770–775.

Lichstein, K. L., & Morin, C. M. (Eds.). (2000). *Treatment of late-life insomnia.* Thousand Oaks, CA: Sage.

Lichstein, K. L., & Riedel, B. W. (1994). Behavioral assessment and treatment of insomnia: A review with an emphasis on clinical application. *Behavior Therapy, 25,* 659–688.

Lichstein, K. L., Wilson, N. M., & Johnson, C. T. (2000). Psychological treatment of secondary insomnia. *Psychology and Aging, 15,* 232–240.

Mahowald, M. W. (2002). *Assessment and management of sleep disorders in primary care practice.* Retrieved May 18, 2002, from http://www.aasmnet.org/MEDSleep/Products/(RosenG)primarycare.pdf

Mellinger, G. D., Balter, M. B., & Uhlenhuth, E. H. (1985). Insomnia and its treatment: Prevalence and correlates. *Archives of General Psychiatry, 42,* 225–232.

Mimeault, V., & Morin, C. M. (1999). Self-help treatment for insomnia: Bibliotherapy with and without professional guidance. *Journal of Consulting and Clinical Psychology, 67,* 511–519.

Morawetz, D. (1989). Behavioral self-help treatment for insomnia: A controlled evaluation. *Behavior Therapy, 20,* 365–379.

Morgan, K. (2000). Sleep and aging. In K. L. Lichstein & C. M. Morin (Eds.), *Treatment of late-life insomnia* (pp. 3–36). Thousand Oaks, CA: Sage.

Morin, C. M. (1993). *Insomnia: Psychological assessment and management.* New York: Guilford Press.

Morin, C. M. (1996). *Relief from insomnia: Getting the sleep of your dreams.* New York: Doubleday.

Morin, C. M., Colecchi, C., Stone, J., Stood, R., & Brink, D. (1999). Behavioral and pharmacological therapies for late-life insomnia: A randomized controlled trial. *Journal of the American Medical Association, 281,* 991–999.

Morin, C. M., Culbert, J. P., & Schwartz, S. M. (1994). Nonpharmacological interventions for insomnia: A meta-analysis of treatment efficacy. *American Journal of Psychiatry, 151,* 1172–1180.

Morin, C. M., & Espie, C. A. (2003). *Insomnia: A clinical guide to assessment and treatment.* New York: Plenum Press.

Morin, C. M., Hauri, P. J., Espie, C. A., Speilman, A. J., Buysse, D. J., & Bootzin, R. R. (1999). Nonpharmacological treatment of chronic insomnia. *Sleep, 22,* 1134–1156.

Morin, C. M., Kowatch, R. A., & Wade, J. B. (1989). Behavioral management of sleep disturbances secondary to chronic pain. *Journal of Behavioral Therapy and Experimental Psychiatry, 20,* 295–302.

Morin, C. M., Stone, J., McDonald, K., & Jones, S. (1994). Psychological treatment of insomnia: A clinical replication series with 100 patients. *Behavior Therapy, 25,* 159–177.

Morin, C. M., & Wooten, V. (1996). Psychological and pharmacological approaches to treating insomnia. *Clinical Psychology Review, 16,* 521–542.

Murtagh, D. R., & Greenwood, K. M. (1995). Identifying effective psychological treatments for insomnia: A meta-analysis. *Journal of Consulting and Clinical Psychology, 63,* 79–89.

National Heart, Lung, and Blood Institute Working Group on Insomnia. (1999). Insomnia: Assessment and management in primary care. *American Family Physician, 59,* 3029–3038.

Ohayon, M. M., & Roberts, R. E. (2001). Comparability of sleep disorders diagnoses using *DSM–IV* and ICSD classifications with adolescents. *Sleep, 24,* 920–925.

Pallesen, S., Nordhus, I. H., Havik, O. E., & Nielsen, G. H. (2001). Clinical assessment and treatment of insomnia. *Professional Psychology: Research and Practice, 32,* 115–124.

Pillitteri, J. L., Kozlowski, L. T., Person, D. C., & Spear, M. E. (1994). Over-the-counter sleep aids: Widely used but rarely studied. *Journal of Substance Abuse, 6,* 315–323.

Pressman, M. R., & Orr, W. C. (Eds.). (1997). *Understanding sleep: The evaluation and treatment of sleep disorders.* Washington, DC: American Psychological Association.

Rajput, V., & Bromley, S. M. (1999). Chronic insomnia: A practical review. *American Family Physician, 60,* 1431–1438.

Regestein, Q. R., Dambrosia, J., Hallett, M., Murawski, B., & Paine, M. (1993). Daytime alertness in patients with primary insomnia. *American Journal of Psychiatry, 150,* 1529–1534.

Reynolds, C. F., Kupfer, D. J., Buysse, D. J., Coble, P. A., & Yeager, A. (1991). Subtyping *DSM–III–R* primary insomnia: A literature review by the *DSM–IV* Work Group on Sleep Disorders. *American Journal of Psychiatry, 148,* 432–438.

Richardson, G. S. (2000). Managing insomnia in the primary care setting: Raising the issues. *Sleep, 23,* S9–S12.

Riedel, B. W. (2000). Sleep hygiene. In K. L. Lichstein & C. M. Morin (Eds.), *Treatment of late-life insomnia* (pp. 125–146). Thousand Oaks, CA: Sage.

Riedel, B. W., Lichstein, K. L., & Dwyer, W. O. (1995). Sleep compression and sleep education for older insomniacs: Self-help versus therapist guidance. *Psychology and Aging, 10,* 54–63.

Rosen, R. C., Rosekind, M., Rosevear, C., Cole, W. E., & Dement, W. C. (1993). Physician education in sleep and sleep disorders: A national survey of U.S. medical schools. *Sleep, 16,* 249–254.

Sateia, M. J., Doghramji, K., Hauri, P. J., & Morin, C. M. (2000). Evaluation of chronic insomnia. *Sleep, 23,* 243–308.

Schochat, T., Umphress, J., Israel, A., & Ancoli-Israel, S. (1999). Insomnia in primary care patients. *Sleep, 22,* S359–S365.

Schultz, J. H., & Luthe, W. (1969). *Autogenic therapy: Vol. 1. Autogenic methods.* New York: Grune & Stratton.

Smith, M. T., Perlis, M. L., Carmody, T. P., Smith, M. S., & Giles, D. E. (2001). Presleep cognitions in patients with insomnia secondary to chronic pain. *Journal of Behavioral Medicine, 24,* 93–114.

Smith, M. T., Perlis, M. L., Park, A., Smith, M. S., Pennington, J., Giles, D. E., et al. (2002). Comparative meta-analysis of pharmacotherapy and behavior therapy for persistent insomnia. *American Journal of Psychiatry, 159,* 5–10.

Soldatos, C. R., Dikeos, D. G., & Paparrigopoulos, T. J. (2000). Athens Insomnia scale: Validation of an instrument based on ICD–10 criteria. *Journal of Psychosomatic Research, 48,* 555–560.

Spielman, A. J. (1986). Assessment of insomnia. *Clinical Psychology Review, 6,* 11–25.

Spielman, A. J., & Anderson, M. W. (1999). The clinical interview and treatment planning as a guide to understanding the nature of insomnia: The CCNY Interview for Insomnia. In S. Chokroverty (Ed.), *Sleep disorders medicine: Basic science, technical considerations and clinical aspects* (2nd ed., pp. 385–426). Boston: Butterworth-Heinemann.

Spielman, A. J., & Glovinsky, P. B. (1991). Introduction: The varied nature of insomnia. In P. J. Hauri (Ed.), *Case studies in insomnia* (pp. 1–15). New York: Plenum Press.

Spielman, A. J., & Glovinsky, P. B. (1997). The diagnostic interview and differential diagnosis of complaints of insomnia. In M. R. Pressman & W. C. Orr (Eds.), *Understanding sleep: The evaluation and treatment of sleep disorders* (pp. 125–160). Washington, DC: American Psychological Association.

Spielman, A. J., Saskin, P., & Thorpy, M. J. (1987). Treatment of chronic insomnia by restriction of time in bed. *Sleep, 10,* 45–56.

Sproule, B. A., Busto, U. E., Buckle, C., Herrmann, N., & Bowles, S. (1999). The use of non-prescription sleep products in the elderly. *International Journal of Geriatric Psychiatry, 14,* 851–857.

Ström, L., Pettersson, R., & Andersson, G. (2000). A controlled trial of self-help treatment of recurrent headache conducted via the Internet. *Journal of Consulting and Clinical Psychology, 68*, 722–727.

Ström, L., Pettersson, R., & Andersson, G. (2004). Internet-based treatment for insomnia: A controlled evaluation. *Journal of Consulting and Clinical Psychology, 72*, 113–120.

Tate, D. F., Wing, R. R., & Winett, R. A. (2001). Using Internet technology to deliver a behavioral weight loss program. *Journal of the American Medical Association, 285*, 1172–1177.

Walsh, J. K., & Engelhardt, C. L. (1999). The direct economic costs of insomnia in the United States for 1995. *Sleep, 22*, S386–S393.

Walsh, J. K., Muehlback, M. J., Lauter, S. A., Hilliker, N. A., & Schweitzer, P. K. (1996). Effects of triazolam on sleep, daytime sleepiness, and morning stiffness in patients with rheumatoid arthritis. *Journal of Rheumatology, 23*, 245–252.

Ware, J. E., Snow, K. K., Kosinski, M., & Gandek, B. (1997). *SF–36® health survey: Manual and interpretation guide*. Boston: Nimrod Press.

Wetter, D. W., Fiore, M. C., Baker, T. B., & Young, T. B. (1995). Tobacco withdrawal and nicotine replacement influence objective measures of sleep. *Journal of Consulting and Clinical Psychology, 63*, 658–667.

Wetter, D. W., & Young T. B. (1994). The relation between cigarette smoking and sleep disturbance. *Preventive Medicine, 23*, 328–334.

Wilson, K. G., Eriksson, M. Y., D'Eon, J. L., Mikail, S. F., & Emery, P. C. (2002). Major depression and insomnia in chronic pain. *Clinical Journal of Pain, 18*, 77–83.

Wolter, T. D., Hauri, P. J., Schroeder, D. R., Wisbey, J. A., Croghan, I. T., Offord, K. P., et al. (1996). Effects of 24-hour nicotine replacement on sleep and daytime activity during smoking cessation. *Preventive Medicine, 25*, 601–610.

World Health Organization. (1993). *The ICD–10 classification of mental and behavioral disorders*. Geneva, Switzerland: World Health Organization.

Zammit, G. K. (1997) *Good nights: How to stop sleep deprivation, overcome insomnia, and get the sleep you need*. Kansas City, MO: Andrews McMeel.

Zammit, G. K., Weiner, J., Damato, N., Sillup, G. P., & McMillan, C. A. (1999). Quality of life in people with insomnia. *Sleep, 22*, S379–S385.

Zarcone, V. P. (1994). Sleep hygiene. In M. H. Kryger, T. Roth, & W. C. Dement (Eds.), *Principles and practice of sleep medicine* (2nd ed., rev., pp. 542–546). Philadelphia: W. B. Saunders.

III

TREATMENT APPLICATIONS: PEDIATRIC INTERVENTIONS

8

PEDIATRIC PSYCHOLOGY IN PRIMARY CARE

DANIEL L. CLAY AND MARILYN STERN

The growing recognition that a significant proportion of medical visits are precipitated by underlying psychological distress and mental health symptoms has made providing psychological services within community-based primary care practices a necessity. Data have clearly demonstrated that integrating mental health care into primary health care centers leads to better health outcomes and substantial cost savings (Maruish, 2000). Integrating pediatric psychological services within the primary medical care system has also become imperative because pediatric primary care practitioners most often serve as the gatekeepers of mental health services, generally taking on the role of the frontline decision maker with regard to whether a child needs psychological treatment (e.g., Holden & Schuman, 1995; Lavigne et al., 1999). The formal recognition of the subspecialty of developmental–behavioral pediatrics by the American Academy of Pediatrics in 1999 provides additional evidence for the growing recognition of the importance of integrating psychological services and pediatrics (McMenamy & Perrin, 2002). Moreover, as the health care system's priorities change from one of specialty care to primary care, collaboration between pediatricians and psychologists will undoubtedly continue to increase (Riekert, Stancin, Palermo, & Drotar, 1999).

To integrate effectively in the primary care setting, pediatric psychologists must work in conjunction with pediatricians and family practitioners to care for children as they move from infancy to adulthood. Continuity of care ensures timely and comprehensive interventions for both physical health and mental health needs, thereby reducing cost and the development of secondary problems. Although integrating psychological services with primary care medicine is clearly beneficial, the psychologist working within this model is presented with a number of unique challenges and opportunities. The purpose of this chapter is to highlight a number of important issues for the psychology practitioner interested in working in pediatric primary care. First we discuss the unique aspects of the pediatric primary care environment. This is followed by an explanation of the various professional roles of psychologists in this setting. A brief description of the most common conditions encountered is then presented. Next we discuss some of the unique barriers and challenges in working in this environment. Finally, we briefly discuss issues in training to effectively work in pediatric primary care and proactive entry into the role of professional pediatric psychologist in primary care.

WORKING ENVIRONMENT AND NORMS

There are several important aspects of the pediatric primary care environment that may differ from the traditional work environments of practicing psychologists (private practice, community mental health centers, counseling centers, and hospitals). Successfully working in this environment often depends on the extent to which psychologists can adjust to different norms, practices, languages, and roles within the health care setting in general, as well as specifically within pediatrics. Descriptions of many issues related to working in a general health care setting are found in other chapters of this book. As a consequence, the focus in this chapter will be on issues specific to pediatrics.

The role of the psychologist in the pediatric primary care setting is often that of support professional to the primary or attending physician, and often the psychologist serves the needs of the pediatrician as much as the patient. It is important to remember that in most instances the physician is the primary medical service provider and the psychologist assists in providing assessment or ongoing treatment in support of the overall medical care. As a consequence, it is essential for the psychologist to have a working knowledge of medical terminology, the primary care model, and the goals of the physician. Medications are often used in conjunction with mental health treatment, so respect and understanding of the medical model is essential. A thorough knowledge of medications, their uses, and side effects is necessary. Demonstrating this knowledge will also help the pediatric psychologist to gain credibility with the clinic physicians.

Although the psychologist may have a short-term relationship with the family involved in services, the physician often has a long-term, ongoing relationship with the entire family. One must understand that the physician likely will continue to provide medical care to the patient and other family members long after the pediatric psychologist's role has ended. The patient–physician relationship is considered long-term in pediatrics (birth to late adolescence) and often life-long in family practice settings.

Psychological work with children often requires numerous contacts with school personnel, social service workers, daycare providers, and family members. Comprehensive assessment and evaluation of treatment effects often necessitate communication with many individuals. In addition, regular communication with several of these agencies is required to ensure continuity of care. Although there is some expectation that nurses will handle much of the communication, the pediatric psychologist will also be expected to make time for such contacts. And psychologists often are not able to bill for this time, the amount of which for some patients may become substantial. One must be prepared to accept this unpaid time as part of the work (Evers-Szostak, 1998).

Services that are provided in this setting are often short-term, intense, and problem-focused. For example, in one primary care pediatrics clinic 75% of cases annually were seen for five or fewer visits, with the modal number of visits being one and the median number of visits being three (Evers-Szostak, 1998). It is important that interventions be directed at solving the presenting problem, which is different from interventions aimed at insight and self-actualization. As a consequence, psychoeducational, behavioral, and cognitive–behavioral interventions are most widely used within this setting. Effective work with parents—including parent-skills training, psychoeducation regarding development, and helping parents advocate for their children within the community and school systems—is an integral part of providing service. In some instances patients may require more long-term psychological treatment. Although this can be provided in-house, it is important to avoid too many of these cases, because maintaining waiting lists is generally regarded as unacceptable by both families and referring physicians. The expectations are that the psychologist will be available on short notice for everything from a brief, informal consult to a more complicated case requiring comprehensive treatment or immediate intervention. This availability will do much to increase the value of the psychological services provided in the primary care setting. More specific information on treatments is provided in the sections that follow.

As with effective collaboration in any health setting, effective communication is essential for the most effective and efficient care. It is critical that the psychologist communicate clearly with the physician in charge regarding the assessment outcome, diagnosis, prognosis, and treatment plan for each patient. In general, it is better to speak directly with the child's physician, but this is not always possible. Careful documentation should be made available to the physician so he or she can be informed of the treatment and progress of the child. Pediatricians place a high value on prompt feedback after a referral (Evers-Szostak, 1998). It is also important to include the nurses in the communication exchanges because they are often the first line of contact regarding the child when a parent or outside agency calls. Likewise, nurses often coordinate information from various service providers (e.g., speech pathologist, dietitian, physical therapist) and in many ways coordinate the child's care.

ROLES

The roles of the psychologist in pediatric primary care settings generally fall into one of three categories: consultation, assessment, and treatment. Each of these roles is described in more detail later in the chapter. It is useful to think of the services provided by the psychologist in this environment as ranging on a continuum from low involvement to high involvement in care. Table 8.1 lists characteristics of each end of the continuum with examples of services and diagnoses that characterize low and high involvement.

The roles of consultation, assessment, and treatment can all vary on the continuum of involvement. Some cases may only require a brief contact with the patient or staff member (e.g., screening assessment or a brief staff question), whereas others may require many extended contacts over time (e.g., ongoing treatment). Brief contacts may or may not be billable services, but more involved cases should be billed to ensure compensation for time spent on the case. It is important that the involvement in the case be structured in a manner that most benefits the patient, medical staff, and still allows for billing.

Consultation

By its very nature, psychologists working within primary health care settings must practice within a consultative framework and must therefore become familiar with various models of consultation, many of which can be readily applied to the pediatric primary care setting. Three main models of consultation have been identified (Roberts, 1986). These models range across a continuum, with one side characterized by a situation in which

TABLE 8.1
Level of Involvement of the Psychologist in Pediatric Primary Care

Low involvement	High involvement
• Physician controls • Brief or no patient contact • Physician provides primary service • Psychology seen as adjunctive • May be informal • Less likely billable	• Psychologist controls care and informs physician • Extended or multiple patient contacts • Provides primary treatment (therapy) • Services likely billable
Examples: • Brief, informal consult • Interpretation of existing test records • Screen for mental health issues • Brief psychoeducation of physician, nurse, patient	*Examples:* • Ongoing psychotherapy • Monitoring psychological effects of medications • Hospitalizing suicidal patient • Consultation with schools, social service agencies • Inpatient consultation • Adherence problems
Likely diagnoses/problems: • Adjustment disorder • Developmental concerns • Reactive grief • Delayed potty training • Mild behavior problems • Screen for sexual or substance abuse	*Likely diagnoses/problems:* • Attention deficit hyperactivity disorder • Major depression • School phobia • Chronic illness (asthma, diabetes) • Toileting problems • Severe behavior problems

there is minimal collaboration between the pediatrician and psychologist and the other side in which a close collaborative arrangement exists between the professionals, with whom they work in a fully integrated system (e.g., Maruish, 2000). The independent functions model is seen when services of a psychological nature are offered in a noncollaborative fashion, as in the case in which a patient is referred for evaluation and ongoing treatment is not expected. In the indirect service functions model the focus of intervention is often on the health care provider and not on the patient directly, such as in the case when providing services is aimed at helping the health care team reframe its communication style with a patient showing low adherence to a medical protocol. The collaborative team model operates when the psychologist is regarded as an integral member in the health care team treating a patient.

The psychologist operating out of the independent consultant functions model serves the needs of the primary practice pediatrician and not the patient (Strosahl, 2000). The physician, or other health care provider, retains primary control of the patient's care. Often, when the psychologist affiliated with a primary care pediatric unit is given a referral for a patient, the psychologist limits contact to conducting a diagnostic assessment and making specific behavioral recommendations for treatment. Because pediatric primary care practices are busy and results-oriented, psychologists are expected to adopt a quick-paced approach to treatment as well. Operating within this model, the psychologist does not work collaboratively with the pediatrician and instead is in contact with the referring pediatrician at the point of referral and at the end of psychological treatment (Evers-Szostak, 1998).

In the independent function model, it is common for the psychologist to see the patient only once and be uninvolved in follow-up contacts. When a psychologist working in the primary pediatric setting has contact with patients, it is often for short periods of time, usually not more than a 15- to 30-minute session and for no more than about three sessions (Strosahl, 2000). Common service goals in these circumstances might include supporting or possibly improving physician-based interventions, educating patients in some specific adjunct treatment protocol (e.g., relaxation methods), supporting the management of chronic cases in prescriptive treatment, or compliance with medical protocol. In other types of consultation opportunities, the psychologist might provide groups of patients referred by the pediatric practice with short-term, educationally based, and content-limited manual-based programs of treatment such as treatments for depression or panic disorder. Psychologists might also be involved in monitoring at-risk patients by meeting with them at one-month intervals for short sessions.

Primary care pediatric psychologists must also incorporate indirect service models of consultation into their practice. Such an approach might involve consulting with the pediatric physician in helping the physician work more effectively with patients, perhaps suggesting specific plans for implementation of patient management protocols. Psychologists can educate physicians to recognize, for example, depressive symptoms that might exacerbate a patient's medical condition. Indeed, untreated depressed primary care patients use medical services twice as often as their nondepressed counterparts (Simon, Von Korff, & Barlow, 1995). Psychologists can also consult in teaching physicians basic communication skills to facilitate better relationships with patients and thus adherence to treatment. In these cases, the psychologist might not even have any contact with the patients of concern. The nature of these consultative opportunities can range from direct meetings with the physicians to being limited to telephone contact. One of the authors has found that routinely scheduled staff meetings with primary care physicians often offer an opportunity for the pediatric psychologist to serve in this indirect consulting function. One recent example of how this works was when the author (MS) provided additional education to pediatric care physicians in identifying and treating psychosocial risk factors related to the diagnosis of attention-deficit/hyperactivity disorder (ADHD).

The collaborative team model is an approach whereby the pediatrician and primary care pediatric psychologist work together to formulate treatment plans for patients. Ideally, pediatric primary practice psychologists take on positions as behavioral health consultants who integrate practice within a team framework. This approach is more commonly seen in teaching centers as opposed to primary care settings in which time efficiency is given the highest priority and in which team meetings are more difficult to schedule. However, primary care pediatric psychologists can attempt to take this approach under those circumstances when, for example, a pediatric patient's care requires both medical management as well as behavioral interventions (Evers-Szostak, 1998).

Assessment

Assessment plays an important role in providing services in the primary care setting. Assessments conducted by the psychologist can range from brief, informal assessments that involve record or case review with a physician to more extended, formal assessment that can include individually administered tests. Assessment may also serve a number of purposes that can include screening, deriving a diagnosis, treatment planning, determining the effects of treatments (i.e., medication), and determining effectiveness and cost-efficiency of services. In most cases, the physician will be the first line of contact for children requiring assessment, and they will be referred to the psychologist for additional assessment or treatment if the screening by the physician indicates the need for such. It may be useful for the psychology staff and medical staff to discuss screening and come to a general understanding of the screening and referral process. For example, will the physicians use a standard screening protocol for all patients to identify potential problems in areas such as developmental delay, school achievement, social development, sexual or physical abuse, and substance abuse? Or will physicians simply follow up on red flags that emerge throughout the course of standard medical treatment? It may also be helpful to be explicit with the medical providers about exactly what type of assessment is provided by on-site psychologists. For example, will learning disability or IQ assessments be conducted on-site? Clear and consistent expectations for the patient, physician, and psychology service provider will benefit all involved and potentially eliminate negative patient and physician experiences.

Assessment to determine the effects of medication is often requested, especially when stimulant medications are prescribed for ADHD. Assessments such as behavior checklists completed by the parent and teacher, computerized tests of sustained attention and concentration (e.g., Test of Variables of Attention [TOVA]; Leark, Dupuy, Greenberg, Gorman, & Kindeschi, 1996), and parent interviews are often necessary to determine the effectiveness of the type and dose of medication for ADHD. The physician may ask the psychologist to monitor medication effects and make recommendations regarding dosage. It is important for the psychologist to have adequate training and knowledge to perform competently and comfortably in such a role. The other most frequent diagnoses that may require assessment of medication effects and adjunctive psychotherapy are depression and anxiety.

Assessments carried out in this setting tend to be brief and problem-focused. More importance is placed on symptom presence and severity as opposed to more distal variables such as personality. As a consequence, assessment instruments most often used include self-report surveys such as the Child Behavior Checklist (Achenback, 1991; parent, child, and teacher report forms), Children's Depression Inventory (Kovacs, 1992), Children's Manifest Anxiety Scale (Reynolds & Richmond, 1985), Vineland Adaptive Behavior Scales (Sparrow, Balla, & Cicchetti, 1984), and Behavior Assessment System for Children (Reynolds & Kamphaus, 1992). Because of the time involved and often lack of reimbursement, tests such as IQ and achievement tests, the Minnesota Multiphasic Personality Inventory—Adolescent (MMPI–A), and projectives are not usually used. Neuropsychological screening may be conducted on-site by the psychologist, but patients are typically referred to a neuropsychologist for more extensive assessments.

Treatment–Intervention

Treatments provided in this setting tend to be brief, problem-focused, and geared toward reducing symptoms. Patients come to the pediatrician's office because of concerns about development, behavior, school problems, or health. Many of the conditions for which treatment is necessary are described earlier. For cases in which more than one professional is involved in the treatment process (i.e., physician, dietitian, physical therapist), the psychologist's role in treatment will vary depending on the nature and severity of the presenting problem. Treatments or interventions can be aimed at the child and his or her parent, at the school or other system, or at the pediatrician.

Treatments aimed at the child are typically behavioral or cognitive–behavioral in nature, focusing specifically on reducing unwanted behaviors (i.e., aggression) and increasing desirable behaviors (i.e., adherence). In most cases, the typical 50-minute therapy or treatment session is not the norm. Rather, patients are often seen for much shorter sessions, either independent of or in conjunction with a physician visit. There are several empirically supported treatments that use brief, focused treatment strategies for many of the presenting problems described earlier (for a more complete description see Christopherson & Mortweet, 2001, or go to http://www.childclinicalpsychology.org/ for a list of evidence-based treatments). Patients who require more long-term treatment are usually referred to another provider, because psychologists working effectively in the fast-paced, high-volume conditions of primary care must be available to see new patients. As noted earlier, waiting lists are not an acceptable option for many physicians who want their patients seen immediately.

As with any work with children, much of the intervention focus is placed on parents. Interventions may include teaching parenting skills, psychoeducation around developmental issues, helping parents become advocates for the child within the medical and school environments, and helping parents communicate clearly and effectively with the pediatrician. Although family therapy is sometimes used, these cases too are often referred to outside treatment agencies.

Interventions are also aimed at outside agencies such as schools and social service agencies. The psychologist must often educate people in those environments regarding the special needs of the child, especially around health issues. Having effective working relationships with key individuals in these environments is helpful and can reduce the amount of time spent in such instances. Likewise, a thorough knowledge of available community resources is necessary for referring patients for treatment outside the primary practice setting. These providers may include community mental health centers, social service agencies, early education programs, school-based service providers, and private practitioners.

Finally, as discussed earlier under the topic of indirect consultation strategies, many interventions are geared toward the medical staff, primarily the pediatrician. These interventions may include psychoeducation around behavioral, educational, or family systems issues, helping medical staff to work effectively with difficult patients or families, and in some cases helping medical staff to deal with their own countertransference issues. The intervention may be predicated by a direct request of the physician or patient or may arise insidiously out of the need to solve a problem that has developed between a family and the physician. For example, when a child is noncompliant with a medical regimen such as diabetes, the physician and other team members may become angry and punitive toward the patient and his or her parents. Unfortunately, this likely exacerbates the compliance problems. Situations like these require work both with the family around compliance issues and with the medical staff around methods for enhancing compliance while dealing with their own angry feelings.

Because primary care physicians are often the gateway for all health and mental health problems, especially in managed care environments, children present with a wide array of health and mental health problems that require psychological intervention. The most common problems encountered in this setting include behavioral problems, school problems, anxiety, depression, chronic illness, as well as sleep and toileting problems (Evers-Szostak, 1998). These problems fall into four broad categories that are described next: (a) mental health and developmental issues requiring psychological treatment, (b) mental health or developmental issues that require a combination of psychological and medical interventions, (c) primarily medical problems requiring some adjunctive psychological intervention, and (d) somatization problems.

Most psychologists are trained to use the *Diagnostic and Statistical Manual of Mental Disorders* (*DSM–IV*; American Psychiatric Association, 1994) as a diagnostic system for mental illnesses. However, in the primary care setting there are other diagnostic or classification systems that are often used to document health and mental health diagnoses as well as other relevant information. It is essential for the psychologist to have a thorough working knowledge of these other diagnostic and classification systems, both to ensure accurate communication with other health professionals and to ensure reimbursement by third-party payers.

Another widely used classification system to classify disease, functioning, and disability status is the *International Classification of Diseases 9th Edition—Clinical Management* (ICD–9–CM; American Medical Association, 2001). This system is based on work by the World Health Organization, and revisions are overseen by the National Center for Health Statistics and the Health Care Financing Administration in the United States. Many third-party payers base payment on the ICD–9–CM diagnostic codes.

The *Diagnostic and Statistical Manual for Primary Care—Child and Adolescent Version* (DSM–PC–CA; Wolraich, Felice, & Drotar, 1996) was developed as a joint effort by several child health and mental health organizations specifically for use as a classification system in pediatric primary care. Although providing a diagnostic scheme consistent with the *DSM–IV*, the DSM–PC also provides an opportunity to document environmental influences and severity levels while taking into account developmental differences in symptom manifestations. This manual is helpful in differentiating developmental variations within normal ranges from diagnosable disorders. A real strength of the DSM–PC is the ability to document conditions severe enough to cause functional impairment yet below the threshold of diagnosis.

CATEGORIES OF PRESENTING PROBLEMS

The first category of presenting problems typically requires only psychological intervention. They tend to be mild to moderate in severity and uncomplicated by complex environmental or medical issues. Presenting problems typically include depression, anxiety, behavior problems (e.g., oppositional behavior), social skill delay, adjustment disorders, bereavement, and school concerns. Referrals are usually made by the pediatrician, school personnel, or social service agencies. The psychologist has the primary responsibility for planning treatment and implementing it, and the pediatrician is typically kept informed of progress.

Another category of presenting problems typically requires a combination of both psychological and medical treatment, yet the problem is considered a mental health or behavioral problem. These problems tend to be more severe and require the addition of medication to the psychological treatment protocol. Diagnoses include ADHD, severe depression or anxiety, encopresis and enuresis, severe behavioral disorders, and sleep disturbances. The pediatrician is typically the primary health service provider, yet the psychologist plays a substantial supporting role in treating the patient. In most cases, the physician prescribes medication and the psychologist provides adjunctive treatment such as implementing a behavioral treatment or teaching relaxation. In addition, the psychologist may evaluate the effects of the medication and make recommendations to the physician regarding medication type and dosage.

A third category includes primarily medical problems that require both medical and psychological intervention. The primary diagnosis is likely a medical diagnosis, and associated developmental or behavioral issues are typically secondary effects of the health condition. Diagnoses typically include chronic illness (e.g., diabetes, asthma, juvenile arthritis, seizures, cancer, and injury). The pediatrician is the primary care provider and the psychologist serves in an adjunctive or complementary role. A close collaborative working relationship is optimal for these problems. Problems requiring intervention may include adjustment to illness, nonadherence, social impact of the condition, pain, dealing with acute procedures, and impact of illness on school. Interventions may include improving coping, distraction during painful procedures, problem-solving adherence issues, psychoeducation regarding the social impact of the medical conditions, and systems interventions with school and medical systems on behalf of the patient.

The final category involves problems that present as medical problems yet are deemed to have a "psychological" etiology and that require psychological treatment. These problems are often seen as somatic and can include abdominal pain, headaches, pseudoseizures, fatigue, and other physical complaints. Although these presentations are less frequent, they do require a close working relationship between the physician and the psychologist. These families tend to view the problems as medical and may be less open to psychological intervention, so it is important for the pediatrician to continue to serve a significant role in patient management. In cases in which the patient clearly needs long-term treatment, the psychologist may wish to refer the patient elsewhere if necessary.

BARRIERS

Psychologists attempting to integrate within a primary pediatric practice or unit face challenges that in all likelihood they did not encounter or even anticipate during their graduate or postdoctoral training. Psychologists are generally unfamiliar with and are not exposed to the practice issues involved with a primary practice model, especially if it functions as a private practice (Evers-Szostak, 1998). To achieve a meaningful integration of psychological services into primary health care, several obstacles need to be overcome. These obstacles, to name a few, include finance issues, turf struggles, and culture clashes (Strosahl, 2000). Pediatric psychologists must take the time to learn about and ultimately adapt their practice to the primary care setting in which they work. They must become familiar with the unique characteristics of the population with whom they are working, including the norms of the setting as well as the goals and priorities of the health care providers. The working environment, by its very nature, is different from that of the traditional mental health practice environment. A pediatric primary care psychologist stepping into this new environment must be able to work at a rapid pace and become oriented toward producing results. Patient load in a typical work week is generally high, and the opportunity to consider longer term treatment as an option is extremely limited and is, in fact, out of step with the realities of practicing in primary care (Evers-Szostak, 1998).

Because psychologists are most often entering into an already established practice, it is imperative that they take the initiative to understand the demands that primary care pediatric practitioners face. The psychologist has to work effectively at building collaborative relationships and must ultimately be seen as part of an integrated team (e.g., Schroeder, 1999). In addition, it is difficult but essential for psychologists to be assertive yet respectful of professional boundaries.

Aside from the professional turf issues that form barriers to collaborative team building, other barriers to providing primary care pediatric psychology services are apparent. Health care providers must be educated as well as consumers on the benefits of psychological services for children. Many health care providers are essentially unfamiliar with the wide range of services (e.g., diagnostic, evaluative, educational, assessment, and therapeutic) that psychologists can provide to their pediatric patients and their families (e.g., Armstrong et al., 1999). Pediatric practitioners also generally lack the specialized education necessary to address developmental and behavioral concerns in a systematic fashion (e.g., Perrin, 1999).

In addition to barriers faced by pediatric psychologists working in primary care, patient barriers to seeking services in these settings also must be addressed. For example, additional barriers to the effective integration of psychological services within a primary pediatric care practice center around the difficulties often experienced by minority groups in gaining access to and utilization of health and mental health services (Coard & Holden, 1998). Often, the mental health service needs of children from minority backgrounds are not met or are even ignored; yet these children have been identified as at significant risk for long-term impairment when these needs are not met. This situation is complicated by the fact that these children have limited access to health care, which, as noted earlier, is at the front line for mental health prevention efforts. Clearly, the role of race and ethnicity in detecting mental health disorders in pediatric primary care must be considered, and lacking sensitivity to such issues creates a real barrier to integrating psychological and pediatric services. Likewise, socioeconomic status—particularly poverty—is an important consideration that has a direct impact on access to and use of health care services as well as health outcomes in pediatric psychology (Clay, Mordhorst, & Lehn, 2002).

Other patient barriers include financial resources, or lack thereof, cultural values, and differences in views of and expectations for mental health and health services. Language considerations in the case of non-English-speaking groups as well as communication style can also differ greatly as a function of culture (Coard & Holden, 1998). Moreover, minorities continue to be underrepresented in health care provider groups, making these differences between patients and provider more salient. Psychologists, because of the nature of the emphasis placed on interpersonal relations in their training, are sometimes better prepared to understand cultural diversity sensitivities than pediatricians. This background enables psychologists to offer educationally based consultation services for the primary care practitioner interested in improving his or her ability to provide screening and preventive and supportive services to children and adolescents from various minority backgrounds. Understanding the interaction of culture, gender, and sexual orientation on health care seeking and medical regimen adherence and increasing general cultural competency are target areas in which psychologists have some level of expertise and can intervene to minimize the barriers associated with youth of minority backgrounds accessing the mental health and health services that are needed.

Reimbursement of psychological services within the primary care setting is also a significant barrier. A great deal of attention has been paid to this issue nationally (e.g., McMenamy & Perrin, 2002). Although a thorough discussion of these issues is clearly beyond the scope of this chapter, a few critical barriers deserve discussion. Third-party payers often refuse to reimburse for necessary psychological services within primary care settings, especially in managed care plans. In some cases physicians are reimbursed for providing psychological services (e.g., counseling) whereas licensed psychologists are not reimbursed. Psychologists must work closely with pediatric colleagues to ensure that services are provided and billed in a manner that maximizes reimbursement while dealing carefully with associated ethical issues. Likewise, much time can be spent calling teachers, discussing the creation and evaluation of Individualized Education Plans or 504 plans, communicating with social service agencies, communicating with pediatricians, and so forth. As discussed earlier, this time is nearly always exempt from reimbursement yet it is essential for optimal service provision. However, there are some advantages regarding reimbursement. For example, if a referral from the primary care provider is necessary it is much easier to obtain if that individual is just down the hall and the psychologist shares the same support staff. In addition, the use of new Health and Behavior Codes allows psychologists to bill for psychological services provided in support of medical treatment (e.g., diabetes, asthma), and this reimbursement is provided through the medical coverage instead of mental health coverage in managed care plans (American Medical Association, 2002).

TRAINING–PROACTIVE ENTRY

Becoming a pediatric psychologist requires training in applied psychology at the doctoral level. Because of licensure restrictions and a competitive job market, it is important that the training take place in a psychology doctoral training program accredited by the American Psychological Association (APA). Both counseling psychology and clinical psychology programs can offer an excellent foundation for specialization in pediatric psychology. However, there is much variability in training within both counseling and clinical psychology, so it is important to examine programs closely to ensure good training in assessment, treatment, and consultation. Programs vary on a continuum of research at one end and practice at the other, and a program with a scientist–practitioner model or clinical scientist model are best because they value an integration of both science and practice while ensuring development of advanced clinical skills. One should avoid programs that are primarily interested in training researchers because opportunities for clinical training are often limited. Division 54 (Society of Pediatric Psychology) of the APA has developed guidelines for training in pediatric psychology, and a 2003 issue of the *Journal of Pediatric Psychology* has been devoted to training issues.

APA-accredited programs have a curriculum that ensures training in the core areas of psychology (e.g., biological bases of behavior, lifespan development). In addition to these cores, one would benefit from taking elective courses in areas related to work with children and practice in a medical setting. These courses may include advanced child development, developmental psychopathology, health psychology, neuropsychology, consultation, and rehabilitation psychology, among others. Additional specialty courses that would be beneficial include behavior analysis, assessment of learning disabilities, social aspects of disability, family therapy, child–play therapy, psychopharmacology, and developmental neuroscience.

Diverse practicum experiences and good supervision are necessary to develop a foundation of clinical skills and more advanced pediatric psychology skills. Early practica experiences should include experience with a general population of both adults and children in settings such as community mental health centers, counseling centers, and training clinics. Once a good foundation of clinical skills has been established, practica in applied pediatric clinics is essential to gain experience and supervision in the more complex issues faced in such settings. These pediatric specialty clinics may include behavior disorders clinics, ADHD clinics, general pediatrics and family practice primary care clinics, and medical specialty clinics (e.g., hematology–oncology, diabetes, asthma). Likewise, consultation for inpatient services also provides an excellent opportunity to develop and refine consultation skills that will be essential for the successful pediatric psychologist. These experiences will be important in preparing the student to be competitive for the required 1-year internships.

Entering a career in pediatric psychology nearly always depends on procuring a good pediatric psychology internship or postdoctoral training. These internship and postdoctoral training sites often are placed within large medical centers or university hospitals and include rotations in several general and specialty pediatrics clinics. Similar to doctoral training programs, there is much variability in internships and postdocs, so one must look closely at the training and supervision provided at each site. There are general medical–health psychology internships that offer rotations in pediatrics, and there are internships that focus solely on training the pediatric psychologist. A list of child and pediatric psychology training programs, internships, and postdoctoral training programs can be found on the Web at http://www.childclinicalpsychology.org/, and the *Directory of Internship and Post Doctoral Training Programs in Clinical Child and Pediatric Psychology, Volume III* (Simonian & Tarnowski, 1999) is also an excellent resource. Choosing and procuring a good internship is an important springboard into the profession because the development of skills and professional networking on internship are key factors to success.

CONCLUSION

Integrating psychology into pediatric primary care settings has increased in recent years, with collaboration between pediatricians and psychologists leading to more effective and cost-efficient care for children and their families. However, this integration presents several challenges to psychologists working in this setting that require advanced skills. This chapter covers the general aspects of practicing in primary care, but more detailed information and training are needed for those interested in developing the advanced skills necessary to be successful and competent in providing psychology services in pediatric primary care.

REFERENCES

Achenback, T. M. (1991). *Manual for the Child Behavior Checklist/4-18 and 1991 profile*. Burlington: University of Vermont, Department of Psychiatry.

American Medical Association. (2001). *International classification of diseases—9th revision—Clinical modification*. Chicago: Author.

American Medical Association. (2002). *Current procedural terminology manual (CPT)*. Chicago: Author.

American Psychiatric Association. (1994). *Diagnostic and statistical manual of mental disorders* (4th ed.). Washington, DC: Author.

Armstrong, F. D., Harris, L. L., Thompson, W., Semrad, J. L., Jensen, M. M., Lee, D. Y., et al. (1999). The Outpatient Developmental Services Project: Integration of pediatric psychology with primary medical care for children infected with HIV. *Journal of Pediatric Psychology, 24*, 381–391.

Butcher, J. N., Williams, C. L., Graham, J. R., Archer, R. P., Tellegen, A., Ben-Porath, Y. S., et al. (1992). *Minnesota Multiphasic Personality Inventory—A (MMPI–A): Manual for administration, scoring and interpretation*. Minneapolis: University of Minnesota Press.

Christopherson, E. R., & Mortweet, S. L. (Eds.). (2001). *Treatments that work with children: Empirically supported strategies for managing childhood problems*. Washington, DC: American Psychological Association.

Clay, D. L., Mordhorst, M. J., & Lehn, L. (2002). Empirically supported treatments in pediatric psychology: Where is the diversity? *Journal of Pediatric Psychology, 27*, 325–337.

Coard, S. I., & Holden, E. W. (1998). The effect of racial and ethnic diversity on the delivery of mental health services in pediatric primary care. *Journal of Clinical Psychology in Medical Settings, 5*, 275–294.

Evers-Szostak, M. (1998). Psychological practice in pediatric primary care settings. In L. VandeCreek, S. Knapp, & T. L. Jackson (Eds.), *Innovations in clinical practice: A source book* (pp. 325–335). Sarasota, FL: Professional Resource Press.

Holden, E. W., & Schuman, W. B. (1995). The detection and management of mental health disorders in pediatric primary care. *Journal of Clinical Psychology in Medical Settings, 2*, 71–87.

Kovacs, M. (1992). *Children's Depression Inventory.* New York: Multi-Health Systems.

Lavigne, J. V., Gibbons, R. D., Arend, R., Rosenbaum, D., Binns, H. J., & Christoffel, K. K. (1999). Rational service planning in pediatric primary care: Continuity and change in psychopathology among children enrolled in pediatric practices. *Journal of Pediatric Psychology, 24*, 393–403.

Leark, R. A., Dupuy, T. R., Greenberg, L. M., Gorman, C. L., & Kindeschi, C. L. (1996). *T.O.V.A. Test of Variables Attention: Professional manual* (Version 7.0) [Computer software]. Los Alamitos, CA: Universal Attention Disorders.

Maruish, M. E. (2000). Introduction. In M. E. Maruish (Ed.), *Handbook of psychological assessment in primary care settings* (pp. 3–41). Mahwah, NJ: Erlbaum.

McMenamy, J., & Perrin, E. C. (2002). Integrating psychology into pediatrics: The past, the present, and the potential. *Family, Systems and Health, 20*, 153–160.

Perrin, E. C. (1999). Collaboration in pediatric primary care: A pediatrician's view. *Journal of Pediatric Psychology, 24*, 453–458.

Reynolds, C. R., & Kamphaus, R. W. (1992). *Behavior assessment system for children.* Circle Pines, MN: American Guidance Service.

Reynolds, C. R., & Richmond, B. O. (1985). *Manual for the Revised Children's Manifest Anxiety Scale.* Los Angeles: Western Psychological Services.

Riekert, K. A., Stancin, T., Palermo, T. M., & Drotar, D. (1999). A psychological behavioral screening service: Use, feasibility, and impact in a primary care setting. *Journal of Pediatric Psychology, 24*, 405–414.

Roberts, M. (1986). *Pediatric psychology: Psychological interventions and strategies for pediatric problems.* New York: Pergamon Press.

Schroeder, S. (1999). Commentary: A view from the past and a look to the future. *Journal of Pediatric Psychology, 24*, 447–452.

Simon, G., Von Korff, M., & Barlow, W. (1995). Health care costs of primary care patients with recognized depression. *Archives of General Psychiatry, 52*, 850–856.

Simonian, S. J., & Tarnowski, K. J. (1999). *Directory of internship and post doctoral training programs in clinical child and pediatric psychology* (Vol. III). Mahwah, NJ: Erlbaum.

Sparrow, S. S., Balla, D. A., & Cicchetti, D. V. (1984). *Vineland Adaptive Behavior Scales (Survey form).* Circle Pines, MN: American Guidance Service.

Strosahl, K. (2000). The psychologist in primary health care. In A. J. Kent & M. Hersen (Eds.), *A psychologist's proactive guide to managed mental health care* (pp. 87–112). Mahwah, NJ: Erlbaum.

Wolraich, M. L., Felice, M. E., & Drotar, D. (1996). *The classification of child and adolescent mental diagnoses in primary care: Diagnostic and statistical manual for primary care (DSM–PC) child and adolescent version.* Elk Grove Village, IL: American Academy of Pediatrics.

9

PEDIATRIC BEHAVIORAL HEALTH CONSULTATION: A NEW MODEL FOR PRIMARY CARE

JOSEPH R. ETHERAGE

The primary care setting is the "linchpin of the new health care delivery system" (Haley et al., 1998, p. 237), and given the high volume and the incredible variety of patient complaints (Pruitt, Klapow, Epping-Jordan, & Dresselhaus, 1998), pediatric primary care providers have little time for counseling caregivers regarding developmental or psychological problems. Reisinger and Bires (1980) found that on average, pediatricians spent 97 seconds with an infant under five months and 7 seconds with an adolescent providing anticipatory guidance. Despite the lack of time available for addressing developmental and psychological concerns, there is a clear need for primary care, "the de facto mental health system" (Strosahl, 1996, p. 1), to address the needs of the more than 7.5 million children and adolescents

This chapter was authored or coauthored by an employee of the United States government as part of official duty and is considered to be in the public domain. Any views expressed herein do not necessarily represent the views of the United States government, and the author's participation in the work is not meant to serve as an official endorsement.

173

in the United States who display significant psychiatric impairment (Institute of Medicine, 1989, cited in Holden & Schuman, 1995). However, although pediatric primary care providers have been more active in treating children with psychiatric symptomatology, Holden and Schuman (1995) concluded that an estimated "two-thirds of children with diagnosable mental health impairment go undetected within pediatric primary care" (p. 83). A report from the Office of the U.S. Surgeon General concluded "the nation is facing a public crisis in mental healthcare for infants, children and adolescents" (U.S. Public Health Service, 2000, p. 11). Psychologists trained to provide behavioral health care to children and adolescents in the primary care setting have the opportunity to play an integral role in addressing this predicament.

The Air Force Medical Service has made the reengineering of primary care services a top priority (Office for Prevention and Health Services Assessment, 2002). As part of that initiative, the Behavioral Health Optimization Project (BHOP) was initiated to train and place Air Force mental health providers in the primary care setting, "a crucial point of access to provide mental health services" (Office For Prevention and Health Services Assessment, 2002, p. 9). These providers, working as consultants to the primary care manager (i.e., the family practice physician), are referred to as behavioral health consultants (BHCs). All Air Force BHCs, including the BHCs at Malcolm Grow Medical Center, Andrews Air Force Base (AFB), Maryland, began their work nearly exclusively with the adult population. At the end of 2001, the Malcolm Grow Psychology predoctoral internship program systematically extended the BHOP training for their interns to include pediatric work with the advent of a pediatric psychologist working in the medical center's pediatric clinic. The goal of this chapter is to provide an overview of the application of the Air Force BHOP model to the pediatric population and its implementation in a pediatric primary care setting.

HISTORY OF PEDIATRIC PRIMARY CARE PSYCHOLOGY

Psychologists working with a pediatric population have documented formal collaboration with pediatricians since the 1960s. Wright (1967) described a result of this collaboration, the pediatric psychologist: a psychologist able to work comfortably in a medical setting involving higher volume and limited contact time with patients, focusing on prevention efforts, and applying "existing psychological knowledge" to pediatric problems (Wright, 1967, p. 324, 1967). Almost 40 years ago, Smith, Rome, and Freedheim (1967) described a practice of two pediatricians who invited a psychologist to work in their clinic a half a day a week. Contrary to today's growing interest in primary care psychology, Smith and colleagues noted that initially the psychologist was reluctant about seeing patients outside of the traditional mental health clinic or medical setting. This reluctance dissipated, however, as the advantages of seeing patients in the primary care setting were realized: less perceived stigma from being seen in the pediatric clinic, a close relationship between pediatrician and psychologist witnessed by patients, increased availability of records, and a collaborative relationship with the pediatrician (Smith et al., 1967).

Despite these early documented advantages of the psychologist and pediatrician working together in the pediatric clinic and published reports of the merits of working in this setting (Routh, Schroeder, & Koocher, 1983), there have been only a limited number of psychologists who have practiced in pediatric primary care settings (Schroeder, 1997). Schroeder hypothesized that pediatricians and psychologists in nonhospital settings may not have ample opportunity for formal relationships. Hurley (1995) went on to describe a number of challenges that she faced establishing a collaborative practice with a group of pediatricians, including negotiation with the pediatric group, legal and accounting issues, marketing, and the importance of ongoing communication. Although working within the military medical system simplifies some of the financial, legal, and marketing concerns, communication and clear procedures are still essential to successful implementation of primary behavioral health care.

MALCOLM GROW MEDICAL CENTER PEDIATRIC PRIMARY BEHAVIORAL HEALTH CARE

Psychologists currently work in four different primary care clinics at Malcolm Grow Medical Center (MGMC) on Andrews AFB, Maryland. Psychologists have worked in primary care clinics at MGMC since 2000, with work in the medical center's pediatric clinic beginning toward the end of 2001. Psychologists serving as BHCs provide training for the six psychology predoctoral interns at Malcolm Grow Medical Center. Rowan and Runyan (see chap. 1, this volume) provide a detailed overview of the consultation model adopted by the Air Force.

PEDIATRIC CLINIC CHARACTERISTICS

There are approximately 5,500 patients enrolled to the pediatric clinic at MGMC. Pediatric patients from other primary care clinics in the medical center (i.e., the flight medicine clinic, the family practice clinic) are also frequently seen in the pediatric clinic. The clinic averages more than 1,600 patient encounters monthly. The clinic is staffed with five pediatricians and two pediatric nurse practitioners. Two aspects of working in the military environment are both the frequent changes in staffing and the frequent moves of the patient population; a pediatric provider rarely works in the clinic for more than three years. Despite the transitory nature of staffing, the clinic's providers have a history of exceptionally strong working relationships and have welcomed visiting specialists (e.g., cardiology, neurology, developmental pediatrics) into the clinic to follow their enrolled patients needing specialist care. Appointments are typically 15 minutes long, with the pediatric provider averaging approximately 25 patients a day. Before the initiation of behavioral health consultation in the pediatric clinic, providers' options for on-base referral for patients with developmental or psychological concerns were limited to developmental pediatrics, a child–adolescent psychiatrist in the mental health clinic, or a pediatric psychologist in the behavioral medicine clinic. Off-base referral includes a number of civilian providers in the local community or another military facility (e.g., Walter Reed Army Medical Center). Referral to a civilian provider is often complicated by both the inability of the referral system to identify the specialization of civilian pediatric mental health providers and the lack of available appointments to mental health providers in the community. Often parents expressed a preference for being treated by military providers; however, the closest military facility to MGMC providing pediatric mental health services is more than 30 minutes away by car. Both the high workload of the pediatric clinic and the complications involved with referral to mental health specialty providers served to highlight the utility of adding a behavioral health consultant to the primary care team.

INITIATION OF PEDIATRIC BEHAVIORAL HEALTH CONSULTATION

In the course of assisting the pediatric clinic staff with adopting the American Academy of Pediatrics (AAP) Guidelines for evaluating and treating attention-deficit/hyperactivity disorder (ADHD; AAP, 2000, 2001), the author provided an overview of the Air Force's BHOP program and the role of behavioral health consultants, along with an invitation to expand these services to the pediatric clinic. Both clinic leadership and pediatric providers enthusiastically accepted the invitation, and the logistics of starting the behavioral health consultation service were quickly worked out with the support of the entire pediatric clinic staff. Given the positive welcome from the pediatric clinic, the goal was to successfully integrate into the clinic.

DEFINING THE EFFECTIVE PEDIATRIC BEHAVIORAL HEALTH CONSULTANT

There are a number of factors associated with an effective BHC, including personal attributes and a wide range of clinical knowledge and skills. Drotar (1995) provided extensive guidance on consulting with pediatricians in multiple settings, including the primary care setting. Drotar (1995, p. 223) described a number of personal attributes that lead to successful consultation: "respect and tolerance for pediatric colleagues, a strong personal and professional identity, pragmatic orientation, professional commitment, and the ability to manage the inherent stresses and changes of medical settings." In addition to these personal attributes, specific knowledge and skills are important. A strong background in behavioral approaches is essential (Schroeder, 1996); the fast pace of the primary care setting dictates the use of efficacious, problem-focused, efficient strategies. An understanding of behavior related to childhood development is also important. Experience in pediatric behavioral medicine or pediatric psychology is also imperative (Evers-Szostak, 2000); a significant portion of children referred for treatment to the BHC present with solely a medical condition. Initial consultation visits are significantly shorter than typical outpatient mental health intakes, making sharp diagnostic skills vital to differentiating patients appropriate for working in the primary care setting from those needing specialty care. The *Diagnostic and Statistical Manual for Primary Care, Child and Adolescent Version* (DSM–PC; Wolraich, Felice, & Drotar, 1996) was a tool developed in part to facilitate the "collaborative management of children's behavioral and developmental problems by pediatricians and psychologists in primary care settings" (Drotar, 1999, p. 379) and, although not currently in wide use, might serve as an additional tool to aid in diagnosis. The successful pediatric BHC also needs to be familiar with community resources and be able to effectively link patients and families with these resources.

PEDIATRIC BEHAVIORAL HEALTH CONSULTANT'S PRACTICE

The primary challenge of starting pediatric behavioral health consultation at MGMC lay in integrating methods from previously successful pediatric primary care psychologists with the Air Force's BHOP model. BHC services in the pediatric clinic are provided along a continuum of care, as detailed by Rowan and Runyan (chap. 1, this volume). Varied strategies for stratifying and providing pediatric primary care services have been used in civilian settings. Schroeder (1979) described utilizing varied preventive services (i.e., telephone call-ins, brief office visits, and psychoeducational groups) and found in 5 years of follow-up that the "data clearly support the expectation that effective short-term intervention can be offered within the pediatric primary care setting" (Kanoy & Schroeder, 1985, p. 25). Evers-Szostak (2000) described a practice in a pediatric clinic made up primarily of individual care with the number of visits ranging from 1 to 112, albeit with an emphasis on brief interventions. Sanders (1999) described a five-tiered, multidisciplinary primary care model ranging from group presentations and mass media strategies and two levels of brief primary care interventions. The BHOP model reflects a combination of elements from both Schroeder's (1997) and Evers-Szostak's (2000) work. Service types for the BHOP model include behavioral health consultation visits, psychoeducational visits–condition management, and continuity consultation (Office for Prevention and Health Services Assessment, 2002).

BEHAVIORAL HEALTH CONSULTATION VISITS

With primary care as the entry point for all patients receiving care, the pediatric BHC sees patients of extremely varied presenting problems either self-referred or referred through the patient's primary care manager (PCM). Behavioral health consultation visits are brief and general in scope. Matching the pace of the primary care setting, initial and follow-up appointments are scheduled for a maximum of 30 minutes, with follow-up appointments frequently 15 minutes long. Initial consultation visits are offered to all patients, irrespective of presenting problem. During the initial consultation visit the BHC defines the presenting problem and the patient and family either start work with the BHC and the pediatric team or, if the condition requires more intensive evaluation or treatment, are referred to the appropriate specialty service. This mirrors Evers-Svostak's approach (1998); severe psychopathology, child abuse cases (managed by the Air Force's Family Advocacy Program), substance abuse, conduct disorder, and patients requiring thorough psychological testing are referred either to military or civilian specialty care providers. A general rule of thumb for engaging care or coordinating referral care is initiating treatment only for patients for whom it can reasonably be expected that three visits can lead to significant changes, or a start to significant change, in the presenting problem.

INITIAL CONSULTATION VISIT

The initial consultation visit is structured in three phases: the introduction, the assessment, and the intervention. The introduction phase includes both child and parent and lasts less than 2 minutes. Content of the introduction includes an exchange of names and a brief description of the provider's profession and his or her role as a BHC in the clinic, structure and time allotted for the appointment, limits of care (the consultative nature of the appointment), a brief statement regarding reporting requirements and that feedback is given to the patient's provider, and that at the end of the appointment recommendations will be given to possibly include follow-up appointments or referral to specialty care. The following is a sample introductory script:

> Welcome. Let's start with introductions. I'm a behavioral health consultant in the pediatric clinic and a pediatric psychologist by training. I work with the other providers here in situations where being healthy means paying attention not only to physical health but also to emotions and behavior. Whenever your provider is concerned about any of these things, they can call me in to help out. We'll spend about 25 minutes to get a better idea of what's going on and then we'll come up with some recommendations that might help out. We may decide that it would help to have you come back to see me a couple of times if we think it would get some positive momentum going for change. Sometimes, we decide that you might benefit from specialty services and if that's the case, I'll make that recommendation to your provider and help them arrange the referral. After we're done today, I'll go over with your provider the recommendations we came up with so we can make sure we're working together as a team. Also, I'll write a note in your medical record so other providers can follow up on how the plan is going. Finally, I want you to be aware that I have the same reporting requirement as other providers in this clinic to ensure yours, your child's and other's safety. I'll provide you with a brochure giving you more information before you leave if you haven't received one. Any questions before we start?

The assessment phase lasts from 15 to 20 minutes. This phase can take slightly longer than the adult BHOP model because assessment frequently involves questioning the child *and* the parent. For adolescents, a significant portion of the assessment phase frequently is done solely with the patient, with the parent returning for the intervention phase. Using a behavioral model akin to that used by Schroeder (1997) allows for a brief, targeted assessment of the presenting problem. The comprehensive assessment-to-intervention system (CAIS) used by Schroeder and Gordon (2002, pp. 57–58) includes six elements: (a) "the referral question," (b) "the social context," (c) "general areas," (d) "specific areas," (e) "the effects of the problem," and (f) "areas for intervention."

Reflecting an understanding of the referral problem in one sentence begins this focused assessment (e.g., "I understand that Dr. Smith referred you and Thomas here today to help with some toilet training concerns"). The

BHC elicits specific information regarding the type of problem; frequency, intensity, and duration of the problem are ascertained. To better understand antecedents and consequences related to the behavior, the parent or child is frequently asked to recall the last time the problem incident or behavior occurred and then describe the situation as if they were a sports announcer or were watching a video of the situation. Taking a minute to gather this detailed information frequently leads to possible interventions through identifying antecedents and reinforcers–punishers. Next, the BHC identifies all individuals affected by the presenting problem (e.g., the daycare provider caring for the encopretic child) and associated with the presenting problem (e.g., the stepparent with whom the child is being defiant). Any relevant additional information, "general areas," is then queried only as needed, including family mental health history, relevant medical history and medications, academic history, developmental history, and relevant psychosocial stressors (e.g., a parent that is deployed). A broad psychosocial history is not gathered; if the BHC determines that a thorough psychosocial history is needed, this is a clear indication that the patient requires specialty care. If not yet determined, functional impairment is assessed to determine the effects of the presenting problem on the child (e.g., "my child won't sit still and do his homework in the evening and is failing math"). Gathering information on functional impairment can provide an effective benchmark for the effectiveness of an intervention. Finally, possible areas for intervention are identified. Through the course of the interview the BHC assesses possible areas for intervention, including parents, the school, or medical intervention. Once the assessment is completed, and before offering any recommendations, the BHC provides a capsule summary to the family (a minute or less) to confirm that there is a clear understanding of the current problem, factors affecting the problem, functional impairment, and strategies already implemented to ameliorate the problem. If the parent or child provides additional information following this summary, that information is integrated into a final summary statement with changes to any intervention made accordingly.

The intervention is the final phase of the initial consultation visit and takes up to 5 minutes of the initial visit. Interventions vary considerably, but there are a number of characteristics that make up all interventions. First is the decision to either recommend continued care through the primary care setting or refer the patient to specialty care. If referrals are indicated, then this is coordinated with the pediatric provider and support staff. If the patient is appropriate for intervention in the primary care setting, then specific, problem-focused suggestions are made to the patient and parents. All interventions are kept simple and clear. Finney, Riley, and Cataldo (1991) implemented a brief (one to six sessions), targeted behavioral treatment in the primary care setting in an health maintenance organization sample of pediatric patients. Results for problems including behavior problems, toileting problems, physical problems, and school problems led to improvement or resolution for 74% of the 93 children studied. In addition, they also found a decreased use of medical services during the year after treatment.

Parents serve a crucial role in implementing recommendations from the intervention. Kanoy and Schroeder (1985) described the importance of helping parents better understand their child's behavior in terms of "appropriate developmental expectations/behaviors" (p. 16). With this increased understanding, parents and child are given specific recommendations targeted at both increasing desired behaviors and decreasing negative behaviors. A complete description of possible intervention strategies exceed the scope of this chapter; however, Kanoy and Schroeder (1985) summarized simple behavioral recommendations for the most common presenting problems as well as parents' evaluations of those recommendations. Christopherson (1982) also provided a summary of effective interventions on a wide range of topics related to anticipatory guidance (e.g., toilet training), early detection of problems, and managing common behavior problems. To increase the likelihood of following through on intervention recommendations the BHC uses a "behavioral prescription pad"; parents and child leave the clinic with specific recommendations in hand. Handouts are frequently used to provide more detailed information on recommendations. Also sample reward charts and diaries to record frequency of behaviors are also used (e.g., nocturnal enuresis record). The parent and child are able to use intervention recommendations and materials provided to actively work toward goals before a follow-up appointment.

FOLLOW-UP VISIT

The follow-up visit varies from 15 to 30 minutes and begins with a review of the implementation of recommendations made from the intervention during the previous visit. Follow-up visits can also take the form of a telephone consultation. The BHC encourages parents and child to share any progress made. Frequently, recommendations from a previous appointment will include gathering data (e.g., frequency of wetting for nocturnal enuresis) and returning with this information to the follow-up appointment. If there has been no significant change in the presenting problem because parents and child are not completing recommendations, potential barriers to change are addressed. Further follow-up is scheduled with the BHC if the treatment intervention has not been fully implemented, the parent or child has identified a new problem, or the parent or child would like an additional appointment to further review treatment progress. If during the course of the follow-up appointment it becomes apparent that the presenting problem has not responded significantly to the initial intervention or the acuity of the problem has increased, then the BHC coordinates referral to specialty care.

PSYCHOEDUCATIONAL VISITS–CONDITION MANAGEMENT VISITS

Psychoeducational visits or condition management visits are intended for patients seen for three or more times with psychological or medical problems for which longer term management by the primary care team is needed.

Psychoeducational visits are intended for the high-frequency, pediatric primary care populations. At MGMC's pediatric clinic, those complaints mirror those common conditions seen in other primary care clinics, namely disruptive–oppositional behavior and ADHD (Briggs-Gowan, Horowitz, Schwab-Stone, Leventhal, & Leaf, 2000; Costello, 1988; Culbertson, 1996; Mesibov, Schroeder, & Wesson, 1977). To most effectively address this concern, the Boystown Common Sense Parenting program (Burke & Schuchmann, 1996) is offered in the pediatric clinic's conference room on a recurring basis. The program provides specific skills to parents to assist in managing disruptive behavior and encouraging positive behavior and has been implemented at multiple Air Force sites (Thompson, Ruma, Brewster, Besetsney, & Burke, 1997). In conjunction with the psychoeducational program, individual condition management visits are spread over time to assist with implementing skills taught in the psychoeducational program. Condition management visits allow the BHC to work in partnership with the pediatric provider in managing chronic conditions (such as ADHD) more effectively.

Physical problems make up the next most frequent presenting problem, with nocturnal enuresis the most common physical complaint (Costello, 1988). Unfortunately, despite their proven efficacy with a behavioral treatment program, enuresis alarm training is infrequently a covered benefit through insurance plans (Houts, 2000). Through a hospital grant, the BHC in the pediatric clinic is able to provide patients with the use of a enuresis alarm free of cost.

Treatment typically consists of approximately four sessions spread over a 2- to 3-month period, using elements from Azrin's Dry Bed Training protocol (Azrin, Sneed, & Foxx, 1974). Identifying both chronic and frequently presenting problems specific to the primary care clinic allows for the effective targeting of both psychoeducational and continuity visits.

CONSULTATION APPROACH

One of the aspects of the Air Force's BHOP model that differentiates it from previously implemented pediatric primary behavioral health care is that the pediatric primary care provider retains primary responsibility of the patient. There are many implications given the pediatric PCM and not the BHC primary responsibility for the case. The first is that any assessment or intervention needs to be coordinated closely with the PCM. The importance of close communication with the PCM has been addressed by others (Haley et al., 1998; Schroeder, 1997) and is crucial in the BHOP model.

The BHOP consultation model most closely resembles a melding of the indirect functions model and the collaborative team model described by Roberts and Wright (1982). Although the PCM retains responsibility for the patient's care in accordance with the indirect functions model, the BHC and the PCM collaborate on strategies recommended by the BHC and medical interventions implemented by the PCM as used in the collaborative team model. The BHOP consultation model requires both written and oral feedback. A secure e-mail system used by the military medical system and documentation in the medical record serve as the primary means of written feedback for the PCM. Under the plan section of a typical BHC's consultation note, the BHC advises the PCM to reinforce or implement specific strategies recommended by the BHC during the appointment. Oral feedback can take the form of a quick "curbside" consult immediately following a patient visit or may take place during the lunch hour or at the end of the day. The pace of the pediatric primary care setting necessitates concise, problem-focused, jargon-free communication. Evers-Szostak (2000) argued that "truly integrated care" (p. 108) requires that the BHC be available in the pediatric clinic on a full-time basis. However, short telephone consultations are used at times given that currently no BHCs at MGMC work full-time within the primary care setting. In addition, the BHC's pager number is provided with the understanding that other work will be interrupted to answer any PCM's page.

A PEDIATRIC BEHAVIORAL HEALTH CONSULTANTS PRACTICE

The pace of the primary care setting creates real challenges for psychologists accustomed to the traditional outpatient clinic setting. Between scheduled appointments, walk-in appointments, charting, and consultation with PCMs, a full day passes quickly. With the BHC practice in the MGMC pediatric now firmly established, a typical day for a BHC working in the pediatric clinic involves 10 to 12 patient encounters. A review of 239 BHC patient encounters from January to September of 2002 in the MGMC pediatric clinic noted the following primary presenting problems: 27% behavior difficulties and oppositionality, 24% inattention and impulsivity–hyperactivity, 14% elimination disorders, 11% acute psychosocial stressors–mood disturbance, 9% physical complaints (e.g., headache), 5% anxiety, 4% developmental disorders, and 4% other. Ages of patients ranged from 1 to 17 years, with a mean and median of 8 years ($SD = 3$ years), and gender was roughly split. Over this time period the average number of patient visits was approximately 1.5. The following case summaries illustrate a typical busy morning for the BHC in the pediatric clinic.

Case 1

Three-year-old Thomas presented with his mother for initial consultation because he had become physically aggressive toward his 6-month-old younger brother.

The father was an active-duty military member whose job led to the mother being the primary caregiver. Thomas's mother did not feel comfortable leaving him in the same room as his baby brother. She avoided corporal punishment and stated that she used time-outs. Through additional queries, Thomas's mother described a time-out procedure that included her bringing Thomas onto her lap and holding him there for 2 to 3 minutes. During this time, she spoke softly to him, encouraging him to be gentle and care for his younger brother.

Recommendations included using a time-out chair and not providing him attention during the period he is being thus punished because her time sitting with him following his aggression was likely serving as an inadvertent reinforcer. The mother was encouraged to set aside 15 minutes a day for nondirective play with Thomas, increasing her focus on catching him being appropriate with the younger brother and providing praise for this behavior. The PCM was advised to encourage these interventions, and the mother was invited to follow-up with the BHC or the PCM if the problem persisted.

Case 2

John was a 14-year-old with recurrent abdominal pain who had missed 15 days of school in the first two months of the school year and presented for a follow-up appointment with his mother.

Depressive and anxiety symptomatology was absent. The patient had not experienced emesis related to the abdominal pain. Since the two weeks from the initial consultation John missed two days of school the first week following the BHC visit. John's mother had implemented the initial BHC consultant recommendations; when John stayed home from school his mother eliminated any daytime television watching and limited John to either completing class work or resting in bed. In addition, John was introduced to distraction techniques that he reported as somewhat helpful.

In the follow-up session John was introduced to diaphragmatic breathing and his pediatrician dropped in for a minute and again confirmed that there was no known medical etiology for the abdominal pain, that there was no need for worry from a medical perspective, and encouraged John and his mother to continue to follow through with the BHC recommendations. A final follow-up appointment was scheduled with the BHC.

Case 3

Amy was an 8-year-old seen for an initial consultation visit recommended by her pediatrician for ADHD, primarily inattentive type.

Amy was being treated with a psychostimulant that resulted in improved attention in the school setting. She took the medication during breakfast. Amy had no significant behavioral problems at home but her parents frequently became frustrated with her inability to get ready in the morning in a timely manner.

Parents were advised to avoid multistep directions, to help Amy with identifying preparation steps for the night before, to use a kitchen timer to help her get through breakfast in a timely manner, and to establish a daily checklist for morning responsibilities, with rewards for successful completion. The PCM was advised to check on implementation of these strategies during Amy's next appointment.

Case 4

Brandon was a 9-year-old with primary nocturnal enuresis referred by his pediatrician following a physical examination.

Brandon had no significant periods of dryness and was currently using a plastic sheet on the bed and was primarily responsible for self-care and clean-up. His parents described him as a heavy sleeper. There was no diurnal enuresis reported. The parents had not used any form of punishment nor had they systematically used a reward system. Parents had informally used scheduled wakings with only minor effect. There were no significant psychosocial stressors. No medications had been used. Brandon was highly motivated for treatment.

The BHC reviewed the use and rationale of urine alarm treatment with Brandon and his mother. Possible difficulties were identified (i.e., waking nightly to the sound/vibration of the alarm) and plans were identified to improve the likelihood of success. Brandon was given a diary to complete for one week to establish a baseline and identify antecedents and trends before initiation of alarm use. The BHC confirmed with the PCM that there were no other medical concerns and advised the PCM to encourage nightly alarm use during Brandon's next follow-up appointment the next week.

Case 5

Emily was a nearly 5-year-old being followed by her pediatrician for chronic constipation and referred to the BHC for an initial consultation, because she would not have a bowel movement on the toilet.

Emily had a significant history of constipation. She had a limited diet but did have good fluid intake. There was no encopresis. Medical treatment by the pediatrician led to Emily having daily bowel movements. Emily has a history of painful bowel movements but no current pain reported. Currently, she was putting on a pull-up diaper and going into a corner in the living room to have a bowel movement. The mother cleaned up Emily afterward but has become frustrated and somewhat angry with Emily. Parents have not used any strategies but have promised Emily a large reward if she will use the toilet.

Parents were advised to set up a reinforcement schedule for 5 minutes of sitting on the toilet after meals. A sticker chart was set up in the bathroom, along with a kitchen timer. When Emily uses a pull-up for a bowel movement, an overcorrection strategy was suggested. Emily would be included in clean-up and in addition took the trash bag (with dirty pull-up) outside to the trash can after getting cleaned up. The mother was encouraged to minimize displayed affect and attention after Emily has a bowel movement in a pull-up and to provide significant praise for completing sitting time. The PCM also encouraged the recommended sitting times and reviewed the sticker chart at follow-up and provided encouragement. Follow-up was scheduled for two weeks.

Case 6

Adam was a 4-year-old referred by his pediatrician for disruptive behavior in the home.

Adam's mother reported that he was in a preschool program half days, three days per week, with no reported behavior difficulties reported from the teacher. At home, the mother reported that she was "never alone" because he followed her around the house constantly, was very "needy," and was defiant and argumentative at times. Adam's mother found herself frequently raising her voice and using punishment strategies. Adam colored quietly during the appointment and responded eagerly to verbal praise from the BHC. Adam had an 8-month-old sister. His father was active duty military and frequently arrived home late in the evening, spending time with Adam primarily on the weekends. The family was relatively new to the area. The mother admitted to depressive symptoms related to current psychosocial stressors.

Adam's mother was provided with referral information to address her current symptomatology. She was also provided with contact information for an on-base play group, allowing her the opportunity to interact with other mothers and Adam the opportunity for independent play with same-age peers. She was also provided with information on the pediatric clinic's parenting program. The BHC recommended that Adam's mother set up a reward chart for 10 minutes of independent play in the afternoon with playtime increased in successive weeks. Finally, the PCM was advised to encourage the same recommendations, and Adam's mother was advised to follow-up by telephone with the BHC the following week.

CONCLUSION

The Air Force Medical Service has taken active steps to optimize primary care through the addition of BHCs to the primary care team. The addition of behavioral health consultation in primary care has led to the increased availability of services for the pediatric population, increased collaboration with pediatrics and mental health, an excellent training opportunity for psychology interns, and a rewarding experience for the pediatric BHC. Access to standard mental health specialty care can frequently take up to a month. Often the BHC is able to briefly meet a patient and parent the same day they see the pediatric PCM. The pediatric providers and the BHC share a close working relationship, frequently meeting for lunch and spending time together discussing cases at the end of the work day. Through a training program that mirrors the proposed curriculum outlined by Mc-Daniel, Belar, Schroeder, Hargrove, and Freeman (2002), predoctoral interns at MGMC are provided with training in primary care psychology for patients of all ages. Finally, although the opportunity to work in a pediatric primary care setting is demanding, the rewards of working with a large number of children and their parents may serve as a catalyst for the continued growth of pediatric BHCs in primary care.

REFERENCES

American Academy of Pediatrics. (2000). Clinical practice guideline: Diagnosis and evaluation of the child with attention-deficit/hyperactivity disorder. *Pediatrics*, *105*, 1158–1170.

American Academy of Pediatrics. (2001). Clinical practice guideline: Treatment of the school-aged child with attention-deficit/hyperactivity disorder. *Pediatrics*, *108*, 1033–1044.

Azrin, J. H., Sneed, T. J., & Foxx, R. M. (1974). Dry-bed training: Rapid elimination of childhood enuresis. *Behaviour Research and Therapy, 12*, 147–156.

Briggs-Gowan, M., Horwitz, S. M., Schwab-Stone, M., Leventhal, J., & Leaf, P. (2000). Mental health in pediatric settings: Distribution of disorders and factors related to service use. *Journal of the American Academy of Child and Adolescent Psychiatry, 39*, 841–849.

Burke, R., & Schuchmann, L. (1996). *Common sense parenting: Trainer's manual* (2nd ed.). Boys Town, NE: Boys Town Press.

Christopherson, E. R. (1982). Incorporating behavioral pediatrics into primary care. *Pediatric Clinics of North America, 29*, 261–296.

Costello, E. J. (1988). Child psychiatric disorders and their correlates: A primary care pediatric sample. *Journal of the American Academy of Child and Adolescent Psychiatry, 28*, 851–855.

Culbertson, J. L. (1996). Attention deficit hyperactivity disorder and learning disabilities in the pediatrician's office. In R. Resnick & R. Rozensky (Eds.), *Health psychology through the life span: Practice and research opportunities* (pp. 195–207). Washington, DC: American Psychological Association.

Drotar, D. (Ed.). (1995). *Consulting with pediatricians: Psychological perspectives*. New York: Plenum Press.

Drotar, D. (1999). The diagnostic and statistical manual for primary care (DSM–PC), child and adolescent version: What pediatric psychologists need to know. *Journal of Pediatric Psychology, 24*, 369–380.

Evers-Szostak, M. (1998). Psychological practice in pediatric primary care. In L. VandeCreek, S. Knapp, & T. Jackson (Eds.), *Innovations in clinical practice: A source book* (Vol. 16, pp. 325–335). Sarasota, FL: Professional Resource Press.

Evers-Szostak, M. (2000). Integration of behavioral health care services in pediatric primary care settings. In M. Maruish (Ed.), *Handbook of psychological assessment in primary care* (pp. 93–114). Mahwah, NJ: Erlbaum.

Finney, J. W., Riley, A. W., & Cataldo, M. R. (1991). Psychology in primary care: Effects of brief target therapy on children's medical care utilization. *Journal of Pediatric Psychology, 16*, 447–462.

Haley, E. E., McDaniel, S. H., Bray, J. H., Frank, R. G., Heldring, M., Johnson, S. B., et al. (1998). Psychological practice in primary care settings: Practical tips for clinicians. *Professional Psychology: Research and Practice, 29*, 237–244.

Holden, E. W., & Schuman, W. B. (1995). The detection and management of mental health disorders in pediatric primary care. *Journal of Clinical Psychology in Medical Settings, 2*, 71–86.

Houts, A. C. (2000). Commentary: Treatments for enuresis: Criteria, mechanisms, and health care policy. *Journal of Pediatric Psychology, 25*, 219–224.

Hurley, L. (1995). Developing a collaborative pediatric psychology practice in a primary care setting. In D. Drotar (Ed.), *Consulting with pediatricians: Psychological perspectives* (pp. 159–171). New York: Plenum Press.

Kanoy, K. W., & Schroeder, C. S. (1985). Suggestions to parents about common behavior problems in a pediatric primary care office: Five years of follow-up. *Journal of Pediatric Psychology, 10,* 15–30.

McDaniel, S., Belar, C., Schroeder, C., Hargrove, D., & Freeman, E. (2002). A training curriculum for professional psychologists in primary care. *Professional psychology: Research and Practice, 33,* 65–72.

Mesibov, G. B., Schroeder, C. S., & Wesson, L. (1977). Parental concerns about their children. *Journal of Pediatric Psychology, 10,* 15–30.

Office for Prevention and Health Services Assessment, United States Air Force Medical Operations Agency. (2002). *Primary behavioral health care services practice manual* (2nd ed.). San Antonio, TX: Author.

Pruitt, S. D., Klapow, J. C., Epping-Jordan, J. E., & Dresselhaus, T. (1998). Moving behavioral medicine to the "front line": A model for the integration of behavioral and medical sciences in primary care. *Professional Psychology: Research and Practice, 29,* 230–236.

Reisinger, K. S., & Bires, J. A. (1980). Anticipatory guidance in pediatric practice. *Pediatrics, 66,* 889–892.

Roberts, M. C., & Wright, L. (1982). Role of the pediatric psychologist as consultant to pediatricians. In J. M. Tuma (Ed.), *Handbook for the practice of pediatric psychology* (pp. 251–289). New York: Wiley.

Routh, D. K., Schroeder, C. S., & Koocher, G. P. (1983). Psychology and primary health care for children. *American Psychologist, 38,* 95–98.

Sanders, M. R. (1999). Triple p-positive parenting program: Towards an empirically validated multilevel parenting and family support strategy for the prevention of behavior and emotional problems in children. *Clinical Child and Psychology review, 2,* 71–90.

Schroeder, C. S. (1979). Psychologists in a private pediatric practice. *Journal of pediatric psychology, 4,* 5–18.

Schroeder, C. S. (1996). Psychologists and pediatricians in collaborative practice. In R. Resnick & R. Rozensky (Eds.), *Health psychology through the life span: Practice and research opportunities* (pp. 109–131). Washington, DC: American Psychological Association.

Schroeder, C. S. (1997). Conducting an integrated practice in a pediatric setting. In R. J. Illback & C. Cobb (Eds.), *Integrated services for children and families: Opportunities for psychological practice* (pp. 221–255). Washington, DC: American Psychological Association.

Schroeder, C. S., & Gordon, B. N. (2002). *Assessment and treatment of childhood problems: A clinician's guide* (2nd ed.). New York: Guilford Press.

Smith, E. E., Rome, L. P., & Freedheim, D. K. (1967). The clinical psychologist in the pediatric office. *Journal of Pediatrics, 21,* 48–51.

Strosahl, K. (1996). Confessions of a behavior therapist in primary care: The odyssey and the ecstasy. *Cognitive and Behavioral Practice, 3,* 1–28.

Thompson, R. W., Ruma, P. R., Brewster, A. L., Besetsney, L. K., & Burke, R. V. (1997). Evaluation of an air force child physical abuse prevention project using the reliable change index. *Journal of Child and Family Studies, 6,* 421–434.

U.S. Public Health Service. (2000). *Report of the Surgeon General's Conference on Children's Mental Health: A national action agenda.* Washington, DC: Department of Health and Human Services.

Wolraich, M. L., Felice, M. E., & Drotar, D. (Eds.). (1996). *The classification of child and adolescent mental diagnosis in primary care: Diagnosis and statistical manual for primary care (DSM–PC) child and adolescent version.* Elk Grove, IL: American Academy of Pediatrics.

Wright, L. (1967). The pediatric psychologist: A role model. *American Psychologist, 22,* 323–325.

10

A CONCEPTUAL MODEL FOR SCHOOL-BASED PREVENTION PROGRAMS IN CHILDREN AND ADOLESCENTS IN THE NEXT FRONTIER

DAWN K. WILSON AND JOEL E. WILLIAMS

Clinicians and health care providers are becoming increasingly concerned with providing adequate health care to children and adolescents. A number of health professionals are advocating for comprehensive pediatric prevention programs and school-based health centers. Although treatment in primary care settings is the hallmark of clinical health psychology, other approaches such as school-based prevention programs can complement the medical model of health care. Such programs have the potential to decrease or reduce future illnesses and chronic diseases, most of which are manifested later in the adult years. For example, school-based programs that facilitate establishing healthy behaviors during childhood and adolescence have the potential to prevent morbidity and mortality in adulthood (Kaplan & Friedman, 1997).

The behavioral health problems that children and adolescents face include obesity, unhealthy diet, physical inactivity, smoking, substance abuse, and teenage pregnancy. The highest rates of obesity are observed in the United States and parts of Europe, and the persistence of obesity in childhood into adulthood has been consistently demonstrated in all populations studied (Micic, 2001). Obesity has increased dramatically in children and adolescents in recent years. The age-adjusted prevalence of overweight from the Third National Health and Nutrition Examination Survey, 1988 to 1994, among White children (ages 6–11) was 9.1% and among Black children was 15.6% (Triano, Flegal, Kuczmarski, Campbell, & Johnson, 1995). Among White adolescents (ages 12–17) the prevalence of overweight is currently 9.4% and among Black adolescents it is 15.7% (Triano & Flegal, 1998). Conditions commonly associated with obesity are insulin resistance, diabetes mellitus, hypertension, dyslipidemia, cardiovascular disease, gallstones and cholecystitis, sleep apnea and other respiratory disfunctions, and an increased incidence of certain cancers (Pi-Sunyer, 2002). In addition, many of the metabolic and cardiovascular complications and some forms of cancer associated with adult obesity have a childhood onset (Micic, 2001).

A related issue to the increase in obesity rates involves corresponding data indicating a 50% decline in physical activity for youth between the ages of 6 and 16 year old (Taylor, Beech, & Cummings, 1997). National surveys indicate that a substantial number of adolescents have inadequate diets (Newmark-Sztainer, Story, Resnick, & Blum, 1998). Furthermore, epidemiological studies have demonstrated a rise in cigarette smoking and drug use in general (i.e., marijuana, stimulants), but especially among adolescents (Johnston, O'Malley, & Bachman, 1994).

In this chapter we review comprehensive school-based models for primary prevention and treatment of health related illnesses in children. These models incorporate the interrelationships among the child, family, school, community, and pediatrician–health care provider and suggests that a school-based primary care model for children is needed for the future. In addition, we provide policy-based suggestions for increasing access to health care among children and adolescents and argue that primary prevention should become a national priority. An overview of the elements of comprehensive school-based health care programs is provided along with empirical examples of programs that have been effectively implemented and evaluated. Directions for future school-based health care programs and public health policy are also summarized in the conclusion of the chapter.

HISTORY OF SCHOOL-BASED HEALTH PROGRAMS

Paavola and colleagues have provided a historical review of interdisciplinary school practice with respect to the service integration movement and the role of psychologists (Paavola et al., 1996). The social reform movement of the 1960s provided the first link between federal government and child-related policies. The federal policies and laws were targeted at individuals who were neglected, oppressed, or discriminated against on the basis of physical limitation or poor socioeconomic status. In 1978, school-based psychological services expanded significantly, and the benefits of these services were most evident in school districts and communities that previously had minimal support services. By the 1980s, the government-regulated mental health services became redefined as an integrated service delivery model that shifted away from just supporting disadvantaged individuals and allowed services among middle-class families. During this time some states enacted policies that required coordination among many agencies to encourage integrated service delivery for youth programs.

Professional psychologists were not directly part of the legislative process that took place during the social reform movement. As a result a task force involving psychologists was developed to address the broader issues concerning the increasing problems of children. The task force included primarily clinical and school psychologists who adopted a community systems model emphasizing prevention, early intervention, and cost-effectiveness. The task force's primary goal was to form well-integrated programs and services that were accessible and comprehensive in addressing priority needs of children, adolescents, and their families (Paavola et al., 1996). For example, these services focused on participation, partnership, and empowerment of family members with the use of culturally sensitive services. The American Psychological Association (APA) also made a policy statement at this time indicating its support for federal, state, and local government agencies and schools in developing service integration models meeting psychological, educational, and mental health needs of children and their families (Paavola et al., 1996).

The implications of the task force goals for psychologists were to encourage providing comprehensive family-centered services in naturalistic and primary care settings. Thus, the purpose of comprehensive family-centered services was to deliver total health care to children where they were located in the community. For example, these settings included schools, homes, health care sites, and child care sites. Because of this effort by the APA, by 1993 some 500 school-based health clinics were established with coordinated services.

During the past decade school-based health centers have become an increasing presence in society. School-based health care centers are now accountable for meeting standards and providing quality health care (Pastore, Murray, & Juszczak, 2001). These standards include providing comprehensive, continuous, age-appropriate programs for children as well as adolescent-focused prevention and treatment programs. The predominant model for school-based health centers is multidisciplinary, with family and community involvement. These centers offer such services as smoking cessation programs, HIV-testing, and mental health evaluation (Pastore et al., 2001). School-based prevention programs have also targeted diet, physical activity, and substance abuse (Davis, Lambert, Gomez, & Skipper, 1995; Kalnins et al., 1994; O'Neil & Nicklas, 2002; Perry, Kelder, Murray, & Klepp, 1992; Vartianen, Tossavainen, Viri, Niskanen, & Puska, 1991). Thus, school-based health centers continue to be a core element of national health promotion efforts targeted at youth and could potentially affect public health policy.

COMPREHENSIVE MODELS OF SCHOOL-BASED PROGRAMS

Comprehensive school health programs have been proposed by a number of investigators (Allensorth & Kolbe, 1987; Motes, Melton, & Waithe-Simmons, 1999; Story, Newmark-Sztainer, & French, 2002). These models propose that a number of factors that range from interpersonal variables to systems-related factors are important elements of a comprehensive integrated school health program. We have summarized these key model components in Table 10.1.

In a review by Story (1999), a comprehensive, integrated model for obesity prevention was presented. The model consists of interacting components that are proposed to enhance healthy eating and physical activity habits in children and adolescents. The eight components include the school health curriculum, school health services, school environment (i.e., supports for good nutrition), school food services, school health promotion programs, school counseling and psychology programs, school physical education programs, and integrated community and school health promotion programs. Story proposed that this type of integrated model should also include a focus on health education and behavioral skills-building components (Story, 1999). For example, children and adolescents should learn what a healthy diet should consist of and the national recommendations for being physically active and fit. Behavioral skills involve teaching children and adolescents how to monitor diet and physical activity behaviors and how to set and evaluate realistic goals for making long-term lifestyle changes. It is suggested that these elements be integrated into the course curriculum of schools. However, given the high priority of standards of learning, there may be barriers to implementing these diet and physical activity elements without tying them directly to standards of learning. Recent studies also suggest that developing health promotion programs during after-school hours may also be ideal given the need for more structured activities in youth during

TABLE 10.1
Comprehensive School Health Model Components

Reference	School environment	Health services	Family	Community
Story (1999)	School food services P.E. classes Health promotion Vending machines Education (nutrition and P.E.) Behavior skills (nutrition and P.E.)	School counselors Health promotion programs Screening programs (BMI)	Involvement and social support Behavior skills	Resources Campaigns/initiatives
Konu and Rimpela (2002)	Health education Physical environment (i.e., safety, ventilation) Student–teacher relationships Student–student relationships Behavior skills (respect, self-fulfillment, and health)	Preventive model	Home environment Cooperation with school	Physical environment (safety)
Motes et al. (1999)	Education (academic, behavioral, emotional) Teacher involvement Classmate involvement Partnerships and collaboration	School counselors Human service providers Identify high-risk youth Early intervention Technical assistance with Medicaid reimbursement	Family involvement Kinship network	Professionals and organizational involvement Human service providers

(continued)

TABLE 10.1 (Continued)

Reference	School environment	Health services	Family	Community
Tashman et al. (2000)	Collaboration between researchers and schools Researchers form genuine relationships with school staff	Dialogue between researchers and school health service providers Collaboration between researchers and providers Researchers collaborate with providers in intervention evaluation	Partnerships with youth and families	Collaboration between schools and communities Allow involvement from community members and leaders Dissemination of intervention outcomes to the community
St. Leger (1999)	Develop a charter for promoting health with the community Classroom health instruction Healthy school environment (i.e., food services, P.E.) Focus child needs Skill-based education (i.e., coping, problem solving) Professional development for teachers	Comprehensive health programs/services School counseling and psychology programs	Collaboration with parents	Collaboration between the school and all levels of community Integrated community and school health promotion efforts
Elias et al. (1994)	Age-appropriate curriculum, focusing on health promotion Teaching social skills, life skills, decision making, and problem solving Additional health-specific learning (i.e., self-care, fitness, alcohol/drug prevention)	Curricula activities and students services	Curricula involves parental learning, reinforcement, and monitoring	Comprehensive school-, family-, community health services

Brindis and Sanghvi (1997)	Establish linkages with managed care organizations	Increase access to parents and children	Involvement at the state and national levels to influence policy decisions and to develop links with MCOs
	Collaborate with PCPs (i.e., referrals, information sharing)		
	Specify services covered for MCO beneficiaries		
	Offer fee-for-service		
	Become a satellite center for MCO providers		
Armbruster et al. (1999)	Address the needs of students	Demonstrate cost-effectiveness via evaluation of utilization and outcome data	
		Develop relationships, contracts, and partnerships with MCOs	
		Advocate program to MCOs (access issues of students and services offered by SBHCs)	

Note. MCO = managed care organization; PCP = primary care provider; SBHC = school-based health center.

after-school hours when there may be less adult supervision at home (Sallis, Johnson, Calfas, Caparosa, & Nichols, 1997; Wilson & Evans, in press).

St. Leger (1999) proposed a health promotion school-based model that primarily focuses on formal instruction that would promote positive attitudes, values, and health-related behavioral skills (i.e., assertiveness, problem-solving skills). This model also focuses on health education and health promotion strategies that are targeted at schools, neighborhoods, and communities. A number of such programs have demonstrated effectiveness in reducing smoking (Perry et al., 1992), reducing alcohol use (Irwin, 1993), and increasing physical activity (Vartianen et al., 1991). Furthermore, a number of studies now indicate that students who are healthier learn more effectively (Levinger, 1994; National Health and Medical Research Council, 1997; World Bank, 1993; World Health Organization, 1995). Elias et al. proposed a model that advocates for age-appropriate health promotion curriculum focusing on teacher–student relationships, skills building, problem solving, and decision-making techniques (Elias, Kress, Gager, & Hancock, 1994). Family members are integrated into the model by encouraging adoption of health promotion behaviors, monitoring, and reinforcement of their youth's behavioral successes. Konu and Rimpela also proposed a model that integrates environmental supports (safety) for healthy behaviors in conjunction with improving teacher–study relationships, peer relationships, and behavioral skills (Konu & Rimpela, 2002).

Rothman et al. (1994) has also demonstrated the cost-effectiveness of prevention-focused approaches for improving behaviors related to substance abuse, sexuality, and unplanned pregnancy using the following criteria: (a) positive change in behavior, (b) greater than 1 year of behavioral data, (c) school classroom-based, (d) recent results, and (e) having a control group.

Another element of comprehensive school-based programs involves providing school health services (Story, 1999). School health services are essential to health promotion and prevention efforts and should involve the school nurse or central coordinator, who could serve as a liaison with the child's family and health care providers. To enhance prevention efforts these programs could include risk-factor screening programs for identifying children who are at risk for obesity, diabetes, high blood pressure, and cardiovascular disease. National surveys, however, such as the School Health Policies and Programs Study, indicate that only 57% of all middle, junior, and high schools have registered nurses who could implement these proposed health services (Small et al., 1995). In addition, only 37% of these schools offer any type of nutritional services for youth.

Investigators have increasingly focused on understanding the dynamics of improving school health-related environments. Several recent studies have evaluated the impact of altering school food services on eating behaviors in youth. For example, Zive and colleagues evaluated the effect of a school policy intervention in 24 middle schools in San Diego County (Zive, Pelletier, Sallis, & Elder, 2002). Schools were randomly assigned to be involved in changing school policies around child nutrition and physical activity services or to no intervention. The policy-based intervention included principals, nutritional staff, health teachers, physical education teachers, associated student body advisors, parent–teacher association (PTA) presidents, and students. The key elements of the intervention included developing reduced fat food choices in the school cafeteria and vending machines. Students taste-tested the foods that were offered and were involved in the policy changes directly. The students also learned behavioral skills and were involved in creating communication strategies of policy changes. The results demonstrated effective changes in school policies. For example, some schools successfully implemented food service stations that served low-fat snack items, whereas other schools developed low-fat pizzas that were offered as part of the school lunch program. Some of the schools also implemented competitive pricing of healthy snacks versus unhealthy snacks and effectively introduced healthy food selections in vending machines. This study is important in that it sets the stage for other needed efforts in changing policies at the school level. National data suggests that only 8% of schools with vending machines currently offer fruit (Story et al., 2002).

Integrating community and school efforts to improve child nutrition and health is another important component of a comprehensive school-based health program model (Story et al., 2002). For example, parent involvement is essential for enhancing psychosocial supports and environmental changes at home that complement policies implemented at the school level. In addition, community supports and resources could assist by providing financial support to schools for programs and by reinforcing the health messages at their own store locations in the community. Fast food outlets and convenience stores are the biggest environmental competitors for promoting healthy eating in youth. For example, fast food outlets provide about 32% of the meals eaten away from home by adolescents (Lin, Guthrie, & Blaylock, 1996; Lin, Guthrie, & Frazao, 1999a). Recent studies show that compared with the foods eaten at home the foods in fast food establishments are higher in fat and lower in fiber and calcium (Lin, Guthrie, & Frazao, 1999b). Major efforts must be made to develop community support in conjunction with school health programs. Families and schools must work together to educate their children and members of the community on the importance of promoting healthy eating policies. Interventions and policies need to focus on controlling high-fat and high-sugar foods in schools by restricting sales of unhealthy foods in school settings. These efforts should also include developing behavioral skills that will reinforce healthy food choices among adolescents when they are outside of the school environment.

Tashman et al. (2000) proposed a model that integrates the science-practice model into a community-based approach that would promote an active dialogue between researchers and mental health leaders to raise awareness about prevention programs in schools and communities. National meetings are proposed to be one forum for researchers and practitioners to begin to develop interactive relationships. Tashman et al. (2000) highlighted the importance of identifying stakeholders such as youth, families, school staff, clergy, and community leaders in these efforts. An example of collaborative work between schools and researchers involved the Primary Mental Health Project (Cowen, Hightower, Pedro-Carroll, Work, & Haffey, 1996). This program involved creating a system for exchanging information between teachers, school mental health professionals, child health care providers (including preventive services), and school personnel. Some suggestions for collaboration included having school administrators handle the proposal of programs through the school system, while having teachers tailor the programs for students. Parent leaders could also provide input and assistance with programs to make sure that it is acceptable and reinforced by families in the home environment. Others have also reported that involving school principals and influential decision makers in implementing school prevention programs has also improved the implementation of such programs (Rohrbach, 1993). Tashman et al. (2000) also emphasized the importance of evaluating and disseminating the results of school-based prevention programs.

Motes et al. (1999) proposed an ecological model school-based mental health service program that was tested in 20 rural schools. The system involved collaboration between state agencies, local school districts, and local mental health centers. The ecological model included implementing preventive efforts across settings such as classrooms, school, home, and communities. The program also linked services to youth and families to changes in the environment in a natural way and involved multiple change agents such as youth, teachers, parents, classmates, and school-based staff teams. The program conceptualized youth and family functioning in terms of interactions with the broader social environment. Examples of these proposed program components include peer support groups, involving youth in community-sponsored programs such as drama or sports, changing seating arrangements in the classroom, or designing alternative routes for going home to allow greater potential for change. Motes et al. also proposed that school-based programs should focus on high-risk youth who have problems with academic, behavioral, or emotional disorders (Motes et al., 1999). High-risk behaviors could also include drug abuse, aggression, or violence.

Evaluation of this pilot program demonstrated that the program enhanced in-school suspension programs, initiated peer-tutoring programs, developed supportive violence-prevention programs, addressed needs with important transitions for youth, and developed mentoring programs.

Armbruster et al. also proposed a policy-based model for linking school-based health programs to managed care practices (Armbruster, Andrews, Couenhoven, & Blau, 1999). This model defined a school-based health center as a free-standing health clinic in the school setting that provides primary health care services, including treatment of acute and chronic illnesses, as well as providing health screenings and physicals (Flaherty, Weist, & Warner, 1996; Weist, 1997; Weist et al., 1996). Armbruster et al. (1999) argued for developing advocacy programs that integrate the school and community services into managed care agreements. Although several models of partnership exist (Brindis & Sanghvi, 1997; Brindis & Wunsch, 1996; Zimmerman & Reif, 1995), few contractual agreements have been made between school-based health centers and managed care organizations (Brindis & Wunsch, 1996). To strengthen the position of school-based clinics, data on the use of their services, cost, and outcome measures must be generated. Although the primary interests in school-based health centers is to increase access for students in need, the managed care organization's goals are to contain costs and serve only those who are affiliated with their service plan. If data can be generated to document reduction in costs associated with urgent care or the development of preventable illnesses, then this may be one approach to demonstrate the cost-effectiveness of such health centers. Preventive services could include reducing drug abuse, alcohol or tobacco use, depression, suicide, teenage pregnancy, sexually transmitted diseases, accidents, and violence. Marketing the strengths of the centers for decreasing the need for more acute services will also be important to managed care organizations. The primary mechanism for changing health policy will involve convincing state legislatures, state officials, and managed care organizations that school-based health centers are essential in addressing the needs of uninsured children.

EMPIRICAL STUDIES

A number of studies have empirically examined school-based health services programs with respect to usage of services, student satisfaction, and cost-effectiveness (see Table 10.2). For example, Anglin, Naylor, and Kaplan (1996) studied health services usage among 3,818 students (9th to 12th graders) at three schools in Denver, Colorado. The most common diagnoses were emotional problems (29%), health supervision (13%), respiratory problems (11%), reproductive health problems (11%), and substance abuse (8%).

Girls were more likely than boys to use services that included medical providers, mental health, and substance abuse counselors. The rate of health services use was the highest among Hispanics (67%), followed by Whites (62%) and Blacks (61%). One fourth of the students used more than one of the three categories of services (medical, mental health, substance abuse), and visit frequency increased significantly for those who used at least two categories of service. The researchers concluded that schools that have student health centers with a wide variety of health services show greater use of comprehensive health care than those in the general population (based on national prevalence data). Higher frequency of health service use in the schools with health centers may indicate the high need for such youth-related services. This study points to the need for more comprehensive health center services and policies that support school-based health services. School-based health service policies should be implemented on a national level to increase access in youth.

Nabors, Weist, Reynolds, Tashman, and Jackson (1999) assessed adolescent satisfaction with school-based mental services in Baltimore, Maryland (ages 14–19 years; $N = 62$). Students receiving mental health services or counseling were evaluated; however, no information was provided on how the participants were recruited or where they were currently receiving school-based services. Those in upper grades reported greater satisfaction than those in lower grades. Students with higher grades reported less satisfaction than those of lower grades. Grades increased as length of treatment increased. Although overall, students reported high satisfaction with services, students primarily defined satisfaction as being happy with something (42%) or as having their needs met (35%). Adolescents reported the most important reason for being satisfied was having a caring relationship with their therapist (35%), followed by emotional release (31%) and learning coping skills (14%).

In a quasi-experimental study, Nabors and Prodente studied 133 students who were either receiving or not receiving school mental health services (Nabors & Prodente, 2002). The students were 11 to 18 years old and were followed over an 18-month period in Baltimore, Maryland. Adolescents who received mental health services showed a greater increase in satisfaction scores from 6 to 12 months, compared with those not receiving services. A total of 80% of the students reported being highly satisfied with mental health services, and girls had higher satisfaction scores than boys. Adolescents who completed treatment had a high prevalence of protective factors (i.e., social support) at the 18-month follow-up than those who dropped out of the program. Boys also showed a greater decrease in youth risk behaviors if they were receiving mental services compared with boys who were not. No differences in youth risk behaviors were found across the two groups for girls.

TABLE 10.2

Empirical Studies of Effectiveness of School-Based Health Services Programs

Reference	Purpose/design	Population	Findings
Kaplan et al. (1998)	Cost effectiveness of school-based services	Students aged 14–18; 56.7% female; in Denver, CO, schools; no race data, no sample size data	• SBHCs increased likelihood of visits for mental health or substance abuse problems visits • More adolescents with access to SBHC (80.2%) had at least one comprehensive health visit, and those with no access had a lower rate (68.8%) • Students with access to SBHCs were screened for high-risk behaviors at a higher rate. Those with SBCH access had 38 to 55% fewer emergent or urgent care visits
Anglin et al. (1996)	Prevalence of and descriptive data regarding school-based services use	3,818 students in Denver, CO, grades 9–12; between 1988–1992; 53% female; 44% White, 28% Hispanic, 22% Black, 6% Other	• Females were more likely than males to use SBHC services • Rate of use was highest among Hispanics (67%), followed by Whites (62%), Blacks (61%), and Other (55%) • Adolescents with access to SBHCs have a higher use of medical, mental health, and substance abuse counseling services than those in the general population.
Nabors et al. (1999)	Assessment of adolescent satisfaction with school-based services	71 students receiving school-based mental health services or counseling program; aged 14–19; 47 female, 59 Black, 12 White	• Overall, students were satisfied with school-based mental health services • Student satisfaction was higher regarding clinicians with more experience • Juniors and seniors and those with lower class grades reported the most satisfaction • Grades increased as length of treatment increased

(continued)

TABLE 10.2 (Continued)

Reference	Purpose/design	Population	Findings
Nabors and Prodente (2002)	Assessment of adolescent satisfaction with school-based services	133 students (79 receiving SMH services, 54 not receiving SMH); aged 11–18; 2:1 girls to boys; urban, low-income, mostly Black	• 80% were highly satisfied with mental health services, with those perceiving their therapist as warm and caring more likely to report satisfaction, and girls demonstrated higher satisfaction than boys • Adolescents receiving mental health services demonstrated greater improvements in satisfaction scores (from 6 months to 12 months) compared with those not receiving services, and scores decreased for the total sample at 18 months • Adolescents completing 18 months of treatment had more protective factors (i.e., social support) than those who left treatment prematurely
Nutbeam et al. (1993)	Community-based preventive health program	7th graders	▪ Teacher-led programs were less effective than community-led programs ▪ Treatment group demonstrated decreases in smoking behavior ▪ Treatment group demonstrated some decreases in alcohol-related behavior
Perry et al. (1992)	Prevention of smoking behavior in children through school curriculum and community programs	6th graders	▪ Treatment group demonstrated significantly lower smoking rates ▪ Unclear whether the school or community aspects of the intervention had a greater contribution to the reduction in smoking
Gortmaker et al. (1999)	Evaluation of a school-based program for weight control (increasing physical activity and healthy diet)	1,295 6th and 7th grade students (Black, Hispanic, White)	▪ Obesity among girls in the treatment group was reduced ▪ Overall, the intervention reduced television viewing hours in boys and girls ▪ Fruit and vegetable consumption increased for girls in the intervention

Study	Intervention	Population	Findings
Kalnins et al. (1994)	Community development with target population defining and actively involved in health improvement intervention	4th graders	▪ Children planned and implemented approaches to improve a local health problem ▪ Local health problem was identified and defined by the children: drug distribution near the school ▪ Children increased skills in community development, community action, and advocacy ▪ Links with various organizations and community groups were strengthened
Davis et al. (1995)	School-based quasi-experimental, classroom, food service, and parental education intervention with pretest/posttest and control schools	2,018 Navajo and Pueblo children in the 5th grade	▪ Significant knowledge increase in treatment groups ▪ Reduced intake of salt and butter in treatment groups ▪ Decreased intake of high fat foods by Navajo treatment group ▪ Significant change in Navajo treatment group regarding female body image
O'Neil and Nicklas (2002)	4-year school-based intervention to increase high school student intake of fruit and vegetables through school media campaigns, workshops, increased availability of fruits and vegetables and parental involvement	2,213 students from 12 schools in New Orleans, LA; 56% female; 84% White, 4% Black, 12% Other	▪ The majority of students were aware of specific media campaign activities ▪ Self-efficacy for fruit and vegetable intake increased in both the treatment and control groups ▪ Treatment groups demonstrated significant increases in knowledge scores ▪ Treatment groups demonstrated significant increases in fruit and vegetable intake (14% in increase) from baseline to follow-up

Note. SBHC = school-based health center; SMH = school mental health.

In another study, Kaplan, Calonge, Guernsey, and Hanrahan (1998) evaluated the cost-effectiveness of school-based health services in 14- to 18-year-old students in Denver, Colorado. Those with access to school-based health centers were 10 times more likely to have mental health or substance abuse visits. An important finding was that students with greater access to school-based health centers also had 38% to 55% fewer urgent care visits. Those who used the school-based health centers were also more likely to have a higher rate of high-risk behaviors. Overall, this study demonstrates that school-based health services were associated with a reduction in urgent care use, suggesting the cost-effectiveness of such programs and that these services reach high-risk youth.

Several school-based prevention programs are also summarized in Table 10.2 that demonstrate the effectiveness of health promotion programs on improving health behaviors in school children. Nutbeam, Smith, Moore, and Bauman (1993) and Perry et al. (1992) both conducted smoking cessation programs in school-age children (6th and 7th graders) that integrated school-based programs with community-based programs. In both studies, the treatment was effective in decreasing smoking behavior. A number of studies have demonstrated that school-based interventions involving the classroom curriculum, food services, parents, school media campaigns, behavior skills workshops, and availability of healthy foods have resulted in positive changes in dietary intake (Davis et al., 1995; O'Neil & Nicklas, 2002; Zive et al., 2002). School-based prevention programs that have targeted increasing moderate or vigorous physical activity have also been effective in changing students' frequency of physical activity (Baranowski, Anderson, & Carmack, 1998; Gortmaker et al., 1999; Vartianen et al., 1991).

PUBLIC HEALTH POLICIES

Public debates on access to health care have focused on issues of cost containment; the impact on business, governance, financing, and health insurance; and the role of the public and private sector in the health services delivery system (Giachello & Arrom, 1997). Adolescents and minorities, however, have tremendous barriers in accessing or entering the health care system for either preventive care or treatment of health-related illnesses. The lack of health insurance is one of the biggest reasons for the lack of access to health care among youth (Giachello & Arrom, 1997). Although the traditional biomedical model focuses on disease and emphasizes mortality as the primary outcome, alternative models have been proposed that focus on increasing life expectancy and health-related quality of life or the impact of health conditions on function (Kaplan & Friedman, 1997). For example, many adolescent health problems do not affect mortality, but good health care may prevent mortality from chronic illnesses.

Kaplan and Friedman (1997) argued for screening services that would result in preventing major disease outcomes among adolescents. The American Medical Association released a set of Guidelines for Adolescent Prevention Services (see http://www.ama-assn.org/ama/upload/mm/39/gap5 mono.pdf). These recommendations provide a framework for delivering preventive services at relevant developmental stages for early (11–14 years), middle (15–17 years), and late (18–21 years) adolescence. Screening measures include substance use, sexual activity, eating disorders, abuse, school performance, depression, and risk for suicide. This approach also emphasizes parental guidance consultations, and thus involves parents directly in the process. The major priorities of this model include health promotion such as decreasing the prevalence of drug use and increasing the rate of healthy diet and physical activity to prevent morbidity and mortality in the future.

One of the problems with a health care policy for adolescence, noted by Kaplan and Friedman (1997), is that preventive services may not be covered under reimbursement schedules for health care policies. This is because it is easier for providers to be reimbursed for treatment rather than prevention services. Furthermore, few resources are available to support other health care providers in disseminating relevant prevention-related information.

Today, health care policies are needed that specifically address the health needs of youth. These policies may take different forms, as discussed by Kaplan and Friedman (1997). For example, federal and state policies are needed that include coverage for uninsured children. Although coverage for aged and disabled individuals has gone up over the past decade, coverage for youth has decreased. Policies of health care providers need to be expanded beyond vaccine policies and should include standard information concerning prevention of drug abuse and sexually transmitted diseases. Statutory regulation such as tobacco advertising should continue to be a national priority. Many of the mass media campaigns are directed at children and include fast-food marketing (Story et al., 2002). For example, junior high school students are exposed on average to 8 hours per day of media content (Ozer, Brindis, Millstein, Knopf, & Irwin, 1998). Television is a major advertising medium for fast-food restaurants, with 95% of their budget spent on such advertisements (Gallo, 1999). Both cross-sectional and longitudinal studies have demonstrated positive associations between television viewing and the rate of obesity (Robinson, 1999).

The Centers for Disease Control and Prevention recently convened an expert panel on policies and programs for promoting cardiovascular health (2002). The panel formulated a policy statement that proposes to highlight the characteristics of an ideal program to address heart disease and stroke over the next 20 years. The major emphasis of the statement is to advocate early prevention through cardiovascular health promotion programs that focus on public health policies and social and environmental supports of cardiovascular disease prevention. Public policy will include social marketing and media components on a national level. The focus of the community prevention efforts will be on promoting protective factors that may incorporate traditional views of eating and being physically active into a holistic view of health. In addition, resources such as social support, modeling, and community cohesion will be incorporated as a key focus in health promotion programs. Efforts to eliminate economic and racial disparities should be a priority.

To create a population at low risk for cardiovascular disease, a population-wide approach to prevention is required. The panel suggested environmental policies for improving nutritional content of foods at the local, state, and national levels (Centers for Disease Control and Prevention, 2002). Better use of land zoning regulations and environmental supports for community safety will also increase the likelihood for physical activity, especially in underserved areas. Skills for effective leadership, advocacy, and communication need to be included as key elements into the public health workforce and schools of public health. Partnerships are needed at the state health departments and local and regional public health agencies to facilitate cooperation and sharing of resources for chronic disease prevention programs.

The panel suggested that schools need to have a focus on daily health education for all students with a variety of appealing and accessible extracurricular sports and recreation opportunities for all children regardless of athletic abilities (Centers for Disease Control and Prevention, 2002). School facilities will promote policies such as tobacco-free environments and good nutrition and community integrated physical activity opportunities. Walk to school programs could also be promoted by schools and local officials.

Isaccs and Schroeder proposed a number of key elements for successful public health campaigns: (a) credible scientific evidence; (b) advocates committed to their cause; (c) ongoing partnerships with the media; and (d) effective laws and regulation (Isaacs & Schroeder, 2001). Public health professionals should be leaders in developing partnerships and community mobilization for effectively promoting a national cardiovascular prevention policy.

MECHANISMS FOR DEVELOPING SCHOOL-BASED HEALTH PROGRAMS

Armbruster (2002) has summarized important elements for developing and administering school-based mental health programs that provide a model for developing school-based health programs. Seven common elements are outlined that include funding, assessment and resources, program structure, staffing and training, partnership and collaboration, quality assurance, and evaluation. Armbruster suggested that the ecosystem of each school is different and that the integration of these elements will vary depending on the needs and infrastructure of the school. By placing an emphasis on partnership and collaboration, however, school-based programs have the potential to benefit children, families, schools, communities, and managed care organizations. A model for access and early intervention through school-based health programs is a cost-effective approach because it will reduce costly treatment of illnesses that are preventable.

Addressing the cost-effectiveness of developing school-based health programs is important, and Armbuster (2002) has proposed that it is essential to set up a system that allows health evaluations to be reimbursed. Thus, a database for evaluating the program costs and effectiveness should be developed. Community input is also needed, and advocates should be identified to work with managed care organizations. Relationships will need to be developed between local, state, and national organizations to promote school-based health centers.

CONCLUSION

Psychologists need to take an active role in continuing to advance integrated service delivery and school-based prevention programs by conducting research that includes the evaluation of comprehensive school-based health centers. Psychologists should lead multidisciplinary efforts in implementing interagency service programs and involve family, school teachers and administrators, communities, and legislative advocates. Training programs will also have a major role in preparing and supporting the integrated service delivery and school-based prevention programs. For example, the integration of comprehensive school-based models could be incorporated into interdisciplinary training programs involving psychologists, internship programs, practicum and internship placement for psychology students, and coursework involving psychology instructors.

REFERENCES

Allensorth, D. D., & Kolbe, L. J. (1987). The comprehensive school health program. *Journal of School Health*, 57, 409–412.

Anglin, T. M., Naylor, K. E., & Kaplan, D. W. (1996). Comprehensive school-based health care: High school students' use of medical, mental health, and substance abuse services. *Pediatrics*, 97, 318–330.

Armbruster, P. (2002). The administration of school-based mental health services. *Child Adolescent Psychiatric Clinic North America, 11*, 23–41.

Armbruster, P., Andrews, E., Couenhoven, J., & Blau, G. (1999). Collision or collaboration? School-based health services meet managed care. *Clinical Psychology Review, 19*, 221–237.

Baranowski, T., Anderson, C., & Carmack, C. (1998). Mediating variable framework in physical activity interventions. How are we doing? How might we do better? *American Journal of Preventive Medicine, 15*, 266–297.

Brindis, C. D., & Sanghvi, R. V. (1997). School-based health clinics: Remaining viable in a changing health care delivery system. *Annual Review of Public Health, 18*, 567–587.

Brindis, C., & Wunsch, B. (1996). *Finding common ground: Developing linkages between school-linked/school-based health programs and managed care plans.* Sacramento, CA: Report of the Foundation Consortium for School-Linked Services.

Centers for Disease Control and Prevention. (2002). *National action plan for cardiovascular health: A comprehensive public health strategy to combat heart disease and stroke. Expert Panel A: Policy and programs draft report for the first meeting.* Atlanta, GA: Author.

Cowen, E. L., Hightower, A. D., Pedro-Carroll, J. L., Work, W. C., & Haffey, W. G. (1996). *School-based prevention for children at risk: The Primary Mental Health Project.* Washington, DC: American Psychological Association.

Davis, S. M., Lambert, L. C., Gomez, Y., & Skipper, B. (1995). Southwest cardiovascular curriculum project: Study findings for American Indian elementary students. *Journal of Health Education, 26*, S72–S81.

Elias, M. J., Kress, J. S., Gager, P. J., & Hancock, M. E. (1994). Adolescent health promotion and risk reduction: Cementing the social contract between pediatricians and the schools. *Bulletin of the New York Academy of Medicine, 71*, 87–110.

Flaherty, L. T., Weist, M. D., & Warner, B. S. (1996). School-based mental health services in the United States: History, current models and needs. *Community Mental Health Journal, 32*, 314–352.

Gallo, A. E. (1999). *Food advertising in the United States* (Agriculture Information Bulletin No. 750). Washington, DC: U.S. Department of Agriculture, Economic Research Service.

Giachello, A. L., & Arrom, J. O. (1997). Health service access and utilization among adolescent minorities. In D. K. Wilson, J. R. Rodrigue, & W. C. Taylor (Eds.), *Health-promoting and health-compromising behaviors among minority adolescents* (pp. 303–320). Washington, DC: American Psychological Association.

Gortmaker, S. L., Peterson, K., Wiecha, J., Sobol, A. M., Dixit, S., Fox, M. K., et al. (1999). Reducing obesity via a school-based interdisciplinary intervention among youth. *Archives of Pediatric Adolescent Medicine, 153*, 409–418.

Irwin, R. (1993). *Evaluation in the school development in health education project.* Canberra, Australia: University of Canberra.

Isaacs, S. L., & Schroeder, S. A. (2001). *Where the public good prevailed.* Retrieved 2002 from http://www.prospect.org/print/V12/10/index.html

Johnston, L. D., O'Malley, P. M., & Bachman, J. G. (1994). *National survey results on drug use from the Monitoring the Future Study, 1975–1993: Volume I. Secondary school students.* Rockville, MD: U.S. Department of Health and Human Services.

Kalnins, I. H., Ballantyne, C., Quatro, G., Love, R., Sturis, S., & Pollack, P. (1994). School based community development as a health promotion strategy for children. *Health Promotion International, 4,* 269–279.

Kaplan, D. W., Calonge, B. N., Guernsey, B. P., & Hanrahan, M. B. (1998). Managed care and school-based health centers. Use of health services. *Archives of Pediatric Adolescent Medicine, 152*(1), 25–33.

Kaplan, D. W., & Friedman, L. (1997). Health care and health policy for adolescents. In D. K. Wilson, J. R. Rodrigue, & W. C. Taylor (Eds.), *Health-promoting and health-compromising behavior among minority adolescents* (pp. 321–346). Washington, DC: American Psychological Association.

Konu, A., & Rimpela, M. (2002). Well-being in schools: A conceptual model. *Health Promotion International, 17*(1), 79–87.

Levinger, B. (1994). *Nutrition, health and advancement for all.* Newton, MA: Education Development Centre and United Nations Development Programme.

Lin, B. H., Guthrie, J., & Blaylock, J. R. (1996). *The diets of America's children: Influences of dining out, household characteristics, and nutrition knowledge* (Publication no. AER-746). Washington, DC: U.S. Department of Agriculture, Economic Research Service.

Lin, B. H., Guthrie, J., & Frazao, E. (1999a). *Nutrient contribution of food away from home* (Publication no. AIB-720). Washington, DC: U.S. Department of Agriculture, Economic Research Service.

Lin, B. H., Guthrie, J., & Frazao, E. (1999b). Quality of children's diets at and away from home: 1994–1996. *Food Review, 21*(1), 2–10.

Micic, D. (2001). Obesity in children and adolescents—A new epidemic? Consequences in adult life. *Journal of Pediatric Endocrinology and Metabolism, 14* (Suppl. 5), S1345–S1352.

Motes, P. S., Melton, G., & Waithe-Simmons, W. E. (1999). Ecologically oriented school-based mental health services: Implications for service system reform. *Psychology in the Schools, 36,* 391–401.

Nabors, L. A., & Prodente, C. A. (2002). Evaluation of outcomes for adolescents receiving school-based mental health services. *Children's Services: Social Policy, Research, and Practice, 5,* 105–112.

Nabors, L. A., Weist, M. D., Reynolds, M. W., Tashman, N. A., & Jackson, C. Y. (1999). Adolescent satisfaction with school-based mental health services. *Journal of Child and Family Studies, 8,* 229–236.

National Health and Medical Research Council. (1997). *Effective school health promotion—Towards the health promoting school*. Canberra: Commonwealth of Australia.

Newmark-Sztainer, D., Story, M., Resnick, M. D., & Blum, R. W. (1998). Lessons learned about adolescent nutrition from the Minnesota Adolescent Health Survey. *Journal of the American Dietetic Association, 98*, 1449–1456.

Nutbeam, D., Smith, C., Moore, L., & Bauman, A. (1993). Warning! Schools can damage your health: Alienation from school and its impact on health behaviour. *Journal of Pediatrics and Child Health, 29*(Suppl. 1), S287–S301.

O'Neil, C. E., & Nicklas, T. A. (2002). Gimme 5: An innovative, school-based nutrition intervention for high school students. *Journal of the American Dietetic Association, 102*, S93–S96.

Ozer, E. M., Brindis, C. D., Millstein, S. G., Knopf, D. K., & Irwin, C. E. J. (1998). *America's adolescents: Are they healthy?* San Francisco: University of California, San Francisco, National Adolescent Health Information Center.

Paavola, J. C., Carey, K., Cobb, C., Illback, R. J., Joseph, H. M., Jr., Routh, D. K., et al. (1996). Interdisciplinary school practice: Implications of the service integration movement for psychologists. *Professional Psychology: Research and Practice, 27*(1), 34–40.

Pastore, D. R., Murray, P. J., & Juszczak, L. (2001). School-based health center: Position paper of the Society of Adolescent Medicine. *Journal of Adolescent Health, 29*, 448–450.

Perry, C., Kelder, S. H., Murray, D. M., & Klepp, K. I. (1992). Community wide smoking prevention: Long term outcomes of the Minnesota Heart Health Program and the Class of 1989 Study. *American Journal of Public Health, 82*, 1210–1216.

Pi-Sunyer, F. X. (2002). The medical risks of obesity. *Obesity Surgery, 12* (Suppl. 1), 6S–11S.

Robinson, T. N. (1999). Reducing children's television viewing to prevent obesity: A randomized controlled trial. *Journal of the American Medical Association, 282*, 1561–1156.

Rohrbach, L. A. (1993). Diffusion of a school-based substance abuse prevention program: Predictors of program implementation. *Preventive Medicine, 22*, 237–260.

Rothman, M., Ehreth, J., Palmer, C., Collins, J., Reblando, J., & Luce, B. (1994). *The potential benefits and costs of a comprehensive school health education program*. Geneva, Switzerland: Draft Report to the World Health Organization.

Sallis, J. F., Johnson, M. F., Calfas, K. J., Caparosa, S., & Nichols, J. F. (1997). Assessing perceived physical environmental variables that may influence physical activity. *Research Quarterly for Exercise and Sport, 68*, 345–351.

Small, M. L., Majer, L. S., Allensorth, D. D., Farquhar, B. K., Kann, L., & Pateman, B. C. (1995). School health services. *Journal of School Health, 65*, 319–326.

St. Leger, L. H. (1999). The opportunities and effectiveness of the health promoting primary school in improving child health—A review of the claims and evidence. *Health Education Research, 14*(1), 51–69.

Story, M. (1999). School-based approaches for preventing and treating obesity. *International Journal of Obesity and Related Metabolic Disorders, 23*(Suppl. 2), 543–551.

Story, M., Newmark-Sztainer, D., & French, S. (2002). Individual and environmental influences on adolescent eating behaviors. *Journal of the American Dietetic Association, 102*(Suppl. 3), S40–S51.

Tashman, N. A., Weist, M. D., Acosta, O., Bickham, N. L., Grady, M., Nabors, L., et al. (2000). Toward the integration of prevention research and expanded school mental health programs. *Children's Services: Social Policy, Research, and Practice, 3,* 97–115.

Taylor, W. C., Beech, B. M., & Cummings, S. (1997). Increasing physical activity levels among youth: A public health challenge. In D. K. Wilson, J. R. Rodrigue, & W. C. Taylor (Eds.), *Health-promoting and health-compromising behaviors among minority adolescents* (pp. 107–128). Washington, DC: American Psychological Association.

Triano, R. P., & Flegal, K. M. (1998). Overweight children and adolescents: Description, epidemiology and demographics. *Pediatrics, 101,* 497–505.

Triano, R. P., Flegal, K. M., Kuczmarski, R. J., Campbell, S. M., & Johnson, C. L. (1995). Overweight prevalence and trends for children and adolescents. The National Health and Nutrition Examination Surveys, 1963 to 1991. *Archives of Pediatric Adolescent Medicine, 149,* 1085–1091.

Vartianen, E., Tossavainen, K., Viri, K., Niskanen, E., & Puska, P. (1991). The North Karelia youth programs. In D. Nutbeam, B. Haglund, P. Farley, & P. Tillgren (Eds.), *Youth health promotion: From theory to practice in school and community* (pp. 108–136). London: Forbes.

Weist, M. D. (1997). Expanded school mental health services: A national movement on progress. In T. H. Ollendick & R. Prinz (Eds.), *Advances in clinical child psychology* (pp. 318–352). New York: Plenum Press.

Weist, M. D., Paskewitz, D. A., Warner, B. S., & Flaherty, L. T. (1996). Treatment outcome of school based mental health services for urban teenagers. *Community Mental Health Journal, 32,* 149–157.

Wilson, D. K., & Evans, A. E. (in press). Health promotion in children and adolescents: An integration of psychosocial and environmental approaches. In M. C. Roberts (Ed.), *Handbook of pediatric psychology* (3rd ed.). New York: Guilford Press.

World Bank. (1993). *World Development Report 1993, Investing in health.* Oxford: Oxford University Press.

World Health Organization. (1995). *WHO expert committee on comprehensive school health education and promotion.* Geneva, Switzerland: Author.

Zimmerman, D. J., & Reif, C. J. (1995). School-based health centers and managed care health plans: Partners in primary care. *Journal of Public Health Management Practice, 1*(1), 33–39.

Zive, M. M., Pelletier, R. L., Sallis, J. F., & Elder, J. P. (2002). An environmental intervention to improve a la carte foods at middle schools. *Journal of the American Dietetic Association, 102*(Suppl. 3), S76–S78.

IV

WOMEN'S AND MEN'S
HEALTH IN PRIMARY CARE

11

WOMEN'S HEALTH AND THE ROLE OF PRIMARY CARE PSYCHOLOGY

ELLEN L. POLESHUCK

Many of the differences between women and men have direct implications for health. The Institute of Medicine's Committee on Understanding the Biology of Sex and Gender Differences reported, "being male or female is an important basic human variable that affects health and illness throughout the life span. . . . There are clear sex differences that have effects on health and illness from a cellular and molecular level to a behavioral level" (Wizeman & Pardue, 2001, p. xix). Yet oftentimes health care is not designed to meet women's unique needs. Women's "health is a complex function of the interaction of economic, political, cultural, biological, psychological, physiological, spiritual and family factors" (American Psychological Association, 1996, p. 22; see also Heldring, 1998). The primary care psychologist specializing in women's health can work with obstetrician–gynecologists, family practitioners, internists, nurse practitioners, physician's assistants, midwives, and other women's health care professionals to provide

The writing of this chapter was supported in part by NIMH grant T32 MH018911 Institutional National Research Service Award. The author would like to thank Lisa M. Dube-Whitehair, MS, RNC; Susan H. McDaniel, PhD; Elizabeth Naumburg, MD; and Linda Travis, PhD, for their valuable feedback on earlier drafts of this manuscript.

integrative, comprehensive, and sensitive care consistent with women's goals and priorities.

This chapter serves as an introduction to several important issues related to women's health and primary care psychology. An overview is provided to facilitate the primary care psychologist's initiation of collaborative work with other women's health care professionals. A biopsychosocial model is used as a guide to patient care, with an emphasis on how primary care psychologists can use their psychosocial expertise to enhance more traditional biomedical approaches to women's health care. The discussion provides a brief overview of several issues central to women's health, including social stressors, health promotion and disease prevention, life-cycle events, mental illness, and relationship issues. In addition, skills that are beneficial for a primary care psychologist to function effectively as a team member in women's health are reviewed. Examples of collaboration with patients from the author's practice will be used to illustrate some of the issues and skills discussed.

SOCIAL STRESSORS FACING WOMEN

Women are at greater risk than men for many social stressors that have direct implications for health. Two examples of such stressors are partner violence and poverty.

Violence

Women are significantly more likely than men to suffer from certain forms of violence. In 1985, former surgeon general C. Everett Koop identified domestic violence as the largest health problem for American women, causing more injuries than automobile accidents, muggings, and rapes combined (Koop, 1991). Unfortunately there is no evidence to suggest that violence has decreased in the interim years. Although studies vary, approximately 33% of women have been physically or sexually abused in childhood, 25% are victims of domestic violence, 25% have experienced stranger or acquaintance rape, and 69% have experienced at least one traumatic or violent event in their lifetimes (Radford & Russell, 1992; Resnick, Kilpatrick, Dansky, Saunders, & Best, 1993; Russell, 1986; Zerbe, 1999). Women who report experiencing any type of violence demonstrate increased health and mental health problems, health care use, emergency room visits, and health care costs (Commonwealth Fund, 1998; Koss, Goodman, Browne, Puryear Keita, & Felipe Russo, 1994; Misra, 2001). Women who report childhood abuse, rape, and domestic violence are at greater risk for asthma, hypertension, chronic pain, sexually transmitted infections including HIV, unplanned pregnancy, exacerbation of chronic illness, recurrent vaginal infections, and painful and irregular menstruation (Allen, 1995; Breslau, Davis, Peterson, Edward, & Schultz, 1997; Campbell, Kub, & Rose, 1996; Davidson, 1993; Eisenstat & Bancroft, 1999; Laws, 1998; Zerbe, 1999). They are also at greater risk for depression, anxiety disorders, eating disorders, suicide, substance abuse, dissociative disorders, and sexual dysfunction (Allen, 1995; Breslau et al., 1997; Campbell et al., 1996; Davidson, 1993; Zerbe, 1999). In addition, women who report experiencing violence are more likely to seek multiple consultations from medical professionals, undergo major surgical procedures such as hysterectomy, use pain medications and tranquilizers, demonstrate nonadherence to medical regimens, view their health as poor, and report physical disability (Eisenstat & Bancroft, 1999; Laws, 1998).

The primary care psychologist can provide support and education to health care professionals and assessment and intervention to women coping with violence. In fact, health care professionals are often reluctant to assess for women's trauma experiences, with fewer than 10% of physicians consistently assessing for physical or sexual abuse (American College of Obstetricians and Gynecologists, 1995; Wagner, Mongan, Hamrick, & Hendrick, 1995). A primary care psychologist can educate health care professionals about the need for assessment, signs and symptoms of violence in their patients, and strategies to screen for violence. Questionnaires for new patients, articles reviewing relevant information, and informal discussions about violence in regard to specific patients can all be used to introduce the role of violence assessment to health care professionals. Without the necessary resources in place, however, it is unlikely health care professionals will feel comfortable discussing violence with their patients, regardless of their skill level in doing so. Therefore, the primary care psychologist should provide consultation, referral, intervention, and support to patients who disclose violent experiences to their health care professionals. This requires that the psychologist be skilled in working with trauma and violence, including assessment and treatment of posttraumatic stress disorder.

Socioeconomic Status

Socioeconomic status is one of the most powerful predictors of women's health status (Adler & Coriell, 1997). Women are more likely than men to be of lower socioeconomic status, and as socioeconomic status decreases, overall health, including morbidity and mortality, worsens (Adler, Boyce, Chesney, Folkman, & Syme, 1993; Adler & Coreill, 1997). For example, women who are poor and uneducated have 25% higher death rates from breast cancer and 2.8 times higher cervical cancer mortality rates than do women of higher socioeconomic status (U.S. Department of Health and Human Services, 1990). The differences in health status among women of varying socioeconomic status may be related to physiological, psychological, behavioral, and social factors such as health behaviors, use of screening and early detection, access to care, and quality and quantity of treatment received (Adler et al., 1993; Adler & Coreill, 1997). The primary care psychologist can work with health care professionals to identify ways in which socioeconomic status may be related to health care issues for women and their families. Examples include apparent nonadherence with medication (e.g., the inability to afford prescriptions) or to prescribed practices (e.g., a patient does not swim three times weekly because of lack of appropriate clothing or facility access). Primary care psychologists can work with social workers and others to identify resources. For example, a pharmaceutical company may donate medication or the health care professional may identify a less costly alternative. The psychologist can also work with health care professionals to find accessible alternatives to recommended interventions, such as walking rather than swimming for exercise.

DIVERSITY

Race, culture, and sexual orientation directly affect women's health status and health care access. Black women, for example, live an average of 73.8 years, 5.7 years fewer than White women (McNair & Roberts, 1998; National Center for Health Statistics, 1996). Heart disease, lung cancer, breast cancer, diabetes, and AIDS have higher morbidity and mortality rates for Black women than for White women (Dreeben, 2001; McNair & Roberts, 1998; National Center for Health Statistics, 1996). Furthermore, Black women are more likely to have delayed and inadequate prenatal care (Ingram, Makuc, & Kleinman, 1986; La Veist, Keith, & Guitierrez, 1995), and the mortality rate of Black women's infants is 2.4 times the mortality rate of White women's infants (Geronimus, 1992; McNair & Roberts, 1998). Many of the health disparities between Black and White individuals persist even after income, socioeconomic status, and insurance coverage differences are controlled (Weinick, Zuvekas, & Cohen, 2000; Williams, 1999). Research suggests that health disparities exist for other minority women as well, including Latinas, Asian Americans, lesbians, and bisexuals (Diamant, Wold, Spritzer, & Gelberg, 2000; National Center for Health Statistics, 1996; Park & Buechner, 1997). The primary care psychologist can prompt health care professionals to consider the role of race, culture, and sexual orientation when planning their interventions with patients. Education and support can facilitate health care professionals' abilities to provide culturally competent and sensitive care. Identifying issues of physician–patient communication, for example, particularly when there are differences in race and class, can increase health care professionals' awareness. In addition, the primary care psychologist can participate in developing and implementing interventions appropriate for minority patients. Community-based care can be one way to improve significantly minority patient access to services.

MULTIPLE ROLES AND SOCIAL SUPPORT

Women are more likely than men to be responsible for coping with the multiple demands of work, children, ill or disabled family members, elderly parents, and household chores (Dempsey, 2000; Misra, 2001; Perry-Jenkins, 1993). More than half of women who have children under the age of 18 work outside of the home (Swanson, Piotrowkowski, Puryear Keita, & Becker, 1997), and approximately 9% of women report caring for a sick or disabled family member (Commonwealth Fund, 1998). Individuals in caretaker roles are at higher risk for depression (Henry, 2000; Kessler & McLeod, 1984).

Women are often responsible for ensuring that their family members receive appropriate health care. In fact, women who neglect their own routine maintenance and preventative health care (e.g., cancer and blood pressure screening) and their own health maintenance behaviors (e.g., exercise and diet) may well be attending to the health care needs of others. Such women may be more likely to visit the health care professional's office for family members than for themselves. These visits can provide an opportunity to address women's health care needs in addition to those of their family members and to introduce the possibility of psychosocial intervention when indicated. For example, a single mother with three young children who brings in her own mother for arthritis pain can be asked about her health, coping, and support system during her mother's exam. Of note, women with multiple roles may be especially open to family therapy because of its systemic emphasis.

It is important for the primary care psychologist to consider that women who work as women's health care professionals are often no different than the women they treat. Many have multiple roles of their own and, similar to their patients, may neglect their own health care needs. The primary care psychologist can address issues of stress and coping with his or her health care professional colleagues. Education about the importance of self-care and health promotion activities for the health care professional as well as patients can be an important role for the psychologist.

Case Example

Ms. R. was a 40-year-old single woman living with many social stressors.[1] She was receiving a small government stipend for income and spending most of her time caring for the younger four of her six children, ages 1 to 22, and for her uncle who was dying of pancreatic cancer. Her oldest son was in jail. Ms. R. and her family lived in an innercity neighborhood; they had bullet holes in their windows. She had been held up at gun point twice and raped once. She was afraid to sleep soundly because she felt that she needed to stay alert constantly to protect her baby. Ms. R. had not been involved with health care since her youngest child was born. She took the bus (along with her two youngest children) to the closest medical clinic that would accept her federal insurance. Ms. R. met with a nurse practitioner (NP) who had never met Ms. R before, and reported aching joints, swollen hands and feet, headaches, difficulties with sleep, and depression.

The NP recognized the complex nature of Ms. R.'s health status, introduced Ms. R. to the primary care psychologist, and recommended they follow up together. The first meeting was with Ms. R., the clinic social worker, and the psychologist to ensure that Ms. R. was benefiting from all available resources, such as help with transportation, child care, home health care, housing, and food. After the initial meeting, Ms. R. met with the psychologist for psychotherapy, focusing on her feelings of depression, helplessness, and isolation. Stress management and pain management techniques were introduced as well. The psychologist went to a meeting at Ms. R.'s church with Ms. R., the minister, and the choir director, and discussed problems with safety in the neighborhood. The psychologist and the nurse practitioner discussed the ways in which Ms. R.'s health care needs were competing with the many other demands in her life, and they later met together with Ms. R. to develop treatment recommendations. Ms. R. agreed she could engage in several health promotion behaviors, including taking a walk twice daily to drop off and pick up her children at the bus stop, continuing to sing in the church choir, and baking rather than frying when cooking. Although the primary care psychologist could not eradicate the many social stressors contributing to Ms. R.'s difficulties, she was able to offer support, teach skills, strengthen her social support network, facilitate access to resources, and help to coordinate her care in an individualized way.

---

[1] Each of the presented clinical examples has been drawn from the author's practice and modified for the purposes of this chapter and to maintain the privacy and confidentiality of the patients and their families.

HEALTH AND DISEASE IN WOMEN

The primary care psychologist can assist health care professionals by promoting health behavior choices and providing support to patients with illnesses.

Health Promotion and Lifestyle

Attention to behaviors such as exercise, smoking cessation, proper diet, substance use, and routine health care (e.g., cardiovascular risk screening) is central to women's physical and mental health. For example, although it is well-established that regular physical activity is associated with improved physical and psychological functioning and decreased symptoms of disease and chronic illness, 75% of American women are underactive (King & Kiernan, 1997). Primary care psychologists can work with health care professionals to design exercise and physical activity plans that are relevant and realistic for the patient's socioeconomic status, race, culture, and other factors related to her personal situation. They can also play an important role in providing patients and their families support in exploring obstacles to health promotion activities and making positive lifestyle changes.

Chronic and Life-Threatening Illness

As a result of high morbidity and low mortality rates, women are likely to live many years of their lives with illness. In fact, more than 80% of women over 65 live with at least one illness (Blumenthal, Matthews, & Weiss, 1994; Commonwealth Fund, 1993). Although some illnesses are unique to women (e.g., endometriosis, gynecological cancer), other illnesses are more common in women (e.g., autoimmune disorders, gastrointestinal disorders, Alzheimer's disease, and muscular skeletal disorders) or present with different symptoms from men (e.g., HIV infection, coronary heart disease), resulting in misdiagnosis and undertreatment (Kyriakidis et al., 1995; Melnick et al., 1994). The need for appropriate treatment of life-threatening illness is evident. Chronic illness, although not life-threatening, can cause significant pain, disability, and diminished quality of life, requiring comprehensive treatment as well.

The primary care psychologist can play a central role in assessing and treating women and families living with chronic and life-threatening illnesses. Stress is known to be associated with immune and endocrine functioning and is often related to a woman's experience with illness (Hall, Altman, & Blumenthal, 1996). Evaluating the consequences of both the illness and its treatment for patients and their families can assist in developing realistic and appropriate treatment recommendations. Through behavioral treatments and psychotherapy, the psychologist can provide women and their families with support, effective coping skills, positive health behaviors, and adaptive belief systems in coping with illness. In addition, the primary care psychologist can work with the patient and her health care professionals to develop individualized approaches for optimization of quality of life and adherence to biomedical regimens.

Case Example

Ms. T. was a 23-year-old full-time mother. She lived with her 28-year-old partner, their 18-month-old son, and her 4-year-old daughter. Ms. T. had been diagnosed with endometriosis and experienced severe chronic pelvic pain. She underwent three laparoscopies and takes multiple pain medications with only modest relief. Ms. T.'s pain was interfering with caring for her children, maintaining her home, participating in competitive sports, and engaging in sexual intercourse. She called her health care professional's office several times a week, making frequent acute appointments and visiting the emergency department after hours when her pain became unmanageable. Her health care professional approached the primary care psychologist because he was feeling frustrated. He knew Ms. T. was suffering, and she did not seem to improve regardless of intervention.

The psychologist and the health care professional discussed an interdisciplinary approach to pain management with an emphasis on improving function rather than curing the pain. They decided to encourage the patient to take medications consistently and schedule regular appointments to decrease acute calls and visits. The psychologist joined the health care professional and Ms. T. at their next appointment, and Ms. T. agreed to meet with the psychologist for a consultation. Ms. T. was open to altering her expectations, learning pain-management strategies, and examining the implications her pain had on her life and relationships. Her partner attended appointments with her so he could learn to better support her in coping with her pain and learn effective strategies along with her. Ms. T gradually learned techniques that decreased the interference from her pain and found her quality of life and her relationships with her partner and children improved. In addition her phone calls and emergency department visits decreased substantially.

LIFE CYCLE TRANSITIONS

Puberty, pregnancy, and menopause are normal stages of women's development, unrelated to emotional distress for most women. Although most women demonstrate few difficulties, these life cycle changes can be challenging because of the social, biological, hormonal, and emotional changes that occur. These changes therefore create windows of vulnerability, and women are more likely to experience onset or recurrence of mental illness during these transitional periods than during other times in their lives.

Puberty

During puberty, the developmental transition from childhood to adolescence with achievement of adult physical form and reproductive functioning, girls experience physical, emotional, and social changes, and others begin to respond to them differently. Puberty is a time when girls may develop vulnerabilities to social pressures, eating disorders, substance abuse, acquaintance rape, sexually transmitted infections, and unplanned pregnancies. In addition, associations have been found with pubertal hormones and both aggressive behaviors and depressive affect (Graber & Brooks-Gunn, 1998). During puberty girls and their families may benefit from closer monitoring and support by health care professionals, with additional assessment and treatment by primary care psychologists as needed. Interventions such as group therapy, social skills training, family therapy, and psychoeducation on topics such as sexuality and body image may be particularly useful.

Premenstrual Dysphoric Disorder

Approximately 3% to 8% of reproductive-age women experience premenstrual dysphoric disorder (PMDD; Gold, 1997; Zerbe, 1999). Although there continues to be a lack of consensus regarding definition, PMDD is defined by the *Diagnostic and Statistical Manual of Mental Disorders—IV* (DSM–IV; American Psychiatric Association, 1994) as symptoms that significantly interfere with functioning during the premenstrual phase only, such as depression, anxiety, irritability, mood swings, and anhedonia. In contrast, premenstrual syndrome (PMS) has a much higher prevalence and involves transient mood changes that do not significantly impair daily school, work, family, or social functioning or require aggressive intervention. Although genetic, hormonal, endocrine function, and learned factors have been proposed as contributing to PMDD, none have been confirmed. The existing research supports using antidepressants, particularly selective serotonin reuptake inhibitors (SSRIs), as front-line treatment of PMDD (Yonkers & Brown, 1996). However, placebo treatments have also been found to be effective for many women (Freeman & Rickels, 1999; Klebanov & Ruble, 1994; McFarlane, 1998). Many nonpharmacological treatments are effective for PMDD, including group and individual psychotherapy, biofeedback, relaxation therapy, diet, exercise, and dietary supplements (Servino & Gold, 1994; Yonkers & Brown, 1996; Yonkers et al., 1997; Zerbe, 1999). Although there continues to be a need for more research on biopsychosocial models of the experience of menstruation and PMDD (Stanton, Lobel, Sears, & Stein Deluca, 2002), a primary care psychologist can encourage discussion among health care professionals regarding the diagnosis and treatment of PMDD. The psychologist can also provide assessment and nonpharmacological treatment to patients diagnosed with PMDD symptoms.

Menopause

Menopause, commonly defined as the last menstrual period and loss of ovarian activity, raises controversy in regard to its definition, course, and the role of intervention. Women live one third of their lives after ceasing to have reproductive capacity, and the majority of menopausal women report happiness, greater marital harmony, and more enjoyment in life after their children have left home (Zerbe, 1999). Some common complaints associated with menopause are depression, anxiety, joint pain, headaches, insomnia, loss of sexual interest, hot flashes, and vaginal dryness and atrophy; however this cluster of syndromes has not been confirmed by research (Derry, Gallant, & Woods, 1997). In fact, the only symptoms that are reliably associated with menopause are vasomotor symptoms (e.g., hot flashes, night sweats) and vaginal changes (e.g., dryness; Coope, 1996; Derry et al., 1997; Gallant & Derry, 1995). Several studies have found that menopausal women do have increased incidence of dysphoria, depression, irritability, anxiety, concentration and memory problems, and feeling unable to cope (Porter, Penny, & Russell, 1996; Sherwin, 1993; Shimp & Smith, 2000). However, psychosocial factors may be more predictive of depression in midlife women than menopause per se (Stanton et al., 2002). Mechanisms that may exist between menopause and depression remain uncertain, suggesting a need for multifaceted and comprehensive intervention (Ayubi-Moak & Parry, 2002). The primary care psychologist can play a role in assessing the patient's current symptoms and concerns, such as discussing the potential risks and benefits of hormone replacement therapy (HRT) as an option with the patient and health care professional and exploring alternative treatment options for women who do not elect HRT. Stress management, physical activity, and decreasing caffeine and alcohol use may help to reduce menopausal symptoms (Derry et al., 1997; Stanton et al., 2002). In addition, some women find previously resolved issues may resurface during menopause (e.g., ambivalence about not having children, loss of a parent at an early age), and for these women psychotherapy may be beneficial.

Pregnancy and Postpartum Related Issues

Pregnancy and postpartum periods are times of enormous transition and change in women's and families' lives, and women demonstrate greater risk of mental illness during these periods than at other times in their lives (Sharp, 1996; Zerbe, 1999). Regardless of the increased risk, most women adapt extremely well to pregnancy-related changes and do not demonstrate significant difficulties (Lobel, 1998; Stanton et al., 2002). Nevertheless, approximately 14% of pregnant women and 9% of postpartum women experience depression (Evans, Francomb, Oke, & Goldberg, 2001). In addition, a very small number of women experience psychotic and bipolar episodes associated with prenatal and postpartum periods. Although SSRIs are frequently used to treat prenatal and postpartum depressions, many women prefer to minimize or avoid the use of medications while pregnant or nursing. Interpersonal psychotherapy, client-centered psychotherapy, cognitive–behavioral therapy, and psychoeducation including partners are effective treatments for postpartum depression (Cooper & Murray, 1997; Holden, Sagovsky, & Cox, 1989; Misri, Kostaras, Fox, & Kostaras, 2000; O'Hara, Stuart, Gorman, & Wenzel, 2000; Wickberg & Hwang, 1996); several of these treatments are being studied with prenatal depression as well. The primary care psychologist can assist health care professionals in screening pregnant and postpartum patients and can provide assessment and psychotherapy to those experiencing difficulties. Pregnancy checks, obstetrical follow-up visits, and well-child exams all provide opportunities to assess women for prenatal or postpartum depression using written screening questionnaires or asking several brief questions about vegetative symptoms and other depressive symptomotology. There is also preliminary evidence to suggest that psychosocial interventions, such as a group treatment for women identified as at-risk for postpartum depression, may reduce the risk for onset of postpartum depression (Elliott et al., 2000).

Fertility

Infertility, the inability of a couple to conceive after one year of regular sexual intercourse without contraception or the inability to carry a pregnancy to live birth (Office of Technology Assessment [OTA], 1988), is present in approximately 7% of U.S. couples with a woman of child-bearing age (Abma, Chandra, Mosher, Peterson, & Piccinino, 1997). Couples who seek medical treatment for fertility problems engage in a complex process that may involve years of demanding procedures and disappointed hopes, with only a 50% success rate (OTA, 1988). Fertility issues are a couple's health problem, with few other medical problems having as profound an effect for both partners. Although the evidence suggests that there is no impairment in marital functioning as a result of fertility difficulties (Stanton & Danoff-Burg, 1995) and that seeking fertility treatment may in fact be related to increased marital satisfaction (Callan & Hennesey, 1988; Downey & McKinney, 1992), there is substantial variability in the impact it has for women and couples. Health care professionals can benefit from psychologists' support in helping women and couples navigate the complex, emotionally difficult, and ethically involved medical decisions. In addition, psychosocial interventions with women and couples can help with coping strategies, increasing a sense of control, reducing stress, and decision making (McDaniel & Speice, 2001; Pasch & Dunkel-Schetter, 1997; Stanton et al., 2002). For example, encouraging women and couples to identify active coping strategies such as relaxation training and moderate exercise and facilitating couples' decision making regarding what procedures they wish to pursue or not pursue can create a sense of increased empowerment.

Termination and Pregnancy Loss

Elective abortions, miscarriages, and late-term pregnancy losses can affect women and couples in diverse ways. Few women who have an abortion show negative psychological sequelae (Adler et al., 1992; Major et al., 2000). Most recover from miscarriage and pregnancy loss without intervention or significant difficulties within one year (Janssen, Cuisinier, Hoogduin, Kees, & de Graavw, 1996). However, some women who suffer these losses demonstrate symptoms of anxiety, grief, sadness, self-blame, anger, diminished libido, poor sleep quality, and general lack of well-being (Adler & Smith, 1998; Zerbe, 1999). Women and couples who must decide whether to terminate a desired pregnancy with a serious fetal anomaly are faced with a particularly difficult choice. These women are the most likely of those who choose termination to show adverse responses (Adler & Smith, 1998). Miscarriage, termination, and pregnancy loss can be difficult for the health care professional who must work closely with, and provide information, recommendations, and guidance to women. Health care professionals often are uncertain how to help women with losses. In such situations the psychologist can provide validation, education, and support to health care professionals. In addition, for the small proportion of women and couples for whom the loss becomes a crisis experience, the psychologist can provide intervention with grief counseling, couples therapy, and group psychotherapy as indicated.

Case Example

Mr. and Mrs. Z., aged 37 and 39, were a middle-class married couple eager to become parents. They each came from a large family with frequent gatherings for holidays, birthdays, and other events. After four years of fertility treatment and two miscarriages, they became pregnant, successfully completed their first trimester, and announced their news to family and friends. However Mr. and Mrs. Z. learned at 19 weeks that the baby tested positive for Trisomy 18 and were struggling to decide whether to keep or terminate the pregnancy. Mrs. Z. called her physician in tears asking for assistance.

Mr. and Mrs. Z. were offered an urgent appointment with the physician, genetic counselor, and primary care psychologist. Through discussions with their health care team, minister, and parents, they made the difficult choice to terminate the pregnancy through induced labor and delivery. The psychologist followed up with the couple to support them in their grieving process and helped them establish rituals meaningful to them, which involved naming the baby, a remembrance ceremony, and planting a tree at their home in her memory. The psychologist encouraged them to meet with the physician when they later had many questions. The physician who delivered Mr. and Mrs. Z.'s baby felt troubled by and responsible for their sadness. The physician and the psychologist had several conversations about the physician's feelings regarding her difficult role. Meanwhile, the psychologist continued to meet with Mr. and Mrs. Z. for the next year as they tried to move forward with their lives and decide if they wished to try again to become pregnant.

MENTAL HEALTH AND FAMILY ISSUES

Mental Illness

Women are more likely than men to develop certain types of mental illnesses. Depression is two to three more times common in women than men, with a lifetime prevalence rate of 20% to 26% for women versus 8% to 12% for men (Blazer, Kessler, McGonagle, & Schwartz, 1994; Henry, 2000; Kessler et al., 1994; Reiger, Burke, & Burke, 1990; Shapiro et al., 1984). Anxiety disorders are also more common in women than men, with more than 30% of women developing an anxiety disorder at some time in their lives (Henry, 2000). In addition, women are more likely than men to exhibit eating disorders, accounting for 90% of reported cases of anorexia nervosa and bulimia nervosa (Walters & Kendler, 1995).

At least 20% of women who make routine visits to their obstetrician–gynecologist meet criteria for mental health disorders using *DSM–IV* criteria (Spitzer, Williams, Kroenke, Hornyak, & McMurray, 2000). Screening for mental health problems has become more standard within primary care (Zerbe, 1999), and women are as likely to seek help for their mental illness from primary care professionals as they are from mental health professionals (Narrow, Reiger, Rae, Manderscheid, & Locke, 1993). However, patients who present first with physical symptoms can easily have their anxiety or depressive symptoms overlooked. The presence of a primary care psychologist provides a reminder to health care professionals to screen for psychosocial issues, such as the patient who is reporting chronic headaches who may be experiencing significant anxiety and stress. The primary care psychologist can provide crisis consultation to the health care provider when a patient discloses suicidal ideation or other acute symptomotology by determining the level of intervention needed, facilitating psychiatric referrals when appropriate, and providing follow-up care or referral elsewhere as indicated by the woman's needs.

Relationship Issues and Sexuality

Interpersonal relationships and sexual functioning are often overlooked aspects of women's health assessments. Women commonly derive meaning, satisfaction, and growth through their relationships (Baker Miller & Pierce Stiver, 1997). The partner relationship is typically one of the most central and important relationships in a woman's life, and marital status is related to health and mortality (Lasswell, 2002). Marital quality has been found to be associated with women's health as measured by immune, cardiovascular, endocrine, neurosensory, and other physiological factors (Kiecolt-Glaser & Glaser, 1992; Kiecolt-Glaser & Newton, 2001). As Speice and colleagues suggested, "A key component of providing health care for women is the recognition of the importance of these relationships and their associated implications for women's health" (Speice, Farley, & McDaniel, 2000, p. 304).

Sexual issues are important aspects of women's health that are disclosed frequently to the women's health care professional. Commonly presented concerns include low libido; differential expectations for the sexual relationship from their partner; painful intercourse; and trying to navigate heterosexual, bisexual, or lesbian sexual identity development. The primary care psychologist can play an important role in encouraging health care professionals to consider relationships and sexual functioning as important components of their health assessment and to offer suggestions for screening and assessment. The psychologist can also provide couple and family evaluations and interventions, including couples therapy, family therapy, and sex therapy as appropriate.

Case Example

Mrs. P., a 47-year-old married woman, was in for her annual exam. Although she did not bring up any psychosocial concerns spontaneously, when directly assessed she reported low-level chronic depressive symptomotology and relationship dissatisfaction. Although she was reluctant to engage in mental health treatment, she agreed to a consultation with the primary care psychologist.

After the initial meeting, Mrs. P. recognized that she had been distracting herself from some long-standing concerns for years and decided that she might benefit from psychotherapy. Through several months of psychotherapy she was able to understand and address the causes of her depressive symptoms and increase communication with her husband. At termination Mrs. P. acknowledged that she never would have engaged in psychotherapy if her health care professional had not recommended a trusted colleague and that she had benefited from the experience.

PRIMARY CARE PSYCHOLOGISTS' ROLE IN WOMEN'S HEALTH

The skills a primary care psychologist brings are beneficial in any women's health context. Following are several recommendations for primary care psychologists and other mental health professionals seeking to specialize in the area of women's health.

A Collaborative Biopsychosocial Approach

The primary care psychologist in women's health takes a lead role in establishing effective collaboration with a team of health care professionals and others involved in women's health care. Developing an integrated approach to the diagnosis and treatment of physical and mental health problems with health care professionals allows the primary care psychologist to have a clearly defined and mutually agreed on role. Even if team members bring different treatment philosophies, they can share a common purpose and a shared paradigm in approaching their patients' health care (Seaburn, Lorenz, Gunn, Gawinski, & Mauksch, 1996). In this way, the patient is introduced to an integrated biopsychosocial approach to understanding her concerns and her treatment, rather than experiencing conflicting and confusing information and recommendations. The primary care psychologist can collaborate effectively, regardless of whether her or his office is on-site or located outside of the medical office. Good working relationships and regular communication among the health care professionals and others involved facilitates a cohesive and interdisciplinary approach. Community-based collaboration through local organizations such as churches, neighborhood recreation centers, and libraries can also be valuable in allowing the primary care psychologist to assist in linking women with health care services.

Woman-Centered Treatment

Any psychosocial intervention used must be woman-centered and flexible enough to meet the particular needs of the patient and her circumstances. Medical family therapy is one psychotherapy approach that may be particularly effective for women because of its focus on relationships, maintaining a sense of control and autonomy, and collaboration rather than hierarchy between health care professional, patient, and partner (McDaniel & Cole-Kelly, 2003; McDaniel, Hepworth, & Doherty, 1992). Medical family therapy proposes that the primary goals for the patient are to develop agency and communion. Agency (or empowerment) is defined as the ability to make personal choices in dealing with health, illness, and the health care system. Communion (or connection) is the strengthening of emotional and spiritual bonds that can be diminished by illness, disability, and contact with the health care system; it includes a sense of being cared for and loved and supported by a community of family, friends, and professionals. Collaboration reduces the power and hierarchical issues that can exist between health care professional and patient. Progress toward agency, communion, and collaboration allows the patient to maintain her individual autonomy in a relational context.

Interpersonal therapy is also particularly well suited for use in women's health settings. Interpersonal therapy is a brief form of psychotherapy that primarily addresses current emotional and relationship difficulties (Klerman, Weissman, Rounsaville, & Chevron, 1984; Stuart & Robertson, 2003). The goals of treatment in interpersonal therapy are identifying a problem area that may be the source of depression, such as interpersonal disputes, role transition, grief and loss, or interpersonal sensitivity, and developing strategies for coping with the problem area. Interpersonal therapy has been found to be effective for treating depression when compared to wait-list control, antidepressant medication, cognitive–behavioral therapy, and parenting education programs, and has been shown to be an effective treatment for depressed low-income adult women, women with postpartum depression, and adolescent women with depression (Elkin et al., 1989; O'Hara, Stuart, Gorman, & Wenzel, 2000); Rossello & Bernal, 1999; Spinelli & Endicott, 2003).

Group treatment, including group psychotherapy, support groups, multifamily groups, and psychoeducational groups, is another modality that can be particularly beneficial for women. The primary care psychologist with group skills can offer opportunities for women to obtain validation and normalization of their personal experience, facilitate their ability to disclose distressing experiences, improve support systems, increase problem-solving skills and self-esteem, and share their experiences and skills with others (Coons, Morgenstern, Hoffman, Striepe, & Burch, 2004). The primary care setting allows for groups to be cofacilitated by a psychologist and a health care professional, modeling a biopsychosocial conceptualization of the difficulties being discussed. Group treatment can be especially helpful for women who may feel isolated, such as those dealing with fertility problems, pregnancy loss, postpartum depression, and chronic pain. For example, there is evidence to suggest that group treatment may be helpful to couples struggling with infertility (Stewart et al., 1992).

Knowledge Base

The primary care psychologist specializing in women's health needs to be well-versed in several areas of psychology and related fields. Education in both health psychology and family psychology are extremely useful. Specific training in areas such as biofeedback, interpersonal psychotherapy, dialectical behavior therapy, and group psychotherapy also can be particularly beneficial. Familiarity with basics of women's reproductive anatomy; health problems frequently observed in women in primary care settings; and a rudimentary understanding of medications, surgery, and other biomedical interventions will allow the primary care psychologist to have a rough working knowledge when collaborating with patients, families, and professionals. Finally, by attending to current social and policy issues related to women's health the primary care psychologist can be sensitive to how these issues affect their patients and effectively advocate for their patients' needs.

CONCLUSION

Women have specific health care needs that are frequently missed or underserved. Primary care settings provide an excellent opportunity for the psychologist to recognize and remedy some of these needs. Women's health care should be collaborative; family-oriented; interdisciplinary; individualized; and sensitive to sex, gender, racial, cultural, religious, sexual orientation, and socioeconomic issues. Women's health care should consider the woman from the cellular to the behavioral levels, from the individual to the family, community, and social levels. As we continue to grow in our ability to provide accessible and comprehensive women's health care, there are many opportunities for improvement. Future directions include more community-based health care, increased support for prevention-based programs, less distinction between the biomedical and the psychological, parity of coverage by health insurances for mental health treatment, training that specifically prepares psychologists to work in the area of women's health, primary care psychologists' involvement in the education of women's health care professionals, and stronger participation in social advocacy for women's health.

REFERENCES

Abma, J. C., Chandra, A., Mosher, W. D., Peterson, L. S., & Piccinino, L. J. (1997). Fertility, family planning, and women's health: New data from the 1995 National Survey of Family Growth. National Center for Health Statistics. *Vital and Health Statistics, 23,* 1–114.

Adler, N. E., Boyce, T., Chesney, M. A., Folkman, S., & Syme, S. L. (1993). Socioeconomic inequalities in health: No easy solution. *Journal of the American Medical Association, 269,* 3140–3145.

Adler, N. S., & Coriell, M. (1997). Socioeconomic status and women's health. In S. J. Gallant, G. Puryear Keita, & R. Royak-Schaler (Eds.), *Health care for women: Psychological, social, and behavioral influences* (pp. 11–23). Washington, DC: American Psychological Association.

Adler, N. E., David, H. P, Major, B. N., Roth, S. H., Russo, N. F., & Wyatt, G. E. (1992). Psychological factors in abortion. *American Psychologist, 47,* 1194–1204.

Adler, N. E., & Smith, L. B. (1998). Abortion. In E. A. Blechman & K. D. Brownell (Eds.), *Behavioral medicine and women: A comprehensive handbook* (pp. 510–514). New York: Guilford Press.

Allen, J. G. (1995). *Coping with trauma: A guide to self-understanding.* Washington, DC: American Psychiatric Press.

American College of Obstetricians and Gynecologists. (1995). ACOG technical bulletin. Domestic violence, number 209. *International Journal of Gynaecology and Obstetrics, 51,* 161–170.

American Psychiatric Association. (1994). *Diagnostic and statistical manual of mental disorders* (4th ed.). Washington, DC: Author.

American Psychological Association. (1996). Research agenda for psychosocial and behavioral factors in women's health. In *Recommendations from the advisory committee of the psychosocial and behavioral factors in women's health: Creating an agenda for the 21st century conference.* Washington, DC: Author.

Ayubi-Moak, I., & Parry, B. L. (2002). Psychiatric aspects of menopause: Depression. In S. G. Kornstein & A. H. Clayton (Eds.), *Women's mental health: A comprehensive textbook* (pp. 132–143). New York: Guilford Press.

Baker Miller, J., & Pierce Stiver, I. (1997). *The healing connection: How women form relationships in therapy and in life.* Boston: Beacon Press.

Blazer, D. G., Kessler, R. C., McGonagle, K. A., & Schwartz, M. S. (1994). The prevalence and distribution of major depression in a national community sample: The National Comorbidity Survey. *American Journal of Psychiatry, 151,* 979–986.

Blumenthal, S. J., Matthews, K., & Weiss, S. M. (Eds.). (1994). *New research frontiers in behavioral medicine: Proceedings of the national conference* (Publication no. 94-3772). Washington, DC: National Institutes of Health.

Breslau, N., Davis, G. C., Peterson, E. L., Edward, L., & Schultz, L. (1997). Psychiatric sequelae of posttraumatic stress disorder in women. *Archives of General Psychiatry, 54,* 81–87.

Callan, V. J., & Hennessey, J. F. (1988). Emotional aspects and support in in vitro fertilization and embryo transfer programs. *Journal of in Vitro Fertilization and Embryo Transfer, 5,* 290–295.

Campbell, J., Kub, J. E., & Rose, L. (1996). Depression in battered women. *Journal of the American Medical Women's Association, 51,* 106–110.

Commonwealth Fund. (1993). *Commonwealth fund survey of women's health.* New York: Author.

Commonwealth Fund. (1998). *Commonwealth fund survey of health concerns across a woman's lifespan: 1998 survey of women's health.* New York: Author.

Coons, H. L., Morgenstern, D., Hoffman, E. M., Striepe, M. I., & Burch, C. (2004). Psychologists in women's primary care and obstetrics and gynecology: Consultation and treatment issues. In R. Frank, S. H. McDaniel, J. H. Bray, & M. Heldring (Eds.), *Primary care psychology* (pp. 209–226). Washington, DC: American Psychological Association.

Coope, J. (1996). Hormonal and non-hormonal interventions for menopausal symptoms. *Maturitas, 23,* 159–168.

Cooper, P. J., & Murray, L. (1997). The impact of psychological treatments of postpartum depression on maternal mood and infant development. In L. Murray & P. J. Cooper (Eds.), *Postpartum depression and child development* (pp. 201–220). New York: Guilford Press.

Davidson, J. (1993). Issues in the diagnosis of posttraumatic stress disorder. In J. M. Oldham, M. B. Riba, & A. Tasman (Eds.), *Review of psychiatry* (Vol. 21, pp. 141–156). Washington, DC: American Psychiatric Press.

Dempsey, K. C. (2000). Men and women's power relationships and the persisting inequitable division of housework. *Journal of Family Studies, 6,* 7–24.

Derry, P. S., Gallant, S., & Woods, N. F. (1997). Premenstrual syndrome and menopause. In S. J. Gallant, G. Puryear Keita, & R. Royak-Schaler (Eds.), *Health care for women: Psychological, social, and behavioral Influences* (pp. 203–220). Washington, DC: American Psychological Association.

Diamant, A. L., Wold, C., Spritzer, K., & Gelberg, L. (2000). Health behaviors, health status, and access to and use of health care: A population-based study of lesbian, bisexual, and heterosexual women. *Archives of Family Medicine, 9,* 1043–1051.

Downey, J., & McKinney, M. (1992). The psychiatric status of women presenting for infertility evaluation. *American Journal of Orthopsychiatry, 62,* 196–205.

Dreeben, O. (2001). Health status of African Americans. *Journal of Health and Social Policy, 14,* 1–17.

Eisenstat, S. A., & Bancroft, L. (1999). Primary care: Domestic violence. *New England Journal of Medicine, 341,* 886–892.

Elkin, I., Shea, M. T., Watkins, J. T., Imber, S. D., Collins, J. F., et al. (1989). National Institute of Mental Health Treatment of Depression Collaborative Research Program: General effectiveness of treatments. *Archives of General Psychiatry, 46,* 971–982.

Elliot, S. A., Leverton, T. J., Sanjack, M., Turner, H., Cowmeadow, P., Hopkins, J., et al. (2000). Promoting mental health after childbirth: A controlled trial of primary prevention of postnatal depression. *British Journal of Clinical Psychiatry, 39,* 223–241.

Evans, J. H., Francomb, H., Oke, S., & Golding, J. (2001). Cohort study of depressed mood during pregnancy and after childbirth. *British Medical Journal, 323,* 257–260.

Freeman, E. W., & Rickels, K. (1999). Characteristics of placebo responses in medical treatment of premenstrual syndrome. *American Journal of Psychiatry, 156,* 1403–1408.

Gallant, S., & Derry, P. (1995). Menarche, menstruation, and menopause: Psychological research and future directions. In A. Stanton & S. Gallant (Eds.), *The psychology of women's health: Progress and challenges in research and application* (pp. 199–259). Washington, DC: American Psychological Association.

Geronimus, A. T. (1992). The weathering hypotheses and the health of African-American women and infants: Evidence and speculations. *Ethnicity and Disease, 2,* 207–221.

Gold, J. H. (1997). Premenstrual dysphoric disorder: What's that? *Journal of the American Medical Association, 278,* 1024–1025.

Graber, J. A., & Brooks-Gunn, J. (1998). Puberty. In E. A. Blechman & K. D. Brownell (Eds.), *Behavioral medicine and women: A comprehensive handbook* (pp. 51–58). New York: Guilford Press.

Hall, N. R. S., Altman, F., & Blumenthal, S. J. (Eds.). (1996). *Mind–body interactions and disease and psychoneuroimmunological aspects of health and disease.* Orlando, FL: Health Dateline.

Heldring, M. (1998). Integrated primary care for women. In A. Blount (Ed.), *Integrated primary care* (pp. 247–260). New York: Norton.

Henry, J. G. A. (2000). Depression and anxiety. In M. A. Smith & L. A. Shimp (Eds.), *Women's health care: 20 common problems* (pp. 263–301). New York: McGraw-Hill.

Holden, J. M., Sagovsky, R., & Cox, J. L. (1989). Counselling in a general practice setting: Controlled study of health visitor intervention in treatment of postnatal depression. *British Medical Journal, 298,* 223–226.

Ingram, D., Makuc, D., & Kleinman, J. (1986). National and state trends in use of prenatal care, 1970–83. *American Journal of Public Health, 76,* 415–423.

Janssen, H., Cuisinier, M., Hoogduin, K., Kees, A. L., & de Graavw, K. (1996). Controlled prospective study on the mental health of women following pregnancy loss. *American Journal of Psychiatry, 153,* 226–230.

Kessler, R. C., McGonagle, K. A., Zhao, S., Nelson, C. B., Hughes, M., Eshleman, S., et al. (1994). Lifetime and 12-month prevalence of *DSM–III–R* psychiatric disorders in the United States: Results from the National Comorbidity Survey. *Archives of General Psychiatry, 51*, 8–19.

Kessler, R. C., & Mcleod, J. D. (1984). Sex differences in vulnerability to undesirable life events. *American Social Review, 49*, 620.

Kiecolt-Glaser, J. K., & Glaser, R. (1992). Psychoneuroimmunology: Can psychological interventions modulate immunity? *Journal of Consulting and Clinical Psychology, 60*, 569–575.

Kiecolt-Glaser, J. K., & Newton, T. L. (2001). Marriage and health: His and hers. *Psychological Bulletin, 127*, 472–503.

King, A. C., & Kiernan, M. (1997). Physical activity and women's health: Issue and future directions. In S. J. Gallant, G. Puryear Keita, & R. Royak-Schaler (Eds.), *Health care for women: Psychological, social, and behavioral Influences* (pp. 133–146). Washington, DC: American Psychological Association.

Klebanov, P. K., & Ruble, D. N. (1994). Toward an understanding of women's experience of menstrual cycle symptoms. In V. J. Adesso, D. M. Reddy, & R. Fleming (Eds.), *Psychological perspectives on women's health* (pp. 183–221). Washington, DC: Taylor & Francis.

Klerman, G. L., Weissman, M. M., Rounsaville, B. J., & Chevron, E. S. (1984). *Interpersonal psychotherapy of depression*. New York: Basic Books.

Koop, C. E. (1991). Foreword. In M. L. Rosenberg & M. A. Fenley (Eds.), *Violence in America: A public health approach*. New York: Oxford University Press.

Koss, M. P., Goodman, L. A., Browne, A., Puryear Keita, K., & Felipe Russo, N. (1994). *No safe haven: Male violence against women at home, at work, and in the community*. Washington, DC: American Psychological Association.

Kyriakidis, M., Petropoulakis, P., Androulakis, A., Antonopoulos, A., Apostolopoulos, T., Barbetseas, J., et al. (1995). Sex differences in the anatomy of coronary artery disease. *Journal of Clinical Epidemiology, 48*, 723–730.

Lasswell, M. (2002). Marriage and family. In S. G. Kornstein & A. H. Clayton (Eds.), *Women's mental health: A comprehensive textbook* (pp. 515–526). New York: Guilford Press.

La Veist, T. A., Keith, V. M., & Guiterrez, M. L. (1995). Black/white differences in prenatal care utilization: An assessment of predisposing and enabling factors. *Health Services Research, 30*, 43–52.

Laws, A. (1998). Sexual abuse. In E. A. Blechman & K. D. Brownell (Eds.), *Behavioral medicine and women: A comprehensive handbook* (pp. 470–474). New York: Guilford Press.

Lobel, M. (1998). Pregnancy and mental health. In H. Friedman (Ed.), *Encyclopedia of mental health* (pp. 229–238). San Diego, CA: Academic Press.

Major, B., Cozzarelli, C., Cooper, M. L., Zubek, J., Richards, C., Wilhite, M., et al. (2000). Psychological responses of women after first-trimester abortion. *Archives of General Psychiatry, 57*, 777–784.

McDaniel, S. H., & Cole-Kelly, K. (2003). Gender, couples, and illness: A feminist analysis of medical family therapy. In T. Goodrich & L. Silverstein (Eds.), *Feminist family therapy* (pp. 267–280). Washington, DC: American Psychological Association.

McDaniel, S. H., Hepworth, J., & Doherty, W. J. (1992). *Medical family therapy: A biopsychosocial approach to families with health problems*. New York: Basic Books.

McDaniel, S. H., & Speice, J. (2001). What family psychology has to offer women's health: The examples of conversion, somatization, infertility treatment, and genetic testing. *Professional Psychology: Research and Practice, 32,* 44–51.

McFarlane, J. M. (1998). Premenstrual disorders. In E. A. Blechman & K. D. Brownell (Eds.), *Behavioral medicine and women: A comprehensive handbook* (pp. 457–462). New York: Guilford Press.

McNair, L. D., & Roberts, G. W. (1998). In E. A. Blechman & K. D. Brownell (Eds.), *Behavioral medicine and women: A comprehensive handbook* (pp. 821–825). New York: Guilford Press.

Melnick, S., Sherer, R., Louis, T. A., Hillman, D., Rodriquez, E. M., Lackman, C., et al. (1994). Survival and disease progression according to gender of patients with HIV infection: The Terry Beirn Community Programs for Clinical Research on AIDS. *Journal of the American Medical Association, 272,* 1915–1921.

Misra, D. (Ed.). (2001). *Women's health data book: A profile of women's health in the United States* (3rd ed.). Washington, DC: Jacobs Institute of Women's Health and the Henry J. Kaiser Family Foundation.

Misri, S., Kostaras, X., Fox, D., & Kostaras, D. (2000). The impact of partner support in the treatment of postpartum depression. *Canadian Journal of Psychiatry, 45,* 554–558.

Narrow, W., Reiger, D., Rae, D., Manderscheid, R. W., & Locke, B. Z. (1993). Use of services by persons with mental and addictive disorders. *Archives of General Psychiatry, 50,* 95–107.

National Center for Health Statistics. (1996). *Health, United States 1995* (DHHS Publication No. [PHS] 96-1232). Hyattsville, MD: U.S. Public Health Service.

Office of Technology Assessment, U.S. Congress. (1988). *Infertility: Medical and social choices* (Publication No. OTA-BA-358). Washington, DC: U.S. Government Printing Office.

O'Hara, M. W., Stuart, S., Gorman, L. L., & Wenzel, A. (2000). Efficacy of interpersonal psychotherapy for postpartum depression. *Archives of General Psychiatry, 57,* 1039–1045.

Park, J., & Buechner, J. S. (1997). Race, ethnicity, and access to health care, Rhode Island, 1990. *Journal of Health and Social Policy, 9,* 1–14.

Pasch, L. A., & Dunkel-Schetter, C. (1997). Fertility problems: Complex issues faced by women and couples. In S. J. Gallant, G. Puryear Keita, & R. Royak-Schaler (Eds.), *Health care for women: Psychological, social, and behavioral influences* (pp. 187–201). Washington, DC: American Psychological Association.

Perry-Jenkins, M. (1993). Family roles and responsibilities: What has changed and what has remained the same? In J. Frankel (Ed.), *The employed mother and the family context. Focus on women series* (Vol. 14, pp. 245–259). New York: Springer.

Porter, M., Penny, G. C., & Russell, D. (1996). A population-based survey of women's experience of the menopause. *British Journal of Obstetrics and Gynaecology, 103,* 1025–1028.

Radford, J., & Russell, D. E. H. (Eds.). (1992). *Femicide: The politics of woman killing.* New York: Twayne.

Reiger, D. A., Burke, J. D., & Burke, K. C. (1990). Comorbidity of affective and anxiety disorders in the NIMH Epidemiologic Catchment Area program. In J. D. Maser & C. R. Cloninger (Eds.), *Comorbidity of mood and anxiety disorders* (pp. 113–122). Washington, DC: American Psychiatric Press.

Resnick, H. S., Kilpatrick, D. G., Dansky, B. S., Saunders, B. E., & Best, E. (1993). Prevalence of civilian trauma and posttraumatic stress disorder in a representative national sample of women. *Journal of Consulting and Clinical Psychology, 61,* 984–991.

Rossello, J., & Bernal, G. (1999). The efficacy of cognitive–behavioral and interpersonal treatments for depression in Puerto Rican adolescents. *Journal of Consulting and Clinical Psychiatry, 67,* 734–745.

Russell, D. E. H. (1986). *The secret trauma.* New York: Basic Books.

Seaburn, D. B., Lorenz, A. D., Gunn, W. B., Gawinski, B. A., & Mauksch, L. B. (1996). *Models of collaboration: A guide for mental health professionals working with health care practitioners.* New York: Basic Books.

Servino, S. K., & Gold, J. H. (1994). Summation. In J. H. Gold & S. K. Servino (Eds.), *Premenstrual dysphorias: Myths and realities* (pp. 231–248). Washington, DC: American Psychiatric Press.

Shapiro, A., Skinner, E. A., Kessler, L. G., Von Korff, M., German, P. S., Tischler, G. L., et al. (1984). Utilization of health and mental health services: Three Epidemiologic Catchment Area sites. *Archives of General Psychiatry, 41,* 971–978.

Sharp, D. (1996). The prevention of postnatal depression. In T. Kendrick, A. Tylee, & P. Freeling (Eds.), *The prevention of mental illness in primary care* (pp. 57–73). Cambridge, MA: Cambridge University Press.

Sherwin, B. B. (1993). Menopause: Myths and realities. In D. E. Stewart & N. Stotland (Eds.), *Psychological aspects of women's health care: The interface between psychiatry and obstetrics and gynecology* (pp. 227–248). Washington, DC: American Psychiatric Press.

Shimp, L. A., & Smith, M. A. (2000). Menopause. In M. A. Smith & L. A. Shimp (Eds.), *Women's health care: 20 common problems* (pp. 91–131). New York: McGraw-Hill.

Speice, J., Farley, A., & McDaniel, S. (2000). Relational problems. In M. A. Smith & L. A. Shimp (Eds.), *Women's health care: 20 common problems* (pp. 303–320). New York: McGraw-Hill.

Spinelli, M. G., & Endicott, J. (2003). Controlled clinical trial of interpersonal psychotherapy versus parenting education program for depressed pregnant women. *American Journal of Psychiatry, 160,* 555–562.

Spitzer, R. L., Williams., J. B., Kroenke, K., Hornyak, R., & McMurray, J. (2000). Validity and utility of the PRIME–MD Patient Health Questionnaire in assessment of 3000 obstetric–gynecologic patients: The PRIME–MD Patient Health Questionnaire Obstetrics–Gynecology Study. *American Journal of Obstetrics and Gynecology, 183,* 759–769.

Stanton, A. L., & Danoff-Burg, S. (1995). Selected issues in women's reproductive health: Psychological perspectives. In A. L. Stanton & S. J. Gallant (Eds.), *The psychology of women's health: Progress and challenges in research and application* (pp. 261–305). Washington, DC: American Psychological Association.

Stanton, A. L., Lobel, M., Sears, S., & Stein DeLuca, R. (2002). Psychosocial aspects of selected issues in women's reproductive health: Current status and future directions. *Journal of Consulting and Clinical Psychology, 70,* 751–770.

Stewart, D. E., Boydell, K. M., McCarthy, K., Swerdlyk, S., Redmond, C., & Cohrs, W. (1992). A prospective study of the effectiveness of brief professionally-led support groups for infertility patients. *International Journal of Psychiatry in Medicine, 22,* 173–182.

Stuart, S., & Robertson, M. (2001). *Interpersonal psychotherapy: A clinician's guide.* New York: Oxford University Press.

Swanson, N. G., Piotrokowski, C. S., Puryear Keita, G., & Becker, A. B. (1997). Occupational stress and women's health. In S. J. Gallant, G. Puryear Keita, & R. Royak-Schaler (Eds.), *Health care for women: Psychological, social, and behavioral influences* (pp. 147–159). Washington, DC: American Psychological Association.

U.S. Department of Health and Human Services. (1990). *National Center for Health Statistics: Health, United States, 1989* (DHHS Publication no. HS 90-1232). Washington, DC: U.S. Government Printing Office.

Wagner, P. J., Mongan, P., Hamrick, D., & Hendrick, L. K. (1995). Experience of abuse in primary care patients: Racial and rural differences. *Archives of Family Medicine, 4,* 956–962.

Walters, E. E., & Kendler, K. S. (1995). Anorexia nervosa and anorexic-like syndromes in a population-based female twin sample. *American Journal of Psychiatry, 152,* 64–71.

Weinick, R. M., Zuvekas, S. H., & Cohen, J. H. (2000). Racial and ethnic differences in access to and use of health care services, 1977 to 1996. *Medical Care Research and Review, 57,* 36–54.

Wickberg, B., & Hwang, C. P. (1996). Counseling of postnatal depression: A controlled study on a population based Swedish sample. *Journal of Affective Disorders, 39,* 209–216.

Wizemann, T. M., & Pardue, M. (Eds.). (2001). *Exploring the biological contributions to human health: Does sex matter?* Washington, DC: National Academy Press.

Williams, D. R. (1999). Race, socioeconomic status, and health. The added effects of racism and discrimination. *Annals of the New York Academy of Sciences,* 896, 173–188.

Yonkers, K. A., & Brown, W. A. (1996). Pharmacologic treatments for premenstrual dysphoric disorder. *Psychiatric Annals, 26,* 586–589.

Yonkers, K. A., Halbreich, U., Freeman, E., Brown, L., Endicott, J., Frank, E., et al. (1997). Symptomatic improvement of premenstrual dysphoric disorder with sertraline treatment: A randomized controlled trial. *Journal of the American Medical Association, 278,* 983–988.

Zerbe, K. J. (1999). *Women's mental health in primary care.* Philadelphia: W.B. Saunders.

12

WOMEN'S SEXUAL ISSUES IN PRIMARY CARE

MEG I. STRIEPE

This chapter reviews theory, research, and interventions that are currently in the forefront of women's sexual health. A historical review of how women's sexuality has been defined is included to provide the context of how the field is advancing. Case examples based on the author's clinical experience are used to explain various aspects of practice. Throughout the chapter an interdisciplinary collaborative approach, which is fitting for primary care settings, is illustrated. The approach described is based on women's health theory and models of practice (Coons et al., 2002). This collaborative approach can be applied and tailored for any practice environment, including obstetrics–gynecology, family practice, and independent practice. Whatever the setting, it is important to have a network of health care practitioners who communicate and operate with compatible models of care. Furthermore, although the focus of this chapter is on adult women's sexuality, the approach has implications for treating male and female clients across the lifespan.

In addition to the pragmatics of addressing women's sexual health issues this chapter highlights what Belar and Deardorff (1995) defined as the multifaceted role of the clinical health psychologist, including assessment, intervention, and consultation. This chapter provides data and resources to facilitate clinical health psychologists taking a lead role in addressing women's sexual problems. For example, what are the issues and what role does a psychologist play when a physician colleague prescribes any female patient complaining of low desire a trial of testosterone?

Another role of the health psychologist is to practice evidence-based medicine. To date, there is a limited body of empirical literature on the diagnosis and treatment of women's sexual problems. Contrary to scientific method and the tenets of practicing evidenced-based medicine, a range of interventions are being prescribed before establishing a sound understanding of female sexual functioning. The current culture includes promoting bio-medical based treatment for sexual dysfunction (e.g., Berman & Berman, 2000; Urometrics, 2000) and studies investigating the effects of sildenafil (Viagra) on women (Basson, McInnes, Smith, Hodgson, & Koppiker, 2002; Caruso, Intelisano, Lupo, & Agnello, 2001; Kaplan et al., 1999; Laan et al., 2002). The biomedical trend is not surprising given the genesis of how women's sexual functioning has been defined. The next section provides the historical context of how women's sexuality has been defined and examines some of the limitations of the model.

HISTORY OF DEFINING WOMEN'S SEXUAL (DYS)FUNCTIONING

A Medical Model of Sexuality

Masters and Johnson's (1966) human sexual response cycle model (HSRCM) defined sexuality in many disciplines, including medicine and psychology. In fact, the language of the HSRCM is so ingrained it is hard to think about sexual response without framing it in terms of *excitement, plateau, orgasm*, and *resolution phases*. Masters and Johnson (1970) deserve honorable recognition for establishing a model that advanced sexuality as being part of science. Theoretically for psychologists, it moved the field of sex therapy from conceptualizing sexual problems as a manifestation of childhood experiences or trauma to anxieties being the basis for poor sexual performance. As a consequence, the psychological treatments of sexual problems are usually grounded in the tenets of learning theory and behavior therapy.

According to Masters and Johnson, a normal sexual response was defined using a linear model and includes a person going through discrete phases of physiological and anatomical changes. Reaching and experiencing orgasm (primarily assumed to be intravaginally) was defined as a necessary phase to be deemed normal. Kaplan (1979) later modified the model and presented "normal" as three phases—desire, excitement, and orgasm. The pragmatic result was that a phase of desire before arousal got added on to the HSRCM, although it was uncertain about what constituted desire. Subsequently, the American Psychiatric Association's diagnostic criteria as published in the *Diagnostic and Statistical Manual of Mental Disorders* (*DSM–IV*; American Psychiatric Association, 1994) reflect the HSRCM model of normality.

However, current research and clinical practice suggest that the HSRCM and hence the *DSM–IV* (American Psychiatric Association, 1994) categorization is not a definitive model of sexual normality for women (Basson, 1999; see Kaschak & Tiefer, 2001; Ogden, 1999; Striepe, 2002). Identified limitations include that the HSRCM is not gender-specific and assumes orgasm is necessary for normal functioning. It is a linear model based on physical–physiological changes, which does not account for the context in which sexuality happens. Furthermore the *DSM–IV* (American Psychiatric Association, 1994) assumes heterosexual orientation as part of "normal" sexuality and that female functioning parallels male functioning—in other words, penile functioning. As a consequence, penile–vaginal intercourse becomes the referent for sexual performance.

In short, Masters and Johnson's research was based on volunteers and measured physiological changes; it is inappropriate to generalize the findings as normal for all individuals. In general, there is a dearth of empirical research on what can be considered normal for female sexual functioning. The HSRCM is what has defined normality since the 1960s and our current understanding of women's sexual functioning. One of the effects of the current nosology is that it often reinforces the belief that there is something wrong with the woman who presents with a sexual problem.

Despite the limitations of the *DSM–IV* (American Psychiatric Association, 1994), it is the nosology that clinicians are often required to use to receive reimbursement by present insurance policies. Sexual dysfunction for males and females is currently classified into the following four categories: (a) sexual desire disorders, including hypoactive sexual desire and sexual aversion disorder; (b) sexual arousal disorders, including female sexual arousal disorder and erectile disorder; (c) orgasmic disorders, including female and male orgasmic disorder; and (d) sexual pain disorders, including dyspareunia and vaginismus. Psychologists are in a unique position to gather information beyond the diagnostic criteria. Consider the following case.

Case Example 1

Karen, a 28-year-old, single, White woman, went to her gynecologist for help with low sexual desire. Her gynecologist completed a physical exam and checked lab values. The gynecologist noted that her testosterone level was on the low side and prescribed testosterone to boost sexual desire. After

3 months there was no improvement in Karen's level of desire and the gynecologist referred her to the psychologist next door. The psychologist explained the biopsychosocial nature of sexuality and the necessity of a thorough evaluation. Initially Karen was resistant to talking about the problem and wanted the testosterone quick fix she had heard in the media. However, it did not take long for Karen to engage in the evaluation and see other pieces that seemed connected to her low desire. For example, when asked about her sexual identity it became evident that Karen was conflicted about her sexual identity and did not really want to be with her current fiancé. However, she felt tremendous pressure to continue her plans of getting married and had never talked to anyone about her sexual orientation or gender ideology. With this additional piece of data, testosterone alone would not be indicated to help Karen. It appeared that she was trying to be sexual with a man she did not feel sexually attracted to and she did not like her sexual role. As a consequence, the first step of treatment in this case of low sexual desire was to ask about the different aspects of sexuality, including orientation and her ideology of being a sexual female. The gynecologist appreciated receiving the psychologist's report and began consulting with the psychologist when addressing sexual issues.

This example demonstrates the importance of defining sexuality beyond the *DSM–IV* (American Psychiatric Association, 1994) and questioning the assumptions of heterosexuality. It also highlights the value of a clinical health psychologist interfacing with physicians to treat sexual issues. Research indicates that individuals are most comfortable talking to their physicians about sexual issues (Metz & Siefert, 1988) and consequently seek medical help for sexual problems. Today physicians are more pressed than ever to provide quality care with a limited amount of time. This is one of the main reasons sexuality does not routinely get addressed in primary care. Other reasons include discomfort talking about sexuality, preoccupation with treating the disease and not the person, and inadequate training and resources (Merrill, Laux, & Thornby, 1990). Clinical health psychologists can play a key role in informing clients about the multifactorial nature of sexuality and the collaborative nature of treatment.

ASSESSMENT OF SEXUAL PROBLEMS

The Pull for the "Quick Fix"

As indicated in the first case, it is likely that the psychologist or other practitioner will experience a pull from the client, physician, partner, insurance company, and within their own self to "fix" the sexual problem quickly. In addition, clients often come with reams of timely information from the media and Internet, especially in the case of sexual problems, which are not commonly talked about. This is a good opportunity for practitioners to evaluate the resource and teach clients to be wise consumers of health care information. The most important thing for practitioners to know is that to date an isolated cause of women's sexual problems has not been identified.

Hormonal Quick Fixes

The question of hormonal replacement or of hormonal supplementation—for example, testosterone—is a common presenting question. It is beyond the scope of this chapter to review the possible pathways that hormones interact with sexual functioning (see Dennerstein, 1997; Graham & Sherwin, 1993; Sanders, 2001). Nonetheless it is important to collaborate with a physician who works with the woman to tailor a hormonal regimen that works for the client. Currently there is no evidence to predict which style of hormonal therapy—progesterone and/or estrogen—will be best for the woman (Feldman, 2002). Furthermore, the role of progesterone in sexual desire is unclear. In regards to testosterone, Feldman (2002) reported that there is no definition of hypo testosterone in women and no evidence (expect anecdotal) for supplementation in premenopausal women. In some cases, testosterone supplementation in postmenopausal women and women with surgical menopause has been found to be effective in treating sexual dysfunction (Shifren, 2000).

As with other health-related problems, clinical health psychologists are well equipped to handle a complicated etiology. It is recommended that communication between the patient, physician, partner, and other practitioners take place to establish realistic expectations and treatment goals. The good news is that once women start the process of evaluation and treatment planning, including receiving information and playing a role in the decision making, they realize they no longer have to try and do it all alone. Women often report a sense of relief knowing there is help for a sexual problem that is often surrounded by secrecy and shame.

In summary, it is important to have a sound model of women's sexual health to complete an assessment, develop a treatment plan, and practice evidence-based medicine.

Case Example 2

Maria, a 26-year-old Latino woman, came to her primary care clinic for a routine annual exam. Her primary care physician asked if she had any concerns. Maria hesitated, but decided if there was one person who could help her it was her doctor. She proceeded to tell her doctor, "I think there is something wrong with me, maybe it's my hormones, I don't have orgasms anymore." Her doctor felt a little caught off guard, but asked how long she had noticed the problem. Maria stated since the birth of their youngest child 16 months ago. The doctor asked about any problems with pain or lubrication during sexual activity. Maria denied any such problems. The doctor assured her that it is normal to go through such changes after having a baby and told her she seemed stressed and to be patient and just keep trying.

With this information in the *DSM–IV* (American Psychiatric Association, 1994), the diagnosis of female orgasmic disorder is indicated. It is important to determine if a sexual problem is lifelong or acquired and situational or generalized. For instance, to ask Maria if she had an orgasm without her husband—for example, "do you experience orgasm when masturbating?" Explicit questions about the subjective experience of being sexual are needed to render an accurate diagnosis. In this case, it would be important to rule out hypoactive sexual desire disorder, acquired with her husband. It would also be important to rule out abuse in the relationship. This example illustrates how consequential it is to gather the specifics based on the context in which the problem occurs. Gathering specifics about the context of being sexual requires talking about sex.

SEXUALITY: A MISSING DISCOURSE

Sex. How is it you respond to the word? This is the place practitioners need to start. Specialized therapy for sexual issues may start with asking clients the question, "What comes to mind when you hear and see the word *sex?*" The clients' response gives an indication of what and how they associate with the word. More often than not sex is assumed to mean penile–vaginal intercourse, and women seeking help for sexual problems respond with descriptors that have a negative valence—for example, painful, obligation, messy, tired, boring, yuck (Striepe, 2002). In contrast, their goals for therapy are to feel positive about being sexual and be full of sexual desire.

The recent U.S. surgeon general's *Call to Action to Promote Sexual Health and Responsible Sexual Behavior* (Satcher, 2001) advances the importance of defining sexuality beyond dysfunction. The report stated,

> Sexual health is not limited to the absence of disease or dysfunction, nor is its importance confined to just the reproductive years. It includes the ability to understand and weigh the risks, responsibilities, outcomes and impacts of sexual actions and to practice abstinence when appropriate. It includes freedom from sexual abuse and discrimination and the ability of individuals to integrate their sexuality into their lives,

derive pleasure from it, and reproduce if they so choose. (Satcher, 2001, p. 1)

This definition lays down a foundation that supports *sex* as being more than an act and not about needing to please a partner. In addition there is not one "normal" way to be sexual, and people have choices in how they want to express their sexuality. Applying this definition to female sexual functioning results in an understanding that is counter to the current zeitgeist that female sexuality is a risk.

Thus when working with issues of sexuality it is important that the practitioner has done some self-reflection on personal beliefs, values, and experiences. For example, how a practitioner feels about gay, lesbian, bisexual, or transgender individuals and their sexual preferences or the topic of sadomasochist practices will influence how a person is assessed. Thus before assessing people with sexual problems it is recommended that practitioners evaluate their own assumptions and comfort level to prevent making judgments. This is not to say that practitioners need to agree with all the diverse ways people are sexual, but as responsible and ethical providers of care it is necessary to know biases and deal with them to prevent the patient from receiving misinformation or suboptimal treatment. It is also important to know that different ways of being sexual can be healthy and considered normal. Defining sex as part of health requires a paradigm shift.

A "NEW VIEW" OF WOMEN'S SEXUAL HEALTH

Choosing women's sexual *health* versus *dysfunction* was deliberate and purposeful because health is the cornerstone of the collaborative approach and new view classification of women' sexuality (Kaschak & Tiefer, 2001) described in this section. Consistent with the theorems of health psychology (Belar & Deardorff, 1995), it is hoped that the emphasis on health will underscore the complexity of sexuality and displace the current pathological interpretations of female sexual problems. The new view campaign is an independent grassroots organization and includes researchers, clinicians, educators, and advocates of women's health working to advance the area of female sexuality (Kaschak & Tiefer, 2001). The new view approach is consistent with a scientist–practitioner's model of women's sexual health. It is based on a critique of empirical evidence, and the application generates clinical applications that support practicing evidence-based medicine. See Exhibit 12.1 for the new view classification system (see Kaschak & Tiefer, 2001).

It is recommended that the new view classification system guide the collection of assessment data that is critical for diagnosis and treatment

EXHIBIT 12.1
Women's Sexual Problems: A New Classification

Sexual problems, which the Working Group (Tiefer) on a New View of Women's Sexual Problems defines as discontent or dissatisfaction with any emotional, physical, or relational aspect of sexual experience, may arise in one or more of the following interrelated aspects of women's sexual lives.

I. *Sexual problems as a result of sociocultural, political, or economic factors*
A. ignorance and anxiety as a result of inadequate sex education, lack of access to health services, or other social constraints:
1. lack of vocabulary to describe subjective or physical experience;
2. lack of information about human sexual biology and life-stage changes;
3. lack of information about how gender roles influence men's and women's sexual expectations, beliefs, and behaviors;
4. inadequate access to information and services for contraception and abortion, sexually transmitted disease prevention and treatment, sexual trauma, and domestic violence;
5. sexual avoidance or distress because of perceived inability to meet cultural norms regarding correct or ideal sexuality, including
a. anxiety or shame about one's body, sexual attractiveness, or sexual responses;
b. confusion or shame about one's sexual orientation or identity or about sexual fantasies and desires;
6. inhibitions as a result of conflict between the sexual norms of one's subculture or culture of origin and those of the dominant culture;
7. lack of interest, fatigue, or lack of time as a result of family and work obligations.

II. *Sexual problems relating to partner and relationship*
A. inhibition, avoidance, or distress arising from betrayal, dislike, or fear of partner; partner's abuse or couple's unequal power; or partner's negative patterns of communication;
B. discrepancies in desire for sexual activity or in preferences for various sexual activities;
C. ignorance or inhibition about communicating preferences or initiating, pacing, or shaping sexual activities;
D. loss of sexual interest and reciprocity as a result of conflicts over commonplace issues such as money, schedules, or relatives, or resulting from traumatic experiences—for example, infertility or the death of a child;
E. inhibitions in arousal or spontaneity as a result of partner's health status or sexual problems.

(continued)

planning. Consider the application of the new view continuing the case of Maria in case example 2.

When asked about her partner and relationship, Maria reported that she did not really want a second child but her husband refused to use birth control. She also felt pressured to be sexual with him because if she did not he would complain publicly about her being "frigid" and threaten her emotionally and financially, saying "I will find another woman and you can

EXHIBIT 12.1 (Continued)

III. Sexual problems as a result of psychological factors
  A. sexual aversion, mistrust, or inhibition of sexual pleasure due to:
      1. past experiences of physical, sexual, or emotional abuse;
      2. general personality problems with attachment, rejection, cooperation, or entitlement;
      3. depression or anxiety.
  B. sexual inhibition as a result of fear of sexual acts or of their possible consequences—for example, pain during intercourse, pregnancy, sexually transmitted disease, loss of partner, loss of reputation.

IV. Sexual problems due to medical factors
  Pain or lack of physical response during sexual activity despite a supportive and safe interpersonal situation, adequate sexual knowledge, and positive sexual attitudes. Such problems can arise from
  A. numerous local or systemic medical conditions affecting neurological, neurovascular, circulatory, endocrine, or other systems of the body;
  B. pregnancy, sexually transmitted diseases, or other sex-related conditions;
  C. side effects of many drugs, medications, or medical treatments;
  D. iatrogenic conditions.

Note. From *Women's Sexual Problems: A New Classification*, by Leonore Tiefer. Reprinted with permission of Leonore Tiefer, convenor of New View campaign, http://www.fsd-alert.org/manifesto.html

go live elsewhere." Maria further explained that she felt it was her role to please him sexually and he stated that if she did not have an orgasm that she is rejecting him. Furthermore since the birth of her baby, Maria reported feeling fatigued and "blue." She stated that she takes care of all the domestic duties. However, when asked Maria reported she has sexual fantasies and has masturbated since the birth of her baby and finds this very pleasurable. She reported she has never told anyone because she thought this was a way of cheating on her husband, with the thinking that if she masturbated she certainly would not have any sexual desire or orgasms left over for him.

With this clinical data, the diagnosis of female orgasmic disorder is still present but it is acquired and situational in that the problem only happens with her husband. The complexity of sexuality becomes apparent, and there is self-report data that Maria does not have biomedical complications with orgasm, given she masturbates and finds the experience pleasurable. It also appears that she has low sexual desire toward her husband. In this case, it is necessary to further determine the context in which she is "trying" to be sexual and to further understand why she cannot say no to her husband. It is also necessary to assess for abuse, because for some women saying no to sex places them at risk for abuse.

The unfortunate outcome of prescribing interventions without an adequate evaluation is that underlying factors that can affect sexual functioning are missed—for example, adhering to a conventional feminine role of needing to please a partner, can result in repeated negative sexual experiences and only make the problem worse. With this in mind it is important to state that women's sexual experiences take place in a patriarchal society, which means that women as strong as they may appear in other facets of their life are often set up to have powerless experiences when being sexual. Be aware that although the experience may not register as a trauma on a measurement or a practitioner's own internal scale, only the client can define the nature of the incident. Furthermore, physical manifestations may be the initial complaint in cases of trauma. During the evaluation, it is critical to use the narrative as a diagnostic tool—that is, listen for what is and what is not there and assess for traumatic sexual experiences. Screening explicitly for domestic violence is helpful because it gives the message that the practitioner identifies psychosocial issues as part of health. However, individuals who have experienced a type of trauma are not always able to identify their experiences as "traumatic," including experiences of rape and sexual coercion. Furthermore, a practitioner who is quick to label the person with a diagnosis or invalidate the person's experience can be repeating a traumatic pattern without being aware of it. When trauma is part of the picture, obtaining the woman's permission to talk to other team members about possible triggers in the medical setting or the patient–practitioner relationship can help prevent retraumatization or exacerbation of symptoms. Thus the trust between the practitioner and client is critical in the evaluation process to ensure privacy and maintenance of healthy boundaries.

The Role of the Psychiatrist and Psychopharmacology

In this case, Maria indicated having symptoms of depression, which is common among women who report sexual problems (Feldman, 2002; Raymond, 2002). Collaborating with a psychiatrist is often indicated to evaluate if the use of medications is indicated, differentiating sexual side effects because of medications and the interaction of mood disorders. Furthermore, consistent with a collaborative approach the role of the psychiatrist is to offer information regarding the side effects of medications and guide the woman in making the choice that best meets her needs. For example, it may be most beneficial for a woman to aggressively treat a depression rather than choose a less effective medication that has fewer sexual side effects. Untreated depression or anxiety can lead to sexual problems. Raymond (2002) recommended explaining that a psychiatric medication is not a quick fix for sexual problems and that the possible side effects need to be asked about explicitly during follow-up visits.

Treatment

Establishing a trusting rapport and completing a thorough assessment, which covers the aspects outlined in the new view, starts the process of treatment. The permission limited information specific suggestions intensive therapy (PLISSIT) model (Annon, 1976; Rosser, Coleman, & Ohmans, 1993) is an interdisciplinary model of care that can further guide practitioners in assessing and treating female sexual issues.

The Permission Limited Information Specific Suggestions Intensive Therapy Model of Intervention

The first step of the PLISSIT model is to obtain permission from the client to talk about sex. This can be done in a number of ways and may depend on the context of the interaction. Just as it is important to establish boundaries with any relationship, when addressing issues of sexuality the boundaries need to be clear, and this can be done during the first step. Each practitioner needs to complete this step with the client.

The second step is to give limited information. Often this step is effective in helping solve sexual problems, because women receive little information about pleasurable sex. For instance, premenopausal women often request lubrication to help ease physical discomfort when being sexual with a partner. She may not realize her own capacity to produce lubrication with stimulation. Providing a limited amount of information on how her body lubricates when aroused can help.

The third step, specific suggestions, includes detailed information specific for the person's presenting problem. To continue the case given earlier, providing specific suggestions on how the client can discover what stimulation feels good may help with lubrication. Including the partner is recommended. Another example of a specific suggestion is suggesting a client take time to learn self-massage to become more aware of bodily sensations.

The final step is intensive therapy with a practitioner who is specialized in sexuality. Exhibit 12.2 lists excellent resources in this subject.

One strength of the PLISSIT model is that it supports interdisciplinary intervention. For example, it may be that the physician is completing the first step of the model and offering information, especially because women are more likely to seek help for their medical concerns (Coons, Morgenstern, Hoffman, Striepe, & Buch, in press). However, it is recommended that each provider repeat the permission step and discuss the boundaries of confidentiality. Especially when working with an interdisciplinary model, it is vital that the patient understand how information is shared and with whom and how she is a part of that process. Standard practice should include telling women how the team communicates and how she will receive feedback and not be "talked" about without discussing it with her first. This serves four important functions: (a) The woman is informed and is in a better position to communicate with her physician; (b) she gains a greater understanding of how a sexual problem is multifaceted; (c) she becomes a collaborative member of the team and is responsible for making decisions about her care; and (d) modeling effective communication with the client and other team members facilitates continuity of care.

CONCLUSION

The combination of the definition of sexual health and the new view classification system establishes a model of female sexual health to guide your work as a scientist–practitioner. A major limitation is that to date there is little empirical research on the application of the model. However in general there is little empirical data on women's sexuality. It is recommended that as clinical health psychologists we practice evidence-based medicine, including knowing the theory that guides our work.

REFERENCES

Annon, J. S. (1976). *Behavioral treatment of sexual problems: Brief therapy*. Oxford: Harper & Row.

American Psychiatric Association. (1994). *Diagnostic and statistical manual of mental disorders* (4th ed.). Washington, DC: Author.

Basson, R. (1999, October). *Use of an alternative model of women's sexual response cycle to address low sexual desire*. Paper presented at New Perspectives in the Management of Female Sexual Dysfunction, Boston University School of Medicine, Boston.

Basson, R., McInnes, R., Smith, M., Hodgson, G., & Koppiker, N. (2002). Efficacy and safety of sildenafil citrate in women with sexual dysfunction associated with female sexual arousal disorder. *Journal of Women's Health and Gender-Based Medicine, 11,* 357–365.

Belar, C. D., & Deardorff, W. W. (Eds.). (1995). *Clinical health psychology in medical settings: A practitioner's guidebook.* Washington, DC: American Psychological Association.

Berman, J., & Berman, L. (2000). *For women only.* New York: Henry Holt.

Caruso, S., Intelisano, G., Lupo, L., & Agnello, C. (2001). Premenopausal women affected by sexual arousal disorder treated with sildenafil: A double blind, placebo controlled study. *British Journal of Obstetrics and Gynecology, 108,* 623–628.

Coons, H. L., Morgenstern, D., Hoffman, E., Striepe, M., & Buch, C. (2002). Psychologists in women's primary care and obstetrics and gynecology: Consultation and treatment issues. In *Primary care psychology.* Washington, DC: American Psychological Association.

Coons, H. L., Striepe, M. I., Poleshuk, E., Braverman, A., Olken, J., Hoffman, E., et al. (2002, February). *Interdisciplinary care in women's health: Five models of practice.* Symposium conducted at the American Psychological Association's 2001 Women's Health Conference—Enhancing Outcomes in Women's Health: Translating Psychosocial and Behavioral Research into Primary Care, Community Interventions, and Health Policy, Washington, DC.

Dennerstein, L., Randolph, J., Taffe, J., Dudley, E., & Burger, H. (1997). Sexuality, hormones and the menopausal transition. *Maturitas, 26,* 83–93.

Feldman, J. (2002, February). Can't I just take Viagra?: Biomedical assessment and interventions in female sexual desire disorder. In M. Striepe (Chair), *Women's sexual health: An interdisciplinary treatment approach to low desire.* Symposium conducted at the American Psychological Association's 2001 Women's Health Conference—Enhancing Outcomes in Women's Health: Translating Psychosocial and Behavioral Research into Primary Care, Community Interventions, and Health Policy, Washington, DC.

Graham, C. A., & Sherwin, B. B. (1993). The relationship between mood and sexuality in women using an oral contraceptive as a treatment for premenstrual syndrome. *Psychoneuroendocrinology, 18,* 273–281.

Kaplan, H. S. (1979). *Disorders of sexual desire.* New York: Brunner/Mazel.

Kaplan, S. A., Reis, R. B., Kohn, I. J., Ikeguchi, E. F., Laor, E., Te, A. E., et al. (1999). Safety and efficacy of sildenafil in postmenopausal women with sexual dysfunction. *Urology, 53,* 481–486.

Kaschak, E., & Tiefer, L. (Eds.). (2001). *A new view of women's sexual problems.* Binghamton, NY: Hawthorne Press.

Laan, E., Van Lunsen, R. H. W., Evererd, W., Riley, A., Scott, E., & Boolell, M. (2002). The enhancement of vaginal vasocongestion by sildenafil in healthy premenopausal women. *Journal of Women's Health and Gender-Based Medicine, 11,* 357–365.

Masters, W. H., & Johnson, V. E. (1966). *Human sexual response.* Boston: Little, Brown.

Masters, W. H., & Johnson, V. E. (1970). *Human sexual inadequacy*. Boston: Little, Brown.

Merrill, J. M., Laux, L. F., & Thornby, J. I. (1990). Why doctors have difficulty with sex histories. *Southern Medical Journal, 83*, 613–617.

Metz, M. E., & Siefert, M. M. (1988). The frequency of sexual problems among family patients. *Family Practice Residency Journal, 7*, 122–129.

Ogden, G. (1999). *Women who love sex: An inquiry into the expanding spirit of women's erotic experience* (Rev. ed.). Cambridge, MA: Womenspirit Press.

Raymond, N. (2002, February). Psychiatric assessment and intervention in female hypoactive sexual desire disorder. In M. Striepe (Chair), *Women's sexual health: An interdisciplinary treatment approach to low desire*. Symposium conducted at the American Psychological Association's 2001 Women's Health Conference—Enhancing Outcomes in Women's Health: Translating Psychosocial and Behavioral Research into Primary Care, Community Interventions, and Health Policy, Washington, DC.

Rosser, B. S., Coleman, E., & Ohmans, P. (1993). Safer sex practices and reduction of unsafe sex among homosexually active men: A new therapeutic approach. *Health Education Research, 8*(1), 19–34.

Sanders, S., Graham, C. A., Bass, J. L., & Bancroft, J. (2001). A prospective study of the effects of oral contraceptives on sexuality and well-being and their relationship to discontinuation. *Contraception, 64*(1), 51–58.

Satcher, D. (2001). *The surgeon general's call to action to promote sexual health and responsible sexual behavior*. Washington, DC: U.S. Department of Health and Human Services.

Shifren, J. L. (2000). Transdermal testosterone treatment in women with impaired sexual function after oophorectomy. *New England Journal of Medicine, 343*, 682–688.

Striepe, M. (2002, February). A women's sexual health group for treatment of low sexual desire. In M. Striepe (Chair), *Women's sexual health: An interdisciplinary treatment approach to low desire*. Symposium conducted at the American Psychological Association's 2001 Women's Health Conference—Enhancing Outcomes in Women's Health: Translating Psychosocial and Behavioral Research into Primary Care, Community Interventions, and Health Policy, Washington, DC.

Urometrics. (2000). *An answer to FSD*. St. Paul, MN: Author.

13

MEN'S HEALTH IN PRIMARY CARE: FUTURE APPLICATIONS FOR PSYCHOLOGISTS

COREY J. HABBEN

It is often noted that the majority of medical research before the past two decades was conducted largely by men and mostly on male subjects, which led to regrettable gaps in understanding of women's health and illness. The women's health movement and feminist scholarship enriched medicine by advancing the study of gender and health beyond the biomedical model that had regularly excluded gender as a variable and used men in epidemiological research as the scientific standard for all people (Sabo & Gordon, 1995). Today, women represent 63% of participants enrolled in clinical research funded by the National Institutes of Health; the U.S. Department of Health and Human Services has a separate Office of Women's Health; most medical textbooks have distinct sections devoted to women's health; and most major medical centers include women's health clinics (Simon, 2002).

Ironically, the tremendous strides made in advancing the study of gender and health have not led to similar advances in the understanding of men's health. Although men had previously dominated epidemiological research as participants and investigators, the study of gender and health recently has predominantly focused on women's health and, at least in relative terms, practically ignored men's health (Courtney, 2001; Good, Sherrod, & Dillon, 2000; Lee & Owens, 2002). A search of the MEDLINE medical research database using the keywords "women's health" and "men's health" reveal startling disparities. From 1966 to February 2002, "women's health" resulted in 8,633 entries whereas "men's health" resulted in 184 (a ratio of 47 : 1). A similar search of the entire PsycINFO psychology research database from 1872 to February 2002 resulted in 687 "women's health" entries and 94 "men's health" entries (a ratio of more than 7 : 1). In contrast, few medical centers include separate men's health clinics, and no distinct federal office of men's health currently exists. Funding of research reflects similar disparities; although age-adjusted mortality rates are higher for men dying of prostate cancer than for women dying of breast cancer (National Center for Health Statistics, 2002), prostate cancer research receives less than half as much funding as does breast cancer research (National Cancer Institute, 2000). Although comparisons too often lead to politically charged and even antagonistic discourse, it is nonetheless apparent that the study of men's health is not nearly as well-developed as is the study of women's health (both in medicine and psychology).

This is particularly discouraging when one reviews the data related to mortality and leading causes of death. Men have historically died at an earlier age than women, currently with a life expectancy that is 5 years shorter than that of a woman born at the same time (National Center for Health Statistics, 2002). Of the top 10 leading causes of death, men die from every single cause of death at a higher rate than women. Stated more specifically, the age-adjusted death rates per 100,000 population are greater for men in each of the 10 leading categories (heart disease, cancer, cerebrovascular diseases, chronic lower respiratory diseases, accidental deaths, diabetes mellitus, influenza/pneumonia, suicide, chronic liver disease/cirrhosis, and homicide; National Center for Health Statistics, 2002).

CAUSES OF MALE MORTALITY: BIOLOGICAL VERSUS BEHAVIORAL

Stillion (1995) proposed an eight-stage hierarchy that categorized various causes of death into varying degrees of causality from "totally inescapable" to "totally controllable." For example, stage 1 included causes of death that were entirely biological or genetic, such as an individual inheriting the dominant gene for Huntington's disease. Stage 8 included causes of death that were almost entirely the result of human choice or behavior, such as suicide. This conceptualization is helpful as one reviews the 10 leading causes of death as it relates to men. The greatest disparities between men and women for the leading causes of death exist under the categories of suicide, with a 4.5 : 1 male-to-female ratio; homicide with a 3.3 : 1 ratio; accidental deaths (particularly motor vehicle-related deaths) with a 2.2 : 1 ratio; and chronic liver disease and cirrhosis with a 2.2 : 1 ratio. All of the remaining causes of death have less than a 2 : 1 ratio (National Center for Health Statistics, 2002). Although it would be impossible to accurately quantify the extent to which biology versus behavior affects these various causes of death, it would be safe to assume that the causes of death that affect the highest *ratio* of men (compared with women) are the categories that are most influenced by behavior and personal choice.

Personal choice plays a much greater role with respect to suicide than does biology, even though biology is certainly a variable that can affect one's potential risk for suicide. Although people do not choose to be murdered, murder is nevertheless more a behavior-based cause of death than a biological one. Accidental deaths, particularly motor vehicle-related deaths, are affected to a great extent by the degree of risk behavior engaged in by the driver. Male drivers involved in motor vehicle-related crashes are roughly twice as likely as female drivers to be intoxicated with a blood alcohol concentration of 0.10% or greater (National Highway Traffic Safety Administration, 2001). Although chronic liver disease and cirrhosis have causes that are mostly biological (such as hepatitis C), one of the leading causes of liver disease and cirrhosis is chronic alcohol abuse. Men are more likely than women (57% vs. 38%, respectively) to be identified as regular drinkers (National Center for Health Statistics, 2002). The leading causes of death that have the smallest male-to-female ratios, including cerebrovascular disease, (1.02 : 1 male-to-female ratio), diabetes mellitus (1.2 : 1), and influenza/pneumonia (1.3 : 1) are largely more affected by biological factors than behavioral. In contrast, the leading causes of death with the highest male-to-female ratios (i.e., suicide, homicide, and accidental deaths in particular) are all deaths that can be prevented through changes in behavior. The psychology of men plays a major role in the ultimate health of men.

VARIABLES AFFECTING MEN'S HEALTH

A 1996 review of the men's health literature by Lloyd (2001) outlined three primary features to men's health. First, men's health is affected by *biology*, such as is the case with prostate and testicular cancer or the varying hormonal factors that affect men's and women's susceptibility to heart disease and strokes (Simon, 2002). Second, men's health is affected by *risk and risk-taking behavior*. Risk-taking behavior can span a wide range of behaviors, such as drug and alcohol abuse, cigarette smoking, unsafe sexual practices, poor diet, reckless driving, increased exposure to dangerous environments, violent behavior, and a number of other behaviors. Risk-taking behavior can also include less obvious behaviors such as avoidance or underutilization of health care. Third, men's health is affected by *masculinity*; that is, the sociocultural and psychological process of learning and adhering to the standards of becoming a man. This can play a significant role in the rules that men live by to govern their behavior and can also serve as a detriment to men's health. A helpful review of masculine gender role stressors and men's health is provided by Good et al. (2000).

It should be noted that men's health is not affected by either biology or risk-behavior or masculinity; in most cases, it is a varying combination of all three factors. Consider the example of heart disease, the leading cause of male mortality and a disease that kills men at a 1.5 : 1 male-to-female ratio. Men have lower levels of estrogen than women and higher levels of testosterone, two hormonal differences that serve to modify biological susceptibility to heart disease (Simon, 2002). One of the largest single behavioral risk factors for heart disease is cigarette smoking. Although the gap has narrowed in recent years, men still smoke cigarettes more frequently than do women (National Center for Health Statistics, 2002). Even masculinity plays a role in male heart disease. Three psychosocial components often associated with traditional masculinity (i.e., lack of adequate social support, type A behavior, and underutilization of health care) are associated with greater risk for coronary heart disease (Helgeson, 1995). In considering social support and underutilization of health care, adult men (18–64 years of age) are twice as likely to have no health care visits to a doctor's office, emergency department, or home visit within the past 12 months, as well as twice as likely as adult women of the same age range to have no usual source of health care (National Center for Health Statistics, 2002). Men are also less likely than women to seek out psychotherapy (Good, Dell, & Mintz, 1989; Wilcox & Forrest, 1992) and more likely to terminate therapy prematurely (Hetzel, Barton, & Davenport, 1994; Moore & Haverkamp, 1989). This speaks to the inherent problem with men's health and men's greater likelihood of dying earlier and in greater numbers from all of the leading causes of death: For whatever reason, men are not being adequately helped by the medical doctors and psychologists who could play major roles in facilitating changes on the biological, behavioral, and psychological level.

PSYCHOLOGISTS' ROLE IN IMPROVING MEN'S HEALTH

Are there variables that affect heart disease whereby psychologists can facilitate positive change in men? Consider each of the three examples of risk factors discussed in examining men's higher rates of heart disease. Psychologists often serve as the primary clinician in helping an individual quit smoking, and innovations in smoking cessation treatment are leading to increasingly positive outcomes. Psychologists also serve as integral sources of social support, particularly for men who often have fewer close relationships from which to receive support. A good psychologist would be effective in modifying rigid standards and rules that contribute to the so-called type A personality. Furthermore, one of the most basic functions of a health psychologist (or, ideally, any psychologist) is to facilitate greater compliance with medical treatment. This should include preventative treatment, such as regular check-ups. If a psychologist sees a man regularly for therapy and does not check to ensure that he is being seen by a medical doctor for a yearly physical, then an important part of care is being ignored.

Given this, heart disease is more affected by biology and less by behavior than other causes of death such as suicide, homicide, and accidental deaths. The latter causes of death also, as previously mentioned, represent the causes that lead to the highest age-adjusted rates of mortality compared with women. One can only wonder if the rates of completed suicide would be lower for men (and, subsequently, at lower male-to-female ratio than the current 4.5 : 1) if more of these men received the supportive and directive care of a psychologist. Similarly, one can only hypothesize what the substance abuse rates would be if men were receiving more treatment from psychologists. It would be safe to assume that more successful and widespread treatment would lead to lower mortality rates related to suicide, homicide, accidental (e.g., motor vehicle-related) deaths, and chronic liver disease and cirrhosis. Similarly, more successful and widespread treatment for smoking cessation would most likely lead to lower mortality rates related to heart disease, lung cancer, and chronic obstructive pulmonary disease.

On a more basic scale, psychologists en masse could have a significant impact on men's health and male mortality merely by increasing the likelihood of men being seen by their medical doctors for preventive check-ups, early intervention during the early stages of disease or illness, and treatment of chronic conditions. To put it simply, many of the imbalances in men's health and mortality as it compares with women's health and mortality are influenced by behavioral or controllable variables—variables over which psychologists can have a significant amount of influence. In many ways, psychologists need to work more like de facto primary care providers for men if any significant changes are to be seen in male mortality rates.

This leads to a difficult question: Whose responsibility is it to ensure that more men see a clinician and continue with treatment? The answer is that the responsibility is both the clinician's and the patient's, although too many psychologists fall into the trap of blaming the male patient and avoiding shared responsibility for treatment failures. As previously noted, men are less likely than women to present for therapy and continue with treatment. It has been noted elsewhere that many men who do present to therapy often do not do so on their own but instead are urged by a partner, recommended by employers, referred by a physician, or ordered by the court (Allen & Gordon, 1990). Yet many elements used regularly in psychotherapy (such as sharing emotions, discussing vulnerabilities, admitting the need for help, and sharing intimate details with a relative stranger) can seem rather foreign to some men and may even lead to early termination. Although common, it is not necessarily appropriate to label such a male patient as "resistant" or "unwilling to make the necessary changes."

Regardless of what got the male patient in the office, one of the psychologist's goals should be to keep any man who would benefit from therapy coming to the office. This may mean adapting one's style, even if only initially, to "fit" more with the patient's needs. Heesacker and Prichard (1992) have provided some suggestions regarding therapy approaches with men, some of which may seem rather counterintuitive to many therapists. Male clients should initially be allowed to tell stories without being reprimanded for avoiding emotional expression. In addition, therapists should be more comfortable with male silence and acting out in therapy. Finally, biblio-, audio-, and video-therapy have been found to be important and beneficial as therapy supplements for men. Using an approach more familiar to many men, such as setting goals, providing homework, and using lists or diagrams, may be initially less foreign to men than talking through problems and emotions (Allen & Gordon, 1990). Men and women often exhibit different styles of communication (Tannen, 1990), and psychologists need to be aware of these differences and make the proper adjustments to communicate effectively. Although men ultimately need to adapt to therapy, the psychologist also needs to adapt to the male patient. This can be as simple as increasing access to treatment through extended office hours. This is integral in working with men, the overwhelming majority of whom work full-time.

CASE EXAMPLE

Frank was a 52-year-old male who was referred to a psychologist by his primary care physician. On initial presentation, Frank was cooperative but businesslike and somewhat guarded ("The main reason I am here is because my doctor told me it might help, and I'll do anything"). He acknowledged that he usually does not visit a doctor, but he decided to set up an appointment with his primary care physician after he began to experience frequent tension headaches that were becoming increasingly debilitating. He also complained that his chronic low back pain has gotten worse over the past year or so. His sleep has been poor for at least the past year ("I can't remember the last time I had a good night's sleep"). When asked how he has been dealing with this, he replied that he "usually just needs to get away from everybody for a while" and that "sometimes I just need to have a few beers and relax." When asked for further clarification, he indicated that he does not drink daily, but he will binge drink "once or twice a month."

Frank recognized that his headaches and back pain tended to get worse as his stress increased. Within the past year, he experienced a significant increase in work overtime hours ("I have to do this because we have a lot of financial problems"), the cross-country relocation of twin sons who had begun college, and the accidental death of a close friend in an automobile accident. Frank decided to see a doctor after his back pain and headaches made work difficult. He also commented that his father died of a heart attack by age 55, and "I can't let that same thing happen to me because my family needs me." (Frank had recently been prescribed antihypertensive medication to treat high blood pressure.)

Frank was initially skeptical of seeing a psychologist because "I'm not the type of guy who cries and talks about his feelings." He prided himself as a problem-solver ("I prefer to deal with things on my own") and he added that he did not want to be seen as a "whiner." He also remarked several times that he placed a high value on being "a good father, a good husband, and a good worker." Following an initial evaluation, the psychologist began with a psychoeducational focus with an emphasis on the mediating relationship between stress and physical health, as well as clarifying and modifying assumptions about therapy. Frank seemed to become invested in therapy when he viewed it as "teaming up with an expert" to work toward the shared goal of improving physical health (particularly, managing pain and headaches) by identifying and expanding better strategies for managing stress. He remarked that, using his preferred approach, he viewed stress and physical pain as "problems" that he would like to better "solve" so that he could be "an even better father, husband, and worker."

Therapy was initially more practical and didactic, with a focus on more utilitarian interventions such as relaxation training. As he became more comfortable and invested in the process of therapy, he became more willing to examine the relationship of stress, emotions, and physical health. He identified that some of his choices for managing stress (such as binge drinking or isolation) might only have served to exacerbate stress and impair physical functioning. This seemed to make him much more willing to consider new strategies, such as identifying and expressing emotions to others, using more adaptive and less destructive coping strategies, maintaining compliance with recommended medication regimens, and following up regularly with his primary care physician.

Through this process, Frank revealed himself to be a more expressive man than he had initially characterized himself to be (e.g., becoming tearful when talking about the death of his friend or beaming proudly when talking about his sons) and learned to share these emotions more readily with his family and friends (particularly when he was feeling overwhelmed with stress). Within 3 months, Frank had returned to more normal sleep, experienced few tension headaches, and experienced minimal lower back pain. He continued to drink occasionally, although he did so in moderation. He remarked that his life continued to be stressful, although he "has more tools and better tools to work with the stress." He became more compliant with his medical treatment and continued with yearly physical exams with his primary care physician. Near the end of treatment, Frank expressed genuine surprise and appreciation that "not only do I feel better physically, but I actually began to look forward to therapy."

CONCLUSION

For some men, as with Frank, it is essential to join the patient where he is (i.e., taking a more problem-solving and practical approach initially) rather than attempting to "change" the patient to adapt to therapy (i.e., demanding that the patient identify and express emotions or share vulnerability early on in therapy). Many men will continue coming to see a psychologist if they feel it is serving a benefit. It is often beneficial to take the approach that you are helping your patient "be a better man" by the work you set out to do. A psychologist can play a major role by helping the patient become more educated about his health, modifying his risk-related behaviors, increasing his compliance with medical treatments and preventive check-ups, and serving as an outlet for support and guidance. The psychologist who shares the role of primary care clinician with a medical doctor will not only help a patient become a better man; with the proper interventions, this patient will also become a healthier man.

REFERENCES

Allen, J. A., & Gordon, S. (1990). Creating a framework for change. In R. L. Meth & R. S. Pasick (Eds.), Men in therapy: The challenge of change (pp. 131–151). New York: Plenum Press.

Courtney, W. H. (2001). Counseling men in medical settings: The six-point HEALTH plan. In G. R. Brooks & G. E. Good (Eds.), New handbook of psychotherapy and counseling with men: A comprehensive guide to settings, problems, and treatment approaches (pp. 59–91). San Francisco: Jossey-Bass.

Good, G. E., Dell, D. M., & Mintz, L. B. (1989). Male role and gender role conflict: Relations to help seeking in men. Journal of Counseling Psychology, 36, 295–300.

Good, G. E., Sherrod, N. B., & Dillon, M. G. (2000). Masculine gender role stressors and men's health. In R. M. Eisler & M. Hersen (Eds.), *Handbook of gender, culture, and health* (pp. 63–81). Mahwah, NJ: Erlbaum.

Heesacker, M., & Prichard, S. (1992). In a different voice, revisited: Men, women, and emotion. Special Issue: Mental health counseling for men. *Journal of Mental Health Counseling, 14,* 274–290.

Helgeson, V. S. (1995). Masculinity, men's roles, and coronary heart disease. In D. Sabo & D. F. Gordon (Eds.), *Men's health and illness: Gender, power, and the body* (pp. 68–104). Thousand Oaks, CA: Sage.

Hetzel, R. D., Barton, D. A., & Davenport, D. S. (1994). Helping men change: A group counseling model for male clients. Special issue: Counseling men. *Journal for Specialists in Group Work, 19,* 52–64.

Lee, C., & Owens, R. G. (2002). Issues for a psychology of men's health. *Journal of Health Psychology, 7,* 209–217.

Lloyd, T. (2001). Men and health: The context for practice. In N. Davidson & T. Lloyd (Eds.), *Promoting men's health: A guide for practitioners* (pp. 3–34). New York: W. B. Saunders.

Moore, D., & Haverkamp, B. E. (1989). Measured increases in male emotional expressiveness following a structured group intervention. *Journal of Counseling and Development, 67,* 513–517.

National Cancer Institute. (2000). *FY2000 NCI Fact Book.* Rockville, MD: 2000.

National Center for Health Statistics. (2002). *Health, United States, 2002 with chartbook on trends in the health of Americans.* Hyattsville, MD: Author.

National Highway Traffic Safety Administration. (2001). *Traffic safety facts 2000: Alcohol.* Washington, DC: Author.

Sabo, D. S., & Gordon, D. F. (1995). Rethinking men's health and illness: The relevance of gender studies. In D. Sabo & D. F. Gordon (Eds.), *Men's health and illness: Gender, power, and the body* (pp. 1–21). Thousand Oaks, CA: Sage.

Simon, H. B. (2002). *The Harvard medical school guide to men's health.* New York: Free Press.

Stillion, J. M. (1995). Premature death among males: Extending the bottom line of men's health. In D. Sabo & D. F. Gordon (Eds.), *Men's health and illness: Gender, power, and the body* (pp. 46–67). Thousand Oaks, CA: Sage.

Tannen, D. (1990). *You just don't understand: Women and men in conversation.* New York: Ballantine Books.

Wilcox, D. W., & Forrest, L. (1992). The problems of men and counseling: Gender bias or gender truth? *Journal of Mental Health Counseling, 14,* 291–304.

V

INFORMATION TECHNOLOGY APPLICATIONS FOR PRIMARY CARE

14

TELEHEALTH AND HEALTH PSYCHOLOGY: EMERGING ISSUES IN CONTEMPORARY PRACTICE

RAYMOND A. FOLEN, LARRY C. JAMES, MARK VERSCHELL, AND JAY E. EARLES

The distribution of psychologists and other health professionals in the United States and in other countries is disproportionately concentrated in urban settings and areas of higher socioeconomic status. Against this background, the use of telecommunications technology to provide primary and specialty health care to unserved and underserved populations has grown exponentially over the past decade (Armstrong, 1998; Bashshur, Sanders, & Shannon, 1997; Coiera, 1997; Maheu, Whitten, & Allen, 2001), and economic viability of this treatment modality is relatively strong (Darkins & Cary, 2000; Puskin, 2001). The use of telecommunications and technology to provide health information and health care across distances is most consistently being referred to as *telehealth* (Nickelson, 1998), although several

This chapter was authored or coauthored by an employee of the United States government as part of official duty and is considered to be in the public domain. Any views expressed herein do not necessarily represent the views of the United States government, and the author's participation in the work is not meant to serve as an official endorsement.

experts in the field believe that the term will eventually be replaced by *e-health* (Maheu et al., 2001).

Psychologists working in rural areas or extending their services to unserved populations are often acutely aware of the isolation and limited resources available to both provider and patient. In recent years, the inventive use of telehealth technology to bridge these resource gaps has been applied to an ever-expanding number of clinical settings. This chapter presents the history of telehealth and describes a number of telehealth applications appropriate to psychology. Technical requirements are discussed and matched to infrastructures available at remote sites. Essential safety, privacy, and liability concerns are also addressed.

TELEHEALTH BEGINNINGS

The telephone was the first technological advancement used to provide health care over distances. When Alexander Graham Bell accidentally spilled battery acid on himself when making the world's first telephone call, little did he realize that his message "Watson, come here I want you" made history as the world's first telehealth consultation (Sivaswamy & Kumar, 2002). As is often the case with new technologies, the expansion and acceptance of this communications medium was nothing short of remarkable. Whereas in 1877 outdoor telephone service had a range of 3 miles, within a year technological advances allowed for call switching over hundreds of miles. What is not widely known is the role medicine played in the development of the venerable instrument. In 1879, during a measles epidemic, a Massachusetts physician was concerned that replacement operators were unfamiliar with the names of local subscribers and recommended a numeric system of phone identification, which was subsequently implemented (Pion, 2000). By 1900, there were 1.4 million telephones in service (Kurzweil, 1999), and by 1918 that number had reached 10 million. Calls to physicians during this time primarily addressed acute health concerns, and the doctor was able to use the technology to determine if a home visit was required. The "plain old telephone service" (POTS) continues to be the primary mode of two-way telecommunications in the country, with more than 95% of homes having phone service.

Following Gugelielmo Marconi's development of the directional radio antenna in the early 1900s, similar advances were being made in radio communications. Americans owned 600,000 radios in 1922, up from 50,000 a year earlier. By 1925, four million homes owned radios and more than 400 stations provided entertainment and information. Early in its burgeoning popularity, health information and government health bulletins were broadcast on a regular basis to the listening populace (M. Smith, 2003).

The advent of television ushered in a technology embraced more rapidly than radio. Only 2 out of every 10,000 families owned television sets in 1946, but within the decade that number jumped to 72% of all American households (Kurzweil, 1999). Advertisements offering remedies for common ailments soon became a regular part of the new medium, and in 1951 the television industry adopted the *U.S. Code of Practices for Television Broadcasters (2004)*, which, among other things, established general standards for medical advertising.

The use of television as an important aid in medical education made its debut at the 1949 American Medical Association convention in Atlantic City, New Jersey. Physicians attending the convention were given the opportunity to observe surgical procedures on an innovation called the color television set. Large groups of physicians and the press watched the procedures in an auditorium filled with 16-inch color televisions. The reported response "was tremendous . . . some people were fainting, when they witnessed the realism of surgery delivered through the power of color images" (TVHistory.TV, 2003). Surgeons performing the procedures addressed the audience in real time, responding to questions passed along by a moderator via a two-way "Q&A link" (thewritingworks.com, 2003). By 1953, the nation's first series of open-circuit continuing medical education clinics had begun (Castle, 1963).

In 1959, the University of Nebraska heralded in the use of advanced telecommunications when it began using two-way, closed-circuit television to extend mental health services to remote areas not served by psychiatric centers (Wittson, Affleck, & Johnson, 1961; Wittson & Benschoter, 1972). In a study comparing four televised group therapy treatments with four that were nontelevised, Wittson and colleagues found that patients "readily accepted" the televised treatment modality.

The use and study of telecommunications technology to provide primary and specialty health care were slow to develop. In 1965, the Russians created the technology needed to transmit electrocardiogram (ECG) information over a telephone line (Ianushkevichus, 1965). By 1970, telephone-based telehealth began to receive attention in the professional literature, where its utility in such areas as suicide prevention and crisis management (Garell, 1969; Lester & Brockopp, 1970), alcohol treatment (Catanzaro & Green, 1970; Koumans, Muller, & Miller, 1967), and drug therapy monitoring (Solomons, 1968) was reported. Telephone lines were also being used to transmit physiological data, to include EEGs (Bennett & Gardner, 1970a, 1970b; Hanley, Zweizig, Kado, Adey & Rovner, 1969), ECGs (Macfarlane & Lawrie, 1970), pulmonary data (Cooper, Abraham, & Caceres, 1969; Rosner, Abraham, & Caceres, 1969), and heart sounds (Vaules, 1970). Medical record data was also being sent via phone (Allen, 1969; Bykhovskii & Krishchyan, 1968). The telephone was a tool for the education of physicians (Meyer, Hansen, Ragatz, & Mulvihill, 1970), nurses (Hornback, 1969), and patients (Klapper, 1970). Differences in the quality of patient–provider interactions delivered via telecommunications versus in-vivo were also being addressed (Colombotos, 1969). Computers began to take on a more significant role in the diagnostic interpretation of ECGs (Ormrod, Book, & Irving, 1970) and other physiological signals (McAllister & Hochberg, 1970) and, in a novel application, computers were being remotely controlled over telephone to control operant behavior experiments (Uber & Weiss, 1966).

A review of MEDLINE and PsycLIT reveals 28 telehealth/telemedicine articles published in the 1970s, and these addressed the utility of the medium in providing medical services primarily to rural and underserved areas. Examples include services provided to the Sioux Lookout reservation in Ontario, Canada, by physicians located in Toronto (Dunn, Conrath, Action, Higgins, & Bain, 1980) and satellite telehealth provided within Newfoundland (Boehnker, 1979) and Canada (Carey, Russell, Johnson, & Wilkins, 1979). Such services were initiated to address significant problems associated with the scarcity and misdistribution of health services. Telehealth was found to offer a valuable educational and treatment resource that was perceived as positively influencing the quality of care provided at remote sites (Grundy et al., 1977). In a study of more than 1,000 patients seen at a community health center, the telephone was found to be as efficient and effective a means for delivery of remote physician care as the more expensive and technical videoconference (Dunn, Conrath, Bloor, & Tranquada, 1977). The authors found no differences in diagnostic accuracy, diagnostic completeness, or patient attitudes toward treatment, but others (Muller et al., 1977) reported the videoconference superior to the telephone when making diagnostic decisions.

The ability to gather accurate and reliable patient health data at great distances was established by scientists at NASA and Vanderbilt University as they monitored astronaut physiology from space (R. Smith, Stanton, Stoop, Brown, & King, 1975). Early successes in monitoring physiology in space provided the impetus for NASA's subsequent technological achievements in this area (Johnston, Stonesifer, & Hawkins, 1975).

Telehealth applications did not consistently receive a positive reception by providers, however. Although two-way television, radio, and remote telemetry resulted in improved access to health care, equipment unreliability, equipment costs, and increased time required to complete telehealth consultations were viewed as major problematic issues (Fuchs, 1979). Within an innercity primary care setting, staff reactions to pediatric consultation via video telecommunications, although ultimately favorable, were initially met with considerable skepticism, and technical difficulties were described as the main disadvantage to the process (Cunningham, Marshall, & Glazer, 1978). The impact of telehealth on the medical culture was also noted, as the distance relationship between patient and provider transformed the role of the provider from absolute authority to that of member of a health team (Park & Bashshur, 1975).

Advancements in computer technology during the 1980s had a profound effect on society but only a slight one on telehealth. A review of MEDLINE and PsychLIT between 1981 and 1990 revealed only 44 records under telemedicine or telehealth, a modest increase from the 28 listings found in the 1970s. The advancements included transmission of MRI images (E. Gardner, Tokarski, & Wagner, 1990) and further refinements in the provision of clinical services and educational activities, the bulk of these initiatives being conducted by Canadian researchers.

Reports of telehealth and telemedicine increased 10-fold in the early 1990s, and it was the final 5 years of the past millennium that heralded in the age of telehealth. The number of MEDLINE and PsycLIT hits for the period 1995 to 2000 grew to a whopping 3,365, a 1000% increase over the combined reports of the prior two decades. It appears that this trend is continuing, as evidenced by 1,500 records found in the years 2001 to 2002 alone.

By 1998, the Veterans' Administration reported 70,000 teleconsultations per year. In the same year, correctional facilities and supporting programs reported more than 15,000 prison medicine teleconsultations. At that time, 37 states (plus the District of Columbia) were involved in telehealth activities provided across state lines. The largest proportion of telemedicine activity involved provider–patient consultation, with specialist consultation and second opinions of primary importance. This was followed in order by ongoing patient management, medical–surgical follow-up, specialty clinic, medication management, and diagnostic exam interpretation (Grigsby & Brown, 2000). The profound expansion of telehealth activity noted in the 1990s, although capitalizing on significant technology enhancements, was largely fueled by the tremendous increase in federal appropriations earmarked for telehealth. For the past several years, this has exceeded $650 million annually (Jerome et al., 2000).

TELEHEALTH APPLICATIONS
IN PRIMARY CARE

For the health psychologist, telehealth applications in the medical domain are as important as those being developed and researched in the more traditional psychological areas of practice. An extensive examination of telehealth applications in the provision of traditional psychological services can be found in the review by Hilty, Luo, Morache, Marcelo, and Nesbitt (2002). Essential information and resources for the clinician interested in the broader telehealth arena can also be found in an excellent book written by Maheu et al. (2001) and at the Office for the Advancement of Telehealth (OAT) Web site (http://telehealth.hrsa.gov). Some of the current and developing applications relevant to behavioral medicine and health psychology are discussed in this section.

For the health psychologist, some of the most exciting advances in telehealth have to do with preventing and managing medical disorders. Telehealth technologies have been actively incorporated in case management (Jerome et al., 2000), primary prevention, and early disease detection; chronic disease control and symptom management; and personal and social support (Finkelstein & Friedman, 2000). Home health care via telehealth, to include monitoring of patient physiology, has also been found to improve case management, particularly with patients who have limited physical mobility or are living at a distance from the health center (C. Smith et al., 2002).

Adherence to medication regimes can be significantly affected by the use of home medication dispensers, pager reminders, and dispensing devices that record the frequency, time, and effectiveness of medication administration. Devices such as "smart" asthma inhalers track this information and provide a means for easy uploading of the data to a computer database accessible by the patient's provider. Blood glucose and hemoglobin A1C monitors with uploading capabilities are also receiving widespread use (Glueckauf, 2002). An excellent integration of telehealth applications can be found in the comprehensive diabetes treatment program detailed in chapter 6 (this volume).

Patient information, both accurate and misleading, is available on the Internet, as are cyberspace support groups for almost every diagnosable condition. For health providers, it is important to recognize that patients regularly access these sources of information. Alternative forms of treatment, whether discussed with the clinician or not, are being advertised and used, and it is incumbent on the health care provider to direct the patient to accurate and reliable sources of information.

Technological advances now allow health care providers to manipulate medical equipment and tools from great distances. One of the more interesting examples of such use can be found in the provision of biofeedback via telehealth (Earles, Folen, & James, 2001; Folen, James, Earles, & Andrasik, 2001). A multisite study is currently underway to study equivalence of biofeedback via these different treatment modalities.

PRACTICAL CONSIDERATIONS IN THE DELIVERY OF TELEHEALTH BANDWIDTH: WORKING WITH THE AVAILABLE INFRASTRUCTURE

For digital or analog communication to occur, an appropriate communications medium needs to be available. This medium is largely defined by its bandwidth, which is the amount of information that can be carried in a given time period over a wired or wireless communications link. These links may take various forms, and descriptors such as POTS, integrated services digital network (ISDN), and broadband reflect their bandwidth and other characteristics. At any particular site, the communication links make up what may be referred to as the communication infrastructure. In digital systems, bandwidth is expressed as bits (of data) per second (bps). A videophone that works at 32K (bps), for example, has $\frac{1}{12}$ the bandwidth of a videophone that works at 384K. Image quality and the ability to provide services in real time or via delayed store-and-forward modalities are dramatically affected by bandwidth availability. Despite all the communications industry fanfare and active marketing, a large portion of society is limited to bandwidth levels that can be achieved through standard telephone connections, where more than 95% of all homes in the United States have POTS. This medium will typically allow a maximum bandwidth of 57K, whereas actual bandwidth is often considerably less, depending on the quality of the telephone line. It is appropriate for low-bandwidth communication (such as voice) and data transfer at moderate speeds. In many rural locations this is the only means of telecommunication. Video imaging is often limited to store-and-forward processes in which one site might record a high-resolution picture or video clip of a patient and send it over a slow telephone line to be reassembled at the other end for review. ISDN and broadband (which include cable modems and digital subscriber line [DSL] connections), on the other hand, can typically offer reliable bandwidth of up to 384K, which is sufficient for quality two-way videoconferencing and can be used for real-time imaging and review of patient information. The clinician must carefully consider the communications infrastructure available at the remote site and choose equipment and procedures that will work within those limitations. Home monitoring of a patient, for example, will likely require equipment that will work in a low-bandwidth POTS environment, and services provided will need to take such bandwidth limitations into consideration.

The biofeedback project mentioned earlier in this chapter is an example of technology and procedure that matches infrastructure. At Tripler Army Medical Center in Honolulu, where the project is being conducted, the center's area of responsibility ranges over approximately one half of the earth's surface, most of which is water. Flying patients in to receive biofeedback services for a period of 6 to 8 weeks is financially untenable for the center and the patients, many of whom live on remote islands in the Pacific or at locations thousands of miles from the tertiary medical facility. As is true for all remote sites, the maximum bandwidth is limited by the available infrastructure, which in this case is likely to be a POTS line. Taking these limitations into consideration, the health psychologists at Tripler developed the means by which biofeedback services could be delivered via this medium. The biofeedback system developed used one POTS line for videoconferencing using videophone equipment that conforms to the H.324 communications protocol standard for low-bandwidth video and voice communication. This standard produces reasonably good audio and pixilated, low-quality video that is adequate for the purposes of monitoring and interacting with the patient. Clinicians report that low-quality video can easily be tolerated, whereas low-quality audio will result in significant dissatisfaction for both clinician and patient.

A second phone line is used to establish a computer-to-computer link. Once this link is established, the clinician controls the computer and biofeedback programs located at the remote end. In this manner the clinician is able to see and talk with the patient while simultaneously controlling the remote computer and viewing the biofeedback signals that are being presented at the remote site. Total equipment costs are approximately $10,000 (see Folen et al., 2001, for a detailed description of the required equipment). Equipment expenses are quickly recouped and, most important, patients who would otherwise not be served are receiving these specialty care services with good result. Higher bandwidth, as it becomes available at the remote sites, can be used to improve the videotelephone quality. The biofeedback equipment works satisfactorily with connections of 14.4K or better, so existing phone lines that produce signals of moderate quality are adequate for this task.

SAFETY AND LIABILITY CONCERNS

Providing services via telehealth technologies requires reliable backup and appropriate emergency procedures at the remote site. Should a patient report imminent suicidality and walk out of the telehealth session, for example, the clinician must be able to immediately contact appropriate personnel at the remote site. Other potential circumstances, such as power failures at either the remote or primary sites, necessitate the need for backup personnel at the remote site.

Telehealth is still in its infancy, and there are few legal precedents established for medical, let alone health psychology, services provided via this venue. As a result, increased legal exposure is likely. For those working in federally qualified health centers or other federally recognized organizations, it may be possible to receive legal protection under the Federal Tort Claims Act. In any event, well-rehearsed procedures that address anticipated clinical scenarios should be established. Clinicians should be familiar with state, federal, and—when relevant—international laws that regulate licensing and credentialing requirements for out-of-district health care providers. Legal precedents for remote licensure have yet to be established, so health care providers must often obtain licensure in each telehealth locale as well as credentialing at each individual health care facility (Edelstein, 2001). Unfortunately, national and international licensing and credentialing standards may be slow to develop. For example, recent legislation introduced by the U.S. Federation of State Medical Boards to facilitate the provision of telehealth services across state lines was countered by new legislation from a number of states requiring full and unrestricted licensure for out-of-state health care providers.

HEALTH INSURANCE PORTABILITY AND ACCOUNTABILITY ACT OF 1996: CONFIDENTIALITY AND PRIVACY

Unintentional and malicious disclosure of patient health care information is a significant risk associated with telehealth care. Patients' rights to control the use and disclosure (i.e., privacy) and protect unauthorized access to (i.e., confidentiality; Ware, 1993) their sensitive personal information may be compromised by transmission across electronic information networks, which have inherent and often unknown security vulnerabilities. Although state laws governing the use and disclosure of health care records are relatively inconsistent (see the Health Privacy Project Web site at http:// www.healthprivacy.org/underresources/statereports for a comprehensive 50-state survey of health privacy statutes), most health care providers have been required to comply with the privacy regulations outlined by the federal Health Insurance Portability and Accountability Act of 1996 (HIPAA) since April 2003 (Edelstein, 2001; Kumekawa, 2001; Pritts, Goldman, Hudson, Berenson, & Hadley, 1999). HIPAA privacy rules, which pertain to individually identifiable health care information transmitted in any format (i.e., electronic, paper, and oral), will have a significant impact on telehealth providers, who will be held accountable for maintaining administrative and physical safeguards to protect the confidentiality of health information and to protect against unauthorized access. A preliminary study by the Advanced Technology Institute, an agency funded by OAT at the Department of

Health and Human Services (DHHS), Health Resources and Services Administration, has outlined the following unique privacy concerns for telehealth providers:

1. a need for a heightened level of concern for patient privacy in the telemedicine environment, especially where patient visits are occurring in real-time;
2. the potential for more complicated informed consent requirements under HIPAA that could inhibit obtaining the necessary patient consent signatures, which are necessary before initiating telehealth activities;
3. the presence of outsiders or nonclinical people in teleconsultations, including nonclinical technicians, camera people, schedulers, and so forth, located on either side of a telemedicine consultation or at the site of a service provider, either physically or via the technology they support;
4. clinical personnel who may not be visible or observable by the patient in a teleconsultation;
5. patient information that is transmitted in electronic and physical forms on a regular basis across organizations and political (state and national) borders;
6. patient information routinely stored electronically or physically at each of the sites involved in the encounter, often unintentionally, but may not be protected by policies or procedures as effectively as information used in onsite encounters.

Another complex concern for telehealth providers is the fact that HIPAA privacy regulations preempt state laws only when they are in conflict with or provide less stringent privacy protections than federal regulatory requirements (Kumekawa, 2001). Under these circumstances, telehealth providers will likely have to resolve a confusing array of state privacy standards. OAT recommends that providers and their sponsoring agencies develop specific administrative procedures, physical safeguards, and technical mechanisms to address these increasingly challenging privacy standards (OAT, 2000). Risk management should be a key component of every telehealth agency's administrative activities, and should at the least lead to the designation of a privacy officer, procedures for obtaining patient consent for all disclosures of protected health care information, and the training of employees about security issues and how to provide the minimum amount of information necessary. Physical safeguards should focus on placing computers with sensitive information away from public areas and locking rooms or cabinets that store sensitive information. Technical security mechanisms would include the use of computer and network passwords, data encryption, and digital signatures to limit access to and protect medical record information.

COMFORT WITH TECHNOLOGY

There are many opportunities to expand or extend one's practice options by embracing telehealth technologies, but the technology may take some getting used to. When using low-bandwidth teleconferencing, for example, clinicians who are used to broadcast (TV) quality images are often put off initially by the video quality limitations inherent in the POTS lines and H.324 protocols. It is the authors' experience, however, that clinicians soon recognize that the low-bandwidth information provided is nevertheless adequate for clinical decision making and the implementation of appropriate treatments.

EQUIPMENT COSTS

As telehealth equipment becomes less expensive, the use of this treatment modality becomes more viable. Teleconferencing equipment that cost $100K a decade ago can be purchased for $\frac{1}{10}$ the cost today. This is true for telehealth hardware being produced to provide specific medical treatment procedures as well as equipment used for videoconferencing. The health psychologist can easily be seduced, however, by the "more is better" sales pitch. It is important in those circumstances to consider the bandwidth infrastructure available at the remote site as well as ease of access to those systems. The elderly homebound patient may be more compliant with a telehealth intervention provided over the telephone line in his or her own home than with a high-bandwidth teleconferencing intervention available only at a location across town.

REIMBURSEMENT

Although there is little doubt that computer networking and automated electronic systems have simplified and facilitated third-party payment transactions, telehealth providers and their sponsoring agencies should be cautious to avoid infringing on HIPPA privacy regulations and federal and state antifraud, abuse, and self-referral laws (Edelstein, 2001; Kumekawa, 2001). Telehealth sponsoring agencies are responsible for the actions of their third-party business associates, including billing companies and data management firms, because HIPPA privacy standards specify that telehealth agencies must develop a legal agreement with their business partners to safeguard patients' health care information (Department of Health and Human Services, 2001). Moreover, telehealth providers and their sponsoring agencies are required to address situations in which third-party business associates fail to comply with their privacy obligations. Health care providers employed or contracted by broad telehealth networks should also be aware that they might be providing services in states in which the practice of professional fee splitting by nonmedical corporations is prohibited. Similarly, providers working for broad telehealth networks that provide services reimbursable under federal health care programs should carefully examine their sponsoring agencies' referral practices. These providers may violate state and federal antifraud, abuse, and self-referral laws if they are subsidizing their sponsoring agencies' capital/operating costs and are receiving referrals from other providers within the network.

IN-VIVO BIAS

Telehealth improves access to care and appears to be an appropriate treatment modality for an ever-increasing number of preventative measures and remedial treatment interventions. However, clinicians often feel that telehealth procedures are inferior to in-vivo interventions. This is a bias that needs to be examined empirically. It is possible that certain procedures may be more effectively delivered via telehealth. The authors have been surprised to find that a substantial minority of patients who have experienced similar interventions via both face-to-face interactions and telehealth report greater comfort with the telehealth modality. Clinicians have also reported that patients being treated via videophone often appear more focused and receptive than their in-vivo counterparts. Additional investigation is needed to discover the specific procedures, patient characteristics, and clinician qualities that promote telehealth interventions as the primary treatment of choice.

TELEHEALTH VERSUS FACE-TO-FACE TREATMENT: LIMITED OUTCOME DATA

A large number of the studies conducted to date have focused on consumer (patient and provider) acceptance of telehealth. Subjective levels of satisfaction tend to be the yardstick of success, and most adult studies do report high levels of patient satisfaction (Hilty et al., 2002). This is also true for studies conducted with children (Elford et al., 2000) and elderly individuals (Jones, 2001). Clinician interrater reliability is generally high in most studies that compare assessments conducted via telehealth with in-vivo settings (Hilty et al., 2002). Although studies have identified cost–benefit issues, patient satisfaction, quality of life, client outcome, organizational support, and provider satisfaction as important factors, comparisons of telehealth to appropriate face-to-face alternatives have been inadequate (Herbert, 2001). Some effort has been made to assess equivalence of treatment when comparing telehealth to face-to-face treatment in wound assessment (S. Gardner et al., 2001) and weight reduction and lifestyle management programs (James, Folen, & Earles, 2001). Overall, the number of controlled trials examining telecommunication-based interventions remains small, and future research needs to be conducted in larger studies with conceptually meaningful control groups and investigations into the types of telecommunication-based interventions that provide the best match with specific populations (Liss, Glueckauf, & Ecklund-Johnson, 2002).

CONCLUSION

In 1998, Congress established OAT to serve as a catalyst for the wider adoption of advanced technologies in providing health care services and education. Although technologies used in telehealth, such as videoconferencing, the Internet, store-and-forward imaging, and satellite and wireless communications, already exist, OAT points out that the health care industry itself lags significantly behind other industries that have already integrated information systems into their daily routines. The major contribution of telehealth toward the treatment of our rural and urban underserved peoples is yet to be realized. Health psychologists, with their more comprehensive biopsychosocial perspective, can contribute significantly in the development and use of these emerging technologies and the ultimate health of the United States and the world communities.

REFERENCES

Allen, S. I. (1969). The telephone as a computer input–output terminal for medical information. *Journal of the American Medical Association, 208,* 673–679.

Armstrong, M. L. (1998). *Telecommunications for health professionals: Providing successful distance education and telehealth.* New York: Springer.

Bashshur, R. L., Sanders, J. H., & Shannon, G. W. (1997). *Telemedicine: Theory and practice.* Springfield, IL: Charles C. Thomas.

Bennett, D. R., & Gardner, R. M. (1970a). Routine transmission of EEG by telephone from a distant community. *Neurology, 20,* 419.

Bennett, D. R., & Gardner, R. M. (1970b). A model for the telephone transmission of six-channel electroencephalograms. *Electroencephalography and Clinical Neurophysiology, 29,* 404–408.

Boehnker, D. M. (1979). Telemedicine by satellite in Newfoundland. *Educational and Industrial Television, 11*(3), 76–80.

Bykhovskii, M. L., & Krishchyan, E. M. (1968). Transmission of medical information through telephone lines. *Biomedical Engineering, 2,* 307–313.

Carey, L. S., Russell, E. S., Johnson, E. E., & Wilkins, W. W. (1979). Radiologic consultation to a remote Canadian hospital using Hermes spacecraft. *Journal of the Canadian Association of Radiologists, 30*(1), 12–20.

Castle, H. C. (1963). Open-circuit television in postgraduate medical education. *Journal of Medical Education, 38,* 254–260.

Catanzaro, R. J., & Green, W. G. (1970). WATS telephone therapy: New follow-up technique for alcoholics. *American Journal of Psychiatry, 126,* 1024–1027.

Coiera, E. (1997). *Guide to medical informatics, the Internet and telemedicine.* New York: Oxford University Press.

Colombotos, J. (1969). Personal versus telephone interviews: Effect on responses. *Public Health Reports, 84,* 773–782.

Cooper, J. K., Abraham, S., & Caceres, C. A. (1969). Telephone transmission of cardiac and pulmonary data. *Archives of Environmental Health, 19,* 712–718.

Cunningham, N., Marshall, C., & Glazer, E. (1978). Telemedicine in pediatric primary care. *Journal of the American Medical Association, 240,* 2749–2751.

Darkins, A. W., & Cary, M. A. (2000). *Telemedicine and telehealth: Principles, policies, performance and pitfalls.* New York: Springer.

Department of Health and Human Services, Office of Civil Rights. (2001, July). *Standards for privacy of individually identifiable health information.* Washington DC: Author. Retrieved May 12, 2003, from http://aspe.hhs.gov/admnsimp/final/pvcguide1.htm

Dunn, E., Conrath, D., Action, H., Higgins, C., & Bain, H. (1980). Telemedicine links patients in Sioux Lookout with doctors in Toronto. *Canadian Medical Association Journal, 122,* 484–487.

Dunn, E., Conrath, D. W., Bloor, W. G., & Tranquada, B. (1977). An evaluation of far telecommunication systems in primary care. *Health Services Research* (Spring), 19–29.

Earles, J., Folen, R. A., & James, L. C. (2001). Biofeedback using telemedicine: Clinical applications and case illustrations. *Behavioral Medicine, 27*(2), 77–82.

Edelstein, S. A. (2001, October 1). Government regulations of telehealth—A US legal perspective. *Business Briefing: Next Generation Healthcare.* Retrieved May 12, 2003, from http://www.wmrc.com/businessbriefing/pdf/GHealthcare2001/Ref%20Section/13.pdf

Elford, R., White, H., Bowening, R., Ghandi, A., Maddigan, B., & St. John, K. (2000). A randomized, controlled trial of child psychiatric assessments conducted using video conferencing. *Journal of Telemedicine and Telecare, 6*(2), 73–82.

Finkelstein, J., & Friedman, R. H. (2000). Potential role of telecommunication technologies in the management of chronic health conditions. *Disease Management and Health Outcomes, 8*(2), 57–63.

Folen, R. A., James, L. C., Earles, J. E., & Andrasik, F. (2001). Biofeedback via telehealth: A new frontier for applied psychophysiology. *Applied Psychophysiology and Biofeedback, 26,* 195–204.

Fuchs, M. (1979). Provider attitudes toward STARPAHC: A telemedicine project on the Papago reservation. *Medical Care, 17*(1), 59–68.

Gardner, E., Tokarski, C., & Wagner, M. (1990). Telemedicine goes the distance. *Modern Healthcare, 20,* 24–32.

Gardner, S. E., Frantz, R. A., Specht, J. K., Johnson-Mekota, J. L., Buresh, K. A., Wakefield, B., et al. (2001). How accurate are chronic wound assessments using interactive video technology? *Journal of Gerontological Nursing, 27*(1), 15–20.

Garell, D. C. (1969). A hotline telephone service for young people in crisis. *Children, 16,* 177–180.

Glueckauf, R. L. (2002). Telehealth and chronic disabilities: New frontier for research and development. *Rehabilitation Psychology, 47*(1), 3–7.

Grigsby, B., & Brown, N. (2000). *1999 report on U.S. telemedicine activity.* Portland, OR: Association of Telehealth Service Providers.

Grundy, B. L., Crawford, P., Jones, P. K., Kiley, M. L., Reisman, A., Pao, Y. H., et al. (1977). Telemedicine in critical care: An experiment in health care delivery. *Journal of the American College of Emergency Physicians, 6,* 439–444.

Hanley, J., Zweizig, J. R., Kado, R. T., Adey, W. R., & Rovner, L. D. (1969). Combined telephone and radiotelemetry of the EEG. *Electroencephalography and Clinical Neurophysiology, 6,* 323–324.

Herbert, M. (2001). Telehealth success: Evaluation framework development. *Medinfo, 10,* 1145–1149.

Hilty, D. M., Luo, J. S., Morache, C., Marcelo, D. A., & Nesbitt, T. S. (2002). Telepsychiatry: An overview for psychiatrists. *CNS Drugs, 16,* 527–548.

Hornback, M. S. (1969). University sponsored staff education in nursing via a telephone-radio network. *International Journal of Nursing Studies, 6,* 217–223.

Ianushkevichus, Z. (1965). On the transmission of ECG over telephone channel. *Klinicheskaia Meditsina (Moskva), 43,* 143–144.

James, L. C., Folen, R. A., & Earles, J. (2001). Behavioral telehealth applications in the treatment of obese soldiers: A feasibility project and a report on preliminary findings. *Military Medicine, 13*(3), 177–186.

Jerome, L. W., DeLeon, P. H., James, L. C., Folen, R., Earles, J., & Gedney, J. J. (2000). The coming of age of telecommunications in psychological research and practice. *American Psychologist, 55,* 407–421.

Johnston, R. S., Stonesifer, J. C., & Hawkins, W. R. (1975). Development of Skylab medical equipment and flight preparations. *Acta Astronautica, 2*(1–2), 69–84.

Jones, B. N. (2001). Telepsychiatry and geriatric care. *Current Psychiatry Reports, 3,* 29–36.

Klapper, M. S. (1970). Medical information service via telephone (MIST). *Journal of the Medical Association of the State of Alabama, 40,* 257.

Koumans, A. J., Muller, J. J., & Miller, C. F. (1967). Use of telephone calls to increase motivation for treatment in alcoholics. *Psychological Reports, 21,* 327–328.

Kumekawa, J. K. (2001, September 30). Health information privacy protection: Crisis or Common Sense? *Online Journal of Issues in Nursing, 6.* Retrieved May 12, 2003, from http://www.nursingworld.org/ojin/topic16/tpc16_2.htm

Kurzweil, R. (1999). *The age of spiritual machines.* New York: Penguin.

Lester, D., & Brockopp, G. W. (1970). Chronic callers to a suicide prevention center. *Community Mental Health Journal, 6,* 246–50.

Liss, H. J., Glueckauf, R. L., & Ecklund-Johnson, E. P. (2002). Research on tele-health and chronic medical conditions: Critical review, key issues, and future directions. *Rehabilitation Psychology, 47*(1), 8–30.

Macfarlane, P. W., & Lawrie, T. D. (1970). Radio and telephone system for multiple channel transmission of E.C.G.s. *British Medical Journal, 3,* 702–703.

McAllister, J. W., & Hochberg, H. M. (1970). Transmission of medical signals for computer analysis. *Journal of the Association for the Advancement of Medical Instrumentation, 3,* 232–236.

Maheu, M., Whitten, P., & Allen, A. (2001). *E-health, telehealth, and telemedicine: A guide to startup and success.* New York: Jossey-Bass.

Meyer, T. C., Hansen, R. H., Ragatz, R. T., & Mulvihill, B. (1970). Providing medical information to physicians by telephone tapes. *Journal of Medical Education, 45,* 1060–1065.

Muller, C., Marshall, C. L., Krasner, M., Cunningham, N., Wallerstein, E., & Thomstad, B. (1977). Cost factors in urban telemedicine. *Medical Care, 15,* 251–259.

Nickelson, D. (1998). Telehealth and the evolving health care system: Strategic opportunities for professional psychology. *Professional Psychology: Research and Practice, 29,* 527–535.

Office for the Advancement of Telehealth. (2000). *Summary report of the Office for the Advancement of Telehealth Seminar's Privacy, Security, and Confidentiality of Medical Records.* Rockville, MD: Author.

Ormrod, J. K., Book, D. T., & Irving, J. G. (1970). Computer interpretation by telephone of electrocardiograms in the home office of a life insurance company. *Transactions of the Association of Life Insurance Medical Directors of America, 53,* 48–60.

Park, B., & Bashshur, R. (1975). Some implications of telemedicine. *Journal of Communication, 25,* 161–166.

Pion, R. (2000, July). Physician's perspective. *EHealthCoach Monthly*. Retrieved September 24, 2004, from www.ehealthcoach.com/NL-PhysPersJul.asp

Pritts, J., Goldman, J., Hudson, Z., Berenson, A., & Hadley, E. (1999, July). *The state of health privacy: An uneven terrain (a comprehensive survey of state health privacy statutes)*. Health Privacy Project, Institute for Health Care Research and Policy, Georgetown University. Retrieved May 12, 2003, from http://www.health privacy.org/resources/statereports/contents.html

Puskin, D. S. (2001, September 30). Telemedicine: Follow the money. *Online Journal of Issues in Nursing, 6*. Retrieved September 24, 2004, from http://www.nursingworld.org/ojin/topic16/tpc16_1.htm

Rosner, S. W., Abraham, S., & Caceres, C. A. (1969). Telephone transmission of spirograms for computer analysis. *Medical Research Engineering, 8*(1), 18–21.

Sivaswamy, R., & Kumar, J. (2002). Doctors on the Internet—Legal and practical implications. *Eubios Journal of Asian and International Bioethics, 12*, 185–188.

Smith, C. E., Cha, J. J., Kleinbeck, S. V., Clements, F. A., Cook, D., & Koehler, J. (2002). Feasibility of in-home telehealth for conducting nursing research. *Clinical Nursing Research, 11*, 220–233.

Smith, M. (2003). *The history of radio: Early Nebraska radio*. Retrieved September 24, 2004, from http://arc.norfolkne.com/wjaghism.htm

Smith, R. F., Stanton, K., Stoop, D., Brown, D., & King, P. H. (1975). Quantitative electrocardiography during extended space flight. *Acta Astronautica, 2*(1–2), 89–102.

Solomons, G. (1968). Monitoring drug therapy by telephone. *Medical Times, 96*, 205–210.

Thewritingworks.com. (2003). *The Smith, Kline and French (Mobile) Medical Color TV Unit*. Retrieved September 24, 2004, from http://www.thewritingworks.com/nostalgia.html

TVHistory.TV. (2003). *Television history—The first 75 years*. Retrieved September 24, 2004, from http://www.tvhistory.tv/

Uber, D. C., & Weiss, B. (1966). Computer control of operant behavior experiments via telephone lines. *Journal of the Experimental Analysis of Behavior, 9*, 507–513.

U.S. Code of Practices for Television Broadcasters. (2004). Retrieved September 24, 2004, from http://www.tvhistory.tv/SEAL-Good-Practice.htm

Vaules, D. W. (1970). Auscultation by telephone. *New England Journal of Medicine, 283*, 880–881.

Ware, W. (1993). *Lessons for the future: Dimensions of medical record keeping, in health records: Social needs and personal privacy, 43, Task Force on Privacy*. Washington, DC: U.S. Department of Health and Human Services.

Wittson, C. L., Affleck, D. C., & Johnson, V. (1961). Two-way television in group therapy. *Mental Hospitals, 12*(10), 22–23.

Wittson, C. L., & Benschoter, R. (1972). Two-way television: Helping the medical center reach out. *American Journal of Psychiatry, 129*, 624–627.

AUTHOR INDEX

Numbers in italics refer to listings in the references.

Nidich, S., 77
Nielsen, G. H., 127, 149
Nielsen, T. A., 129, 148
Nieto, F. J., 147
Niskanen, E., 194, 213
Nordhus, I. H., 127, 149
Nordlander, R., 79
Norris, S. L., 112, 118
North, F., 79
Novak, R. M., 87, 101
Nutbeam, D., 204, 206, 212, 213
Nygren, A., 79

O'Brien, J. A., 105, 116
Ockene, I. S., 58
Ockene, J. K., 46, 53, 58
O'Connor, C. M., 78
O'Connor, P. G., 59
O'Donohue, W. T., 26
Offord, K. P., 151
Ogden, G., 245, 256
O'Hara, M. W., 227, 232, 238
Ohayon, M. M., 124, 149
Ohmans, P., 253, 256
Oke, S., 227, 236
Oldham, J. M., 235
Oliver, R. L., 44, 58
Olken, J., 255
Ollendick, T. H., 213
O'Malley, P. M., 192, 211
O'Neil, C. E., 194, 205, 206, 212
Oordt, M. S., 26
Orleans, C. T., 26, 57
Ormrod, J. K., 272, 284
Ornish, D., 69, 78, 80
Orr, W. C., 143, 149, 150
Orth-Gomer, K., 65, 80
Osborn, S., 117
Oster, G., 46, 58
Ovalle, K., 109, 117
Owens, R. G., 258, 265
Ozer, E. M., 207, 212

Paavola, J. C., 192, 193, 212
Paillard, M., 123, 148
Paine, M., 122, 149
Palermo, T. M., 155, 171
Pallesen, S., 127, 149
Palmer, C., 212

Pao, Y. H., 283
Paparrigopoulos, T. J., 131, 133, 150
Para, M. F., 99
Pardue, M., 217, 240
Parekh, P., 118
Park, A., 150
Park, B., 273, 285
Park, J., 220, 238
Parry, B. L., 226, 234
Pasch, L. A., 238
Pasick, R. S., 264
Paskewitz, D. A., 213
Passera, P., 118
Pastore, D. R., 193, 194, 212
Patel, C., 79
Pateman, B. C., 212
Paterson, D., 30, 37
Pauley, D. R., 101
Pavliscsak, H., 118
Pease, D. J., 118
Pedro-Carroll, J. L., 200, 210
Pelletier, R. L., 199, 214
Pennington, J., 150
Penny, G. C., 226, 239
Perdices, M., 85, 86, 88, 102
Perlis, M. L., 127, 150
Perrin, E. C., 155, 167, 168, 171
Perry, C., 194, 198, 204, 206, 212
Perry-Jenkins, M., 221, 239
Person, D. C., 134, 149
Peter, R., 64, 80
Peterson, A. L., 122, 147
Peterson, E. L., 219, 235
Peterson, K., 210
Peterson, L. S., 227, 234
Petito, C. K., 86, 102
Petropoulakis, P., 237
Pettersson, R., 56, 59, 145, 151
Peyrot, M. F., 109, 118
Philip, P., 123, 148
Piccinino, L. J., 227, 234
Pierce Stiver, I., 230, 234
Piette, J. D., 118
Pignone, M. P., 10, 26
Pillitteri, J. L., 134, 149
Pinker, S., 111, 118
Pion, R., 270, 285
Piotrokowski, C. S., 221, 240
Pi-Sunyer, F. X., 192
Pitrak, E. M., 87, 101
Poleshuk, E., 255

SUBJECT INDEX

Thiamin deficiency, 30
Thyroid disorders, 30–32, 35
Time management, 109
Tobacco use. *See* Smoking
Transcendental meditation, 70
Transition to assessment, 16
Transition to intervention, 18
Transtheoretical model of health behavior change, 52, 53
Traumas, 34, 36
Treatment refusal, 52. *See also* Compliance with treatment regimen
Triage system, 62, 73–75
Tricyclic antidepressants, 44
Tripler Army Medical Center (TAMC), 107, 111–112, 275–276
Tumors (neoplasts), 30, 33–34
Tuskegee study, 92
Type A personality, 64, 65, 69, 70, 260, 261
Type D personality, 64–65, 69–70

Uremia, 31, 32
U.S. Department of Health and Human Services, 257, 278
U.S. Federation of State Medical Boards, 277

VA Connecticut Healthcare System (VACHS), 47, 48, 55
Veterans' Administration (VA), 4, 273
Viagra, 244
Videotapes, 142, 262
Vineland Adaptive Behavior Scales, 162
Violent behavior
    against women, 218–219
    children and adolescents, 200, 201
    men, 260
Viral infections, 32
Visualization (mental imagery), 109, 110, 141

Weight changes, 35, 36
Weight management
    diabetes, 108, 113
    health psychologist's role, 4, 55
    heart disease, 69, 75
    HIV/AIDS, 97
    telehealth, 145
Women's health, 217–256
    case examples, 222, 224, 228, 230, 245, 247, 250–251
    chronic and life-threatening illness, 223–224
    cultural and racial differences, 220–221
    current research status, 257–258
    future treatment and policy directions, 233
    health promotion and lifestyle, 223
    heart disease risk, 64, 65
    interpersonal relationships and sexual functioning, 230–231, 243–254
    life cycle transitions, 224–229
    menopause, 226
    mental illness, 229–230
    minority women, and HIV/AIDS, 89
    multiple roles and social support, 221–222
    new classification system for sexual problems, 249–254
    pregnancy and postpartum related issues, 227–229
    premenstrual dysphoric disorder, 225–226
    primary care psychologist's role, 231–233
    puberty, 225
    sexual health resources, 254
    social stressors, 218–220
    socioeconomic status, 219–220
    violence, 218–219
World Health Organization, 164

ABOUT THE EDITORS

Larry C. James, PhD, ABPP, is the chief of the Department of Psychology at Tripler Army Medical Center in Honolulu, Hawaii. He was previously the chief of the psychology department at Walter Reed Army Medical Center in Washington, DC. He is certified by the American Board of Professional Psychology in both clinical and health psychology. He has served on the board of directors of the American Psychological Association Division 38 (Health Psychology) and is a fellow of Divisions 12 (Society of Clinical Psychology), 38 (Health Psychology), and 19 (Society for Military Psychology).

Raymond A. Folen, PhD, ABPP, is the chief of the Behavioral Medicine and Health Psychology Service at Tripler Army Medical Center. He is also an associate professor of clinical psychology with Argosy University in Honolulu, Hawaii. Dr. Folen is certified by the American Board of Professional Psychology in clinical psychology. He is past president of the Hawaii Psychological Association and is a fellow of the American Psychological Association Divisions 31 (State Psychological Association Affairs) and 55 (American Society for the Advancement of Pharmacotherapy). In addition, he is recognized as a Distinguished Practitioner by the National Academies of Practice.